Statue of Liberty—Ellis Island Centennial Series

Books in the Statue of Liberty—Ellis Island Centennial Series

Germans in the New World

Germans in the New World

ESSAYS IN THE HISTORY OF IMMIGRATION

Frederick C. Luebke

UNIVERSITY OF ILLINOIS PRESS
Urbana and Chicago

This book is printed on acid-free paper.

Library of Congress Cataloging-in-Publication Data

Luebke, Frederick C., 1927–
   Germans in the New World: essays in the history of immigration/
Frederick C. Luebke.
       p.   cm.—(Statue of Liberty—Ellis Island Centennial series)
   Includes index.
   ISBN 0-252-01680-7 (alk. paper)
       1. German Americans—History.   2. United States—Emigration and
immigration—History.   3. Germany—Emigration and immigration—
History.   4. Germans—Brazil—History.   5 Brazil—Emigration and
immigration—History.   I. Title.   II. Series.
E184.G3L9   1990
973'.0431—dc20   89-35122
                                                           CIP

For Norma

Contents

Acknowledgments

It is impossible, given the character of this book, for me to identify all the intellectual debts that I have accumulated in writing these essays. Editorial assistance is quite another matter. No one has helped me more than my wife, Norma Wukasch Luebke, who through the years generously and graciously has given me the benefit of her professional expertise. I am also pleased to remember the considerable encouragement and editorial advice that I have received from Kathleen Neils Conzen, Roger Daniels, Walter D. Kamphoefner, James M. Bergquist, and Robert E. Knoll. The University of Nebraska–Lincoln, especially its Department of History and Center for Great Plains Studies, has assisted my work in ways too various to list here. I acknowledge all this help with much gratitude.

My thanks also go to the editors and publishers of the following materials for permission to reprint all or parts of my essays here:

Chapter 1: "The Immigrant Condition as a Factor Contributing to the Conservatism of the Lutheran Church—Missouri Synod." *Concordia Historical Institute Quarterly* 38 (April 1965): 19–28.

Chapter 2: "The German-American Alliance in Nebraska, 1910–1917." *Nebraska History* 49 (Summer 1968): 165–85.

Chapter 3: "Legal Restrictions on Foreign Languages in the Great Plains States, 1917–1923." In *Languages in Conflict: Linguistic Acculturation on the Great Plains*, edited by Paul Schach, 1–19. Lincoln: Univ. of Nebraska Press, 1980.

Chapter 4: "The Germans." In *Ethnic Leadership in America*, edited by John Higham, 64–90. Baltimore: Johns Hopkins Univ. Press, 1978. This article appears here under the title "German-American Leadership Strategies Between the World Wars."

Chapter 5: "German Immigrants and American Politics: Problems of Leadership, Parties, and Issues." In *Germans in America: Retrospect and Prospect*, edited by Randall M. Miller, 57–74. Philadelphia: German Society of Pennsylvania, 1984.

Chapter 7: "Images of German Immigrants in the United States and Brazil, 1890–1918: Some Comparisons." In *America and the Germans:*

An Assessment of a 300-Year History, 2 vols., edited by Frank Trommler and Joseph McVeigh, 1: 207–20. Philadelphia: Univ. of Pennsylvania Press, 1985.

Chapter 8: "The German Ethnic Group in Brazil: The Ordeal of World War I." *Yearbook of German-American Studies* 18 (1983): 255–67.

Chapter 9: Sections I, II, VI, and VII of this essay are modified from pp. 387–96 and 403 in my essay "Ethnic Minority Groups in the American West." In *Historians and the American West,* edited by Michael P. Malone, 387–413. Lincoln: Univ. of Nebraska Press, 1983. Much new material has been added.

Introduction

The study of German immigrants and their descendants in America has not attracted the attention of many professional historians. Even though the Germans are one of the most important and arguably the largest of ethnic groups in the United States, their history has been neglected, most persistently perhaps by German Americans themselves. Reasons for this are easy to identify.

First, to be of "German origin" is itself a vague and imprecise concept. German-speaking immigrants have come to America not only from Germany, but also from Austria, Hungary, Russia, Rumania, Yugoslavia, Switzerland, and France. Germany as a political entity was founded only in the latter part of the nineteenth century. German language and culture, which is much more important as a basis for ethnic consciousness than is country of origin, has never been congruent with German nationality.

Second, few ethnic groups in America have been as varied in religious belief, political persuasion, socioeconomic status, occupation, culture, and social character as the German are, despite persistent historic stereotypes to the contrary. Generalizations about the Germans are inevitably hazardous and sure to be disputed. Because they have been so diverse, German Americans have displayed limited unity and no great interest in a common history, at least by comparison to other ethnic groups, such as Poles, Irish, or Norwegians. Their tendency to cultural amnesia has been greatly augmented in the twentieth century by two World Wars in which Germany was identified as a great and evil adversary. For many persons, thoughtless propaganda and the legacy of Hitlerian horrors transformed German identity in this country; it became a source of social discomfort, something they preferred to ignore.

My own interest in the history of Germans in America was originally generated by a desire to understand that segment of immigrant society from which I sprang. Even though my paternal great-grandfather emigrated a century before I was born, my family's ties to German immigrant culture, especially Lutheranism, remained intimate. My maternal grandfather was a clergyman in the Lutheran Church—Missouri

Synod, as were assorted uncles and grand uncles, cousins and second cousins; my father was a teacher in the synod, as were two older brothers and other uncles and cousins. It was a matter of course that I should follow the same path. I attended the appropriate Lutheran college and later served as a teacher in several Lutheran parish schools, a Lutheran high school, and another Lutheran college. German Lutheranism in America was a small world. It seemed self-contained; its influence was pervasive. It needed to be understood.

Received wisdom within the Lutheran Church—Missouri Synod suggested that its history was the lengthened shadow of leaders whose fearless dedication to *reine Lehre*—the pure doctrine promulgated by Martin Luther—carried the church through a series of fierce theological battles to attain its present magnitude. When I had enrolled in a doctoral program at the University of Southern California in the late 1950s, I had an opportunity to study the history of the Missouri Synod—the ethnic institution I knew best—and to place it in the social context provided by the assimilation process that all immigrant institutions must experience.

I perceived a history that differed from the one I had been taught. My reading of history, buttressed by personal experience, led me to conclude that a sociohistorical interpretation offered far more understanding than the traditional emphasis on leaders, theology, and institutional change did.[1] The Missouri Synod, despite its congregational polity, seemed dominated by its clergy. This elite, unlike its rank-and-file members, emigrated primarily for religious reasons and naturally sought to use every means at hand to preserve the doctrinal character of the church in the American environment. This they perceived as a threatening milieu whose assimilative powers seemed irresistible. Reacting defensively, they established programs of German-language maintenance founded on an institutional structure of parochial schools, teachers colleges, and theological seminaries, all buttressed by an effective printing and publishing agency. A by-product of such a closed system was a heightened self-consciousness, an uncompromising isolationism, and a determination to do battle with the enemies of the True Faith. These enemies included the proponents of puritanical moralism, revivalism, rationalism, Wesleyan emotionalism, Catholicism, Masonry, socialists, Forty-eighters, atheists, and sometimes fellow Lutherans of other synods. The product of this initial study, revised and amended, is the first article included in this book. It bears the unwieldy title of "The Immigrant Condition as a Factor in the Conservatism of the Lutheran Church—Missouri Synod."

In 1961 I accepted an appointment to the faculty of Concordia College in Seward, Nebraska, a teacher-education institution of the Missouri Synod. I transferred my doctoral studies in history to the University of Nebraska, where I worked with Professor James C. Olson, whose principal interests were in the history of Nebraska, Indians, and the American West. But I continued with ethnic history and now turned to the political acculturation of the German ethnic group in Nebraska during the last two decades of the nineteenth century.

As I undertook my dissertation research, I quickly discovered that there were no useful patterns for me to follow in the writings of earlier historians of the Germans in America, if I were to avoid the pitfalls of elitism and the morass of filiopietism. Instead, I turned to Lee Benson, who had demonstrated that ethnicity and religion were capable of explaining political behavior on a local level more effectively than socioeconomic factors could.[2] Samuel P. Hays's several articles on the social analysis of political history were especially revealing to me.[3] The work of both historians was enormously helpful as I sought to conceptualize the problem and to develop an appropriate methodology for its solution. The result was a pioneering effort in the application of coefficients of correlation and other methods of quantification to the solution of a historical problem. In 1969 this work was published in revised form as *Immigrants and Politics: The Germans of Nebraska, 1880–1900* (Lincoln: Univ. of Nebraska Press).

In my view, the key to understanding ethnic political behavior lay in assimilation theory. It seemed to me that at a given time and place an immigrant's voting behavior was likely to be correlated closely with the frequency and quality of interpersonal contacts with members of the host society. Thus, for example, a German immigrant in Nebraska who resided in a city or town and who was employed in a craft, business, or profession that involved many contacts with Anglo-American society would be more likely to vote Republican in the late nineteenth century than would a German farmer living in the relative isolation of the countryside. Ethnocultural divergence from the norm could be expected to diminish as the assimilation process ran its course, except when issues such as prohibition, women's suffrage, Sabbatarianism, and the regulation of parochial schools achieved salience among the immigrants. The basic method used to reveal this relationship was the correlation of manuscript census data (which recorded the entire voting population on a township and ward level) with voting data (also on a township or precinct level).

My research in German voting behavior led me to an interest in the effect of World War I on the German ethnic community in the United States. One of the striking aspects of German-American organizational life, I discovered, was that the Germans were very slow, compared to other ethnic groups, to organize themselves on a national scale for any common purpose, political or otherwise. I found no unified German-ethnic organization or association in the late nineteenth century—the National German-American Alliance was not organized until 1901. Although there was at least one useful book on this institution, almost nothing had been published on its state branches. The second article in this book, "The German-American Alliance in Nebraska, 1910–17," is the product of my investigation, on the state level, into the institutional life of the Alliance, which was at best an ill-starred venture whose brief life ended when the United States went to war with Germany. Entirely conventional in concept and method, this article represents no new exercise in the methodology of ethnic history, but it led me directly to a consideration of the problem posed by World War I for American citizens of German birth or descent.

I wished to understand better why people, both immigrants and the native-born, behaved as they did when their government went to war with the ancestral homeland of one of its largest ethnic groups. But before I could analyze the events in the domestic war of 1917 and 1918 against German language and culture, I needed to study the structure of the German-American community and to understand how it was perceived by American society in the decades before the war. Again my debt to Samuel P. Hays was clear: He taught that systematic history required the study of social structure before specific events or a series of events could be analyzed adequately.[4] This approach demanded that the diversity of German America be taken into account; further, this approach assumed that the several components of this subsociety were affected variously by the events of the war. It was an interpretation that was nonquantitative in method, but it nonetheless emerged from the modes of thought and method that governed my earlier study of political behavior. In my view, there was no need to identify fools and culprits or to praise stalwart heroes and martyrs, even though there was no dearth of such figures on either side. The product of this research was my second book, *Bonds of Loyalty: German Americans and World War I* (DeKalb: Northern Illinois Univ. Press, 1974). It was a full-scale effort to understand that most unfortunate chapter in the history of German America.

Unfortunately the war on German language and culture did not end on Armistice Day in 1918. In fact, the most restrictive laws intended to curb the use of and instruction in the German language were enacted by legislatures, mainly in western states, in 1919 and 1921. The history of their enactment and of the legal battles they engendered is treated in "Legal Restrictions on Foreign Languages in the Great Plains States, 1917–23." That such laws were declared unconstitutional by the United States Supreme Court in 1923 should be instructive to contemporary advocates of new restrictive legislation aimed primarily at Spanish-speaking persons concentrated in California, Texas, Florida, and elsewhere.

Like the article that precedes it, "German-American Leadership Strategies between the World Wars" is an extension of my study of the impact of World War I on the German-American community. Early in 1975 while I was engaged in research as a Fulbright fellow in the Institut für Auslandsbeziehungen in Stuttgart, West Germany, John Higham asked me to prepare a paper on German-American leadership for a symposium at Johns Hopkins University. Because, in my opinion, there has been no effective, visible leadership among the Germans in the United States since the beginning of World War II, I felt obliged to consider this topic during the period between the world wars. No effort is made here to analyze the social characteristics of ethnic leaders, the ways in which they differ from the commonalty of the group, or the relationships between the two. Instead, I concentrated on strategies that emerged during the two decades, as leaders sought to help the German-American community recover from the social and psychological ravages wrought upon them by World War I. At first, prominent voices advocated the exercise of political power, much as they had before the war. Following the election of 1928, it became clear that such a plan could never succeed, and a new generation of leaders urged that politics be abandoned in favor of the pursuit of cultural goals. This approach was aborted by the onset of the Great Depression and the rise of the American Nazis, whose strategy of blood and tactics of violence were offensive to the majority of German Americans.

The tricentennial commemoration of the first settlement of German immigrants in the New World in 1983 was the occasion for writing a broadly synthetic view of "German Immigrants and American Politics: Problems of Leadership, Parties, and Issues," prepared for presentation to the German Society of Pennsylvania. In the first part of this essay, I return to the question of ethnic political leadership. In my view, the type of leadership represented by the distinguished and famous Carl Schurz could not attain substantial ethnic-group political goals, given the heterogeneity of the German-American ethnic group and the realities of the American political system. On the other hand, politicians had the potential for accomplishing much for their constituencies, both ethnic and native, provided that they were willing occasionally to sacrifice ethnic ideals in favor of party loyalty. The essay reviews the changing relationships of German Americans, chiefly in the nineteenth century, to the several political parties and the issues, usually ethnocultural, that had salience for them. In the twentieth century, German-American concerns shifted to questions of foreign policy; such issues seem to have dominated the voting behavior of citizens of German heritage, at least when it can be identified in the decades since World War II. At the same time, German ethnic leadership seems to have vanished.

The next series of articles in this book expands the focus of inquiry from the United States to comparisons with the history of Germans who chose to immigrate to other lands—in this case, to Brazil. While working in the collection of materials on *Auslanddeutsche* in the Stuttgart Institut für Auslandsbeziehungen in 1974, I began a study of German immigration to Brazil in order to compare the experiences of German Brazilians in World War I with those of their cousins in the United States. This work eventually culminated in the publication of *Germans in Brazil: A Comparative History of Cultural Conflict during World War I* (Baton Rouge: Louisiana State Univ. Press, 1987). My interest in comparative history resulted in several related studies, three of which are included here.

The first is "Patterns of German Settlement in the United States and Brazil, 1830–1930." Although the two streams of immigration were similar in motivation, in social and cultural characteristics, and in the kinds of ethnic institutions that were created, the differences in the two receiving societies and their physical environments were pronounced. In Brazil the German immigrants tended to create more exclusive, concentrated, rural colonies in which ethnic language and culture could be more readily sustained than in the United States. My purpose here is not to pursue some quantitative methodology, but rather to compare systematically patterns of German settlement in the two countries by contrasting time and rate of immigration, causes and sources of emigration, social characteristics of immigrants, land laws, occupational structures, and the like. The essay was originally prepared for a symposium on comparative aspects of the history of migration organized by Rudolph J. Vecoli and sponsored by the Immigration History Research Center at the University of Minnesota in 1986.

Comparisons of the United States with Brazil are also at the heart of the next essay, "Images of German Immigrants in the United States and Brazil, 1890–1918." Here the focus is on how German immigrants were perceived in the two countries and on how these images contributed to the potential for cultural conflict. There are variations, of course, in the stereotypes that developed in the two countries, but the Germans generally were well received in both. Immigrant perceptions of the host societies were also important. In Brazil the social distance between the immigrants and the host society was greater and the German sense of cultural superiority was keener than in the United States; the potential for cultural conflict was therefore correspondingly increased. This essay was originally prepared for a conference held in Philadelphia in 1983 in commemoration of the tricentennial of German immigration to America; it draws extensively upon both *Bonds of Loyalty* and *Germans in Brazil.* World War I provided the occasion for the release of hidden tensions in both Brazil and the United States. Although the war in Europe commenced in 1914, both the United States and Brazil entered the conflict only in 1917. In both countries the long period of neutrality provided opportunities for the incubation of ethnic tensions. When war was finally declared, both countries understandably displayed much hostility against the Germans in their respective populations. In Brazil, where the German ethnic population posed virtually no threat to national security, the reaction was unusually severe compared to the United States and was climaxed by two series of anti-German riots in several major Brazilian cities. Originally prepared for presentation to the American Historical Association in 1982, "The German Ethnic Group in Brazil: The Ordeal of World War I" is a highly condensed version of *Germans in Brazil.*

Two historiographical essays form the final part of the book. The first, "Turnerism, Social History, and the Historiography of European Ethnic Groups in the United States," interprets the concepts and methods that American historians of immigration have used since Frederick Jackson Turner opened the field early in our century. My purpose here is to suggest, first, that even though Turner's celebrated frontier thesis tended to have an inhibiting effect on the practice of immigration history, the methodology he espoused still remains useful today. Second, Oscar Handlin shifted attention from Turner's environmental forces to the processes of social change that emerge from the interaction between immigrants and the receiving society. Third, advocates of the social analysis of ethnopolitical history laid the foundations for effective comparative analysis in immigration studies. Since then the field has expanded in many directions, but many of the best studies continue to pursue questions relating to social history. Some have been informed by pluralist concepts, others by inquiry into the relationships between ethnicity and class, and at least one synthetic interpretation—John Bodnar's *Transplanted: A History of Immigrants in Urban America* (Bloomington: Indiana University Press, 1985)—transcends both developments. Still others focus on international migration as a social process and in doing so employ a methodology that, like Turner many decades ago, incorporates the environmental variable. The essay concludes with a discussion of ethnic history conceived as the interaction over time of cultural variables with social and physical environments. Although this article evolved out of a paper originally prepared for a seminar sponsored by the American Association for State and Local History, it has been extensively revised and expanded here.

The concluding essay sharpens the focus by emphasizing research and publication on the German experience. Written specifically for this collection, it offers an interpretation of three centuries of German-American history as based on some of the best research conducted in this field during the past two decades. The structure of the essay emerges from the hard data of immigration—who came when for what reasons, where and how they settled, and why. The emphasis is primarily on social factors, immigrant institutions, and the relationships of German-Americans to national affairs. The essay concludes with commentary on topics that, in my view, call for further development. Special attention is given to churches of German immigrant origins, the topic with which this collection of essays begins.

The last two essays summarize the enormous changes that have taken place in the conceptualization and methodology of immigrant or ethnic group history in the United States in recent decades. A half century ago, this field was dominated by Turnerian thought; preeminent among historians of German immigrants in America was Carl F. Wittke, who counted Turner among his professors at Harvard University. A mere glance at the body of Wittke's work, but especially at his synthesis *We Who Built America* (1939; rev. ed. Cleveland: Western Reserve University Press, 1964), reveals what has transpired. His emphasis, even as late as 1964, remained on the contributions of immigrant peoples to America's greatness. The immigrants were so numerous and so influential, Wittke's title announces, that they could claim that America was the fruit of their labors. They had left the confining precincts of Europe for the freedom of America's vast frontiers. There the immigrants were transformed by environmental forces, both physical and social, into buoyant, energetic, innovative, pragmatic, and democratic Americans. But unlike Turner's frontiersmen, they were not stripped entirely of their culture. Much of it remained to contribute to that which is quintessentially American.

In some respects the new immigration history contrasts strongly with the old. Whereas the traditional was assimilationist and stressed the cultural contributions of the newcomers, the new is more often pluralist and focuses on cultural conflict. The old tended to describe individual accomplishment and, drawing upon readily available sources such as letters, speeches, diaries, and other qualitative sources, was unintentionally elitist; the new analyzes the relationships of the ethnic group (i.e., the masses of ordinary people of limited skills in communication) with elements of the receiving society, including other ethnocultural collectivities. It uses quantitative sources, such as census manuscripts, tax lists, city directories, voting data, and other public records. Whereas traditional immigration history tended to perceive unity or homogeneity within an ethnic group, the new analyzes diversity and internal variation.

The new historians of immigration have often used the concepts and methods of the social sciences. This derives partly from their need to analyze social structures as necessary background for understanding historical events. Such an approach was uncommon among traditionalist historians of an earlier time, who more often sought to explain the causes and consequences of specific historical events without fair consideration for the social setting.

In my own case, I discovered early on that extensive reading in traditional studies of German-American history provided me with few tools to analyze immigrant political behavior in a systematic way on a local level or to analyze voter data comparatively. I therefore turned to sociologists and political scientists for help; later I was attracted to the concepts and methods of cultural geographers and anthropologists. Scholars in those disciplines may well abjure any apparent relationship between their work and mine. But in adapting some of their ideas I have intended to supplement rather than to replace traditional concepts and methods in immigration history.

All of the previously published essays presented here are essentially in their original form. I have corrected mistakes that have come to my attention and have made minor revisions. In most cases they were published in journals not widely distributed or in books with titles that, for entirely appropriate reasons, tended to obscure the content of my articles and their relationship to immigration history. They are unified by a style of thought or point of view that seeks to transcend filiopietism and to find the place of German immigrants in the broad context of social history. Collected in the format of this book, they may make a contribution to the history of Germans in the Americas that was not possible when published separately.

NOTES

1. Two books were especially illuminating to me. They were Oscar Handlin, *The Uprooted: The Epic Story of the Great Migration that Made the American People* (New York: Grosset and Dunlap, 1951), of which a revised and enlarged edition was published in 1973 by Little, Brown; and H. Richard Niebuhr, *The Social Sources of Denominationalism* (New York: Henry Holt, 1929).

2. I refer here especially to Benson's *Concept of Jacksonian Democracy: New York as a Test Case* (Princeton: Princeton Univ. Press, 1961) and his extended essay "Research Problems in American History," in *Common Frontier of the Social Sciences*, ed. Mirra Komarovsky (Glencoe, IL: The Free Press, 1957), 113–83.

xxii Germans in the New World

3. At that time I was able to draw upon Hays's "Social Analysis of American Political History," *Political Science Quarterly* 80 (September 1965): 373–94, and his "History as Human Behavior," *Iowa Journal of History* 58 (July 1960): 193–206. Since then these and other essays have been anthologized in *American Political History as Social Analysis* (Knoxville: Univ. of Tennessee Press, 1980.

4. See especially Hays's essays "New Possibilities for American Political History" (1968), pp. 115–16, and "A Systematic Social History" (1971), pp. 146–50 and passim, both published in *American Political History as Social Analysis*.

Germans in the New World

The Immigrant Condition as a Factor Contributing to the Conservatism of the Lutheran Church–Missouri Synod

1

In the twenty-five years that have passed since this article was written, the Lutheran Church—Missouri Synod has undergone wrenching changes that have intensified its conservative character. This essay is reprinted here because it continues to illuminate the sociohistorical sources of contemporary developments in the Missouri Synod, even though other variables have increased in importance as the immigration phase fades in the collective memory. More than that, however, it makes the point, often overlooked by immigration historians, that ethnicity can be made to serve the interests of religion, not merely the reverse. In other words, religion must be taken seriously and on its own terms. This is not to suggest that all immigrant churches have reacted to the processes of assimilation in the same way as did the Lutheran Church—Missouri Synod.

In its present form the article is only slightly modified from what was published in 1965. A more extensive revision—one that would treat substance—would compromise its unity and integrity. For that reason my revision consists only of a few corrections, editorial modifications, and the omission of some notes, a paragraph, and an occasional phrase.

Today [i.e., *circa* 1960], more than one-half century after its immigrant phase came to an end, the Lutheran Church—Missouri Synod has begun to examine its nineteenth-century antecedents with increasing interest and sophistication. The kind of corporate self-knowledge that may be gained through objective historical inquiry has long been obscured by popular, filiopietistic histories and biographies that rarely transcended the obvious, and seldom placed the church and its leaders in the social, economic, political, and cultural surroundings from which men and institutions are inseparable. A number of professionally competent studies have been produced, but generally the Missouri Synod has not given systematic or comprehensive study to its history as a religious institution of an immigrant people.

The reasons for this failure are complex but can be explained partially by the fact that the founders of the Lutheran Church—Missouri Synod (but not its rank-and-file membership) emigrated to America primarily for religious reasons and that they raised up walls of isolation, intentionally and otherwise, to protect the church in its immigrant condition. Its modern conservative character bears witness to the extraordinary success of their enterprise. It is the purpose of this essay to provide a summary view of the church as a nineteenth-century immigrant institution by broadly synthesizing the ideas of several historians and applying them to the Missouri Synod. Frankly interpretive and fragmentary in scope, it is intended to stimulate questions rather than to provide answers.

Among the most perceptive analyses of the hopes and fears, the aspirations and disappointments of immigrant peoples is *The Uprooted* by Oscar Handlin.[1] The author follows the typical experiences of immigrants who left their European homes, most often in peasant villages, to settle in a new, strange, and often bewildering land. Handlin shows how attitudes and thought patterns contributed to religious rigidity, and how many immigrants became much more conservative than did their fellows who remained in Europe.

According to this interpretation, religion became the chief support to the newcomers as they were forced to adjust to the new circumstances in America, as they struggled to save something of the old, familiar ways. Cut loose from the moorings of peasant life, the immigrants found that religion alone seemed to survive the transfer to the United States. Their problem was to reconstruct their way of religious life in the new environment. Accustomed to the unquestioned status of established churches with their universality, hierarchy, old buildings, ancient rituals and traditions, they found the diversity of religious affiliations and the accompanying competition difficult to understand. There was also the disturbingly unfamiliar and oppressive problem of financial support. The latitudinarianism of American religious life also represented a threat to the establishment of the immigrant church. Americans seemed to believe that salvation was a matter of ethical conduct, that any faith or none at all might lead to it. But to many an immigrant, salvation was the reward of faith and suffering, not of good behavior. Hence the newcomer felt that religious institutions had to be protected from this and other debilitating American notions. The only way to guarantee the survival of the immigrant church lay in a complete transfer of the old religious system to the New World, not merely in theology, but in language and customs as well. Thus the immigrant condition led to an aggressive defense of the old pattern, an intolerance of change, and a conservatism more firm than that of the homeland.[2]

Among the major American Protestant denominations, the Lutheran church is clearly a product of these general circumstances. Despite an essential uniformity in doctrine, the several groups emigrating from regions where the Lutheran church was established, whether Germany, Sweden, Norway, or Denmark, all insisted upon their own church organizations. As H. Richard Niebuhr pointed out in his study of denominationalism, each group was dissatisfied with the varieties of Lutheranism that had preceded it, diluted, as they seemed to be, with American ideas and attitudes.[3]

Of the major divisions remaining in American Lutheranism today, the Lutheran Church—Missouri Synod is one of the most conservative and perhaps the most dynamic. To what extent did the immigrant condition contribute to the indelible stamp of conservatism that the church acquired during its formative period in the nineteenth century and has carried to the present day?

The origins of the Missouri Synod are inextricably bound up with the Saxon Germans, numbering more than six hundred, who immigrated as a colony to Missouri via New Orleans in 1839. In contrast to the vast majority of German immigrants, these Saxons left the Old World for the New largely for religious reasons rather than for economic ones. They were part of the "Old Lutheran" protest against the forced union of Lutheran and Reformed congregations in the state church of Saxony. Having endured governmental persecution for their nonconformity, they followed the advice of their spiritual guide, Martin Stephan, to pool their resources for a colonization venture in America.

The social characteristics of the group are striking. Fully 45 percent of the total were female; average age was twenty-five. The group included eight pastors, eleven candidates for the ministry, five teachers, nine merchants, a lawyer, a doctor of medicine, the curator of the Saxon state archives, and other professional persons. A mere 14 percent could be classified as peasants, while 61 percent were craftsmen or mechanics. The common treasury was the equivalent of more than $80,000.[4] Not a band of impoverished peasants fleeing economic constrictions, these Saxons were the products of urban, middle-class culture, and their highly educated leaders were committed to theological principles much more rigid and orthodox than those of the state church from which they fled.

Shortly after the Saxons arrived in St. Louis and established their main colony in rural Perry County, the community was torn by strife. Stephan had succeeded in creating an episcopacy with himself as bishop. Shortly thereafter his world crashed about him as he was accused of adultery. Quickly deprived of his office, Stephan was exiled from the settlement and transported across the Mississippi River to Illinois. Meanwhile, the Saxons became thoroughly distressed over fear that the colony, having banished its bishop, was now without a religious bond— that in the sight of God the group no longer constituted a part of the Kingdom of Grace. Out of this crisis emerged the commanding figure of C. F. W. Walther, who advanced congregationalism as a new principle from which the status of the Saxons within the Christian church could be rationalized. Under Walther, who came to dominate the group by virtue of his exceptional ability and personality, the Saxons became totally committed to a congregational polity, with no small results for their continued religious conservatism.[5]

Walther and his followers then investigated existing Lutheran synods, hoping to find an organization with which they might affiliate. The older groups, they felt, were tainted with liberalism and rationalism. Of the synods that were strongly German in character, only the Ohio Synod operated in the West. But it also was suspect because it was an outgrowth of the older, unionistic Pennsylvania Ministerium. Walther then decided to publish a church paper, *Der Lutheraner*, which he dedicated to the principles of conservative Lutheranism and distributed widely among German Lutheran immigrants throughout the country. He called for the creation of a new Lutheran synod founded on confessional and congregational principles. This was accomplished in 1847 when the German Lutheran Synod of Missouri, Ohio, and Other States was organized in Chicago, with Walther as its first president.

According to Handlin, the peasants' religion was the one pillar that remained steadfast in support of their crumbling house of culture. In the case of the founders of the Missouri Synod, it seems that the opposite was true — German culture with all its trappings was used to perpetuate the theological conservatism. In this case, to paraphrase Richard Niebuhr, religion supplied the energy, the goal, and the motive of the movement whereas cultural factors supplied the occasion and determined the form taken by the religious dynamic.

Thus for the confessional German Lutheran immigrant "the faith of the church [was] its greatest treasure and *raison d'être;* contamination of that faith [was] the church's greatest pitfall."[6] The Lutheran leaders believed, therefore, that every effort had to be made to preserve doctrinal purity in the alien and hostile American environment. Religious isolation was imperative; social and cultural isolation would also contribute mightily to the preservation of the faith.

Fundamental to such a program of isolationism was the development of an educational system. In the same year that the Saxons arrived in Missouri, they took steps to found a preparatory school that would serve to train future pastors. By 1900 the Missourians maintained two large seminaries and a half dozen preparatory schools modeled on the German *Gymnasium*. In addition, two colleges were founded to guarantee a supply of teachers for the parochial schools that the synod urged every local congregation to maintain. These elementary schools in turn supplied students for the preparatory schools, thus completing the circle.

With this closed system the synod defended itself against the greatest threat to its religious isolationism. Its colleges and seminaries flourished in a world apart from the mainstream of American Protestant Christianity. Gradually young graduates, indoctrinated into a theological synthesis formulated by Luther and crystalized by Walther, replaced their elders in positions of leadership, untouched by revivalism, rationalism, the Social Gospel, or whatever else characterized the religious environment at a given moment.

It is no doubt true that when the Missourians established their schools they were also expressing a sense of cultural superiority common to many German immigrants of the nineteenth century. Remembering their own training in the schools and universities of Germany, many of the church's leaders felt contempt for what passed for public education in the Midwest at that time. Still, they were more interested in perpetuating a religious pattern than a cultural one.[7] For a time it was a constitutional provision of the synod that a congregation's admission to membership was conditioned upon the establishment and maintenance of a parish school. Walther reveals the importance he placed on them: "God grant that our German Lutheran Church may retain the gem, its parochial school! For most assuredly, humanly speaking, above everything else, the future of our church in America is dependent upon it. . . . The further careful fostering of our parochial schools is and will remain, after the public ministry, the principal means of our existence and continuance."[8]

Another weapon used to ward off Americanization was the German language. In this the Missouri Synod was no different from other German religious groups. The language of the schools, the theological source books, and the worship services was always German. Here cultural waters ran deep. Even those Germans who were not religiously inclined often harbored a great love for Luther's translation of the Bible and for their incomparable heritage of chorales.[9] Such sentiments naturally slowed the process of Americanization. The entrenchment of the native tongue was abetted also by extreme congregationalism, a polity that facilitated organization along ethnic lines.

By the end of the nineteenth century English still had not made many inroads. The clerical prejudice against it remained strong; many pastors feared that genuine Lutheranism could not thrive in an English-speaking congregation. Here and there such parishes had been founded in the face of opposition by prominent synodical leaders, who publicly declared such doings dangerous. This hostility was augmented by the fact that English-speaking congregations saw no need for parochial schools and did not establish them.[10]

Given the synod's educational system and the role of the German language, the need for a denominational publishing house became obvious.

Textbooks, theological journals, publications for the laity, hymnbooks, and other worship materials, all in German, were needed to preserve immunity against the latitudinarianism and liberalism of American Christianity. By 1869 the synodical printing establishment was a reality; it went on to become a leader among religious publishers.

To many of the nineteenth-century German immigrants, the church's unusual emphasis on theological creed was not of great importance. As Marcus Hansen has pointed out, "The important thing was a place existed where the mother tongue was spoken, where one's compatriots gathered from miles around, where customs were familiar."[11] Around the nucleus of the congregation developed musical organizations, social groups, insurance funds, and even cooperative merchandising agencies. Moreover, the average layman was willing to surrender to the pastor's preeminence in theological matters, both in dogma and in practice, and to follow his leadership. Hence, even though all power was theoretically vested in the congregation of laymen, it was actually the clergy who determined the conservative pattern of the church.

Unlike the European state church system, the American concept of the separation of church and state fostered a spirit of competition among the churches, and competition promoted particularity. In Europe the established churches enjoyed a virtual monopoly; in the United States they had to compete actively for the loyalty of members and for their position in the new and alien society. This generated a high degree of self-consciousness and emphasized the peculiar characteristics of each denomination. Agreements with competitors were minimized, disagreements stressed.[12] For this reason the history of the Lutheran church in America, especially when recounted by its own members, appears to be little more than one dogmatic dispute after another. Because of its origins and early history, the Missouri Synod was always one of the most vigorous and uncompromising of the disputants. Walther always adhered strictly to his principle—"No Union without Unity"—no partnership without fellowship in principle. Not regarded as quibbling or unwarranted polemic, theological warfare was believed to contribute to the strength of the church, its inner unity, and its ministry.[13] With other Lutherans there was at least communication; they were seeking others of like mind to do battle against the enemies of the true faith. But other denominations were quite beyond the pale of fellowship; indeed, they were usually the enemy.

The self-imposed separation of Lutheranism from other branches of Christianity may be observed in what it opposed. With its historic emphasis on *sola fide*, the Lutheran church reacted negatively to the moralism common to American Protestantism. The Puritan heritage, which tended to make religion a matter of right behavior, was manifested in Sabbatarianism, temperance movements, and other reformist tendencies, all of which had little appeal for the German Lutheran immigrant. Rationalism, which pervaded the older Protestant denominations, was likewise repellent. This, after all, is what many of the synod's founding fathers had fled from in Germany.

But there was also a strong antiritualist tendency. Some synodical leaders believed that liturgical practices made undesirable sensory appeals; this, they argued, helped to account for the prominence of Roman Catholicism among false churches. At the same time, emotionalism was especially repugnant to the immigrant German Lutheran pastor, for it was the Methodist frontier missionary, his chief competitor for the immigrant, who made extensive use of revivalist techniques. The result was that Missouri Synod Lutheranism was often spare, austere, and sternly intellectual.

The confessional Lutheran also placed the Masonic orders, the Odd Fellows, and other lodges and secret societies within the religious context. Opposition to these organizations unquestionably stemmed from theological concerns, yet the Missourians recognized that the appeal of the lodges was essentially social and economic. The solution was therefore to fight fire with fire. As early as 1853 an earnest plea was made to all synod members and congregations to establish Christian indigent and disability benefit plans, thereby neutralizing the "ever-increasing grasping seduction of the secret societies."[14]

Moving from the religious environment to the larger sphere of American society, it becomes apparent that here too the German immigrant church had experiences that tended to intensify its isolationism. Caught up in the complex pattern of conflict between native and foreign groups, the churches often received the brunt of chauvinist fears and suspicions. As Richard Niebuhr expressed it, "The newcomers were mostly poor, they were often illiterate, sometimes thriftless, always different in language and customs."[15] Hostility was a natural result as the sense of superiority possessed by the native-born population found opportunity for expression. Assertion by one group evoked a corresponding self-assertion in the other, and ultimately a more deeply rooted sense of solidarity and self-consciousness. The Saxons in Missouri felt a strong nativist disapproval after they arrived in St. Louis.[16] The Know Nothing uproar of the 1850s was essentially an anti-immigrant movement.

In the face of such tensions the clergy were often anxious to remove the sources of friction. Many immigrants led undisciplined lives in the free, individualistic society of the United States. The restraints of family and tradition common to village life in Europe were no longer binding, and the immigrants discovered that their mores by no means coincided with those of Puritan America. Thus when the first missionary to an immigrant group arrived in his new community, he automatically found himself in the vanguard of a reform movement, a clean-up campaign. Irrespective of his past personal inclinations, he was more or less forced by circumstances to forbid pastimes and pleasures among his parishioners that the traditions of his early theological training had condoned.[17] Among these were the beer drinking and dancing that were common to wedding festivities, picnics, and other occasions. Usually the stand taken by the church in these matters was governed by local conditions, although in 1875 one district convention of the Missouri Synod heard a set of formal propositions against operating and visiting saloons.[18]

This tendency to shift toward a sterner conservatism in practice was intensified by the characteristics of the clergymen themselves. A shortage of pastors was perennial, and often German-American communities appealed to the mother country for men to counterbalance the frequent tendency toward intemperance and all sorts of social misery. But the state churches of Europe were unable to respond. If help was to come it had to be undertaken by benevolent associations and individuals. Pastors who were prepared to offer themselves for service in the difficult, primitive conditions of the American West tended to be men of greater zeal and standards of conduct than were their fellows who remained within the comfortable security of a state church.[19] In the case of the German Lutheran synods, this tendency is particularly evident in the large number of men sent to America by Wilhelm Loehe of Neuendettelsau and after 1870 by Friedrich Brunn of Steeden.[20]

Sometimes the government was added to the Lutheran list of hostile groups or agencies. This could flow from any legislation that might affect the church negatively. The Missouri Synod was particularly sensitive about its parochial schools. When, for example, the Wisconsin legislature enacted a law requiring written reports on attendance, enrollment, curriculum, and language of instruction to be submitted annually to the district superintendent of schools, the Lutheran outcry was unrestrained. German Lutherans were never known for active participation in political affairs, yet their response to this threat included a mobilization of public opinion and of votes so thorough that the Republican party, which had sponsored the measure, was thoroughly beaten in the subsequent election of 1890. The offending law was thereupon repealed.

Contacts of still another variety tended to emphasize the particularity and conservatism of the German Lutherans. These were with the so-called Forty-eighters, for whose radical politics, freethinking religion, and nationalist sentiments they had no sympathy whatever. Although there was little ground for their fears, the church fathers imagined their own positions of leadership in the German-American community menaced by these dynamic, culture-conscious refugees of the revolutions of 1848.[21]

Thus no matter which way he turned, the German Lutheran immigrant leader saw potential hostility and harassment. He saw it in fellow Germans such as the Forty-eighters, in fellow Lutherans such as clergy of the Ohio Synod, in fellow Protestants such as the Methodists, and in fellow Christians such as the Catholics; he saw it in lodges and secret societies, in the native-born American population, and sometimes even in the government. Such threats, real or imaginary, produced a self-consciousness of high intensity. Only an uncompromising conservatism, it was believed, could possibly preserve the religious identity of the group. Every possible social, cultural, and theological weapon was to be wielded in the battle for survival.

As the nineteenth century drew to a close, the size and character of the immigration from Germany underwent a significant change. The numbers were decreasing and few of the later arrivals were attracted by "Missourianism." This meant that growth from this source virtually ceased, and as it did, the church's fifty-year history as an immigrant institution gradually terminated. The process of Americanization, so long delayed, began to transform the external features of the synod, even as its obvious German traits faded.

Yet its heart remained untouched. The church owed its origins to theological conservatism; its half-century of experience as an immigrant institution enhanced this tendency. Today, more than another half century later, the Lutheran Church — Missouri Synod continues to be characterized by its historic religious isolationism, but it is now coupled with activity totally adapted to the American environment.

EPILOGUE

In 1969, four years after this essay was published, the historical course of the Lutheran Church — Missouri Synod was altered fundamentally by the election of Jacob A. O. Preus as its president. For at least three decades the leadership of the synod had been vested in men of moderate temperament who were nonetheless thoroughgoing theological conservatives. But they recognized that the synod had been transformed during the preceding half century from an immigrant institution into an American Protestant denomination. They modernized the church as an institution and they made certain limited accommodations in the direction of communication and cooperation with other Lutheran bodies.

Not surprisingly, this gradual movement evoked cries of anguish, beginning in the late 1930s, from ultraconservative clergymen who fervently believed that the adherence of the Missouri Synod to its traditional doctrinal positions was being abandoned by its leaders. Stiffened by a mindset that derives from convictions of infallibility, the synod's internal critics sustained a drum-fire attack, largely by means of privately financed periodicals, on the synodical leadership, its boards, and theologians for what they understood to be a betrayal of God's Truth. They were uncompromising apologists for a seventeenth-century theology, tempered in the nineteenth century in the American forge of the immigrant condition and hammered into shaped by C. F. W. Walther and Franz Pieper, among others. A revered theologian of great power, Pieper had served the synod either as president or as its leading dogmatician at Concordia Seminary in St. Louis from 1887 (when C. F. W. Walther died) to his own death in 1931.

The climax of this movement came in 1969 when the ultraconservatives engineered the election of Jacob A. O. Preus, a young, attractive clergyman of Norwegian antecedents. In my view, Preus's election represents the triumph of the siege mentality I have described as rooted in immigrant experience. But the event must not be divorced from national affairs. Preus, like Richard M. Nixon, who took office in the same year, owed his election in part to the keen distress felt at that time by conservatives of all kinds, political and otherwise, as they watched American students, stimulated by racial injustices and the tragedies wrought by the Vietnam War, indulge themselves in their usually well-intentioned but none-theless destructive excesses.

A second major event in the synod's traditionalist revolution occurred in 1974. To Preus and his supporters, the fountainhead of theological error was to be found in the faculty of Concordia Seminary, then presided over by John Tietjen, a moderate. In the view of the ultraconservatives, Tietjen was protecting teachers of false doctrine and he, like them, had to be removed from office. After many months of maneuvering, Tietjen was suspended from his office in January. His dismissal was followed by a strike of students and a majority of the faculty. In an act of quintessential folly, they symbolized their protest by marching off campus, leaving the institution in the hands of a minority of conservative professors eager to follow the directives of a conservative seminary board. The champions of tradition had won the field without having to convict a single professor of heresy.

Since that time the Lutheran Church—Missouri Synod has been unswerving in its reactionary course. It has suffered a considerable brain drain, as many men and women of talent in the institutional structures of the synod have sought more congenial environments elsewhere. True academic freedom does not exist in its colleges and seminaries. The synod has endured considerable financial problems, although it is arguable whether they are due to doctrinal strife. Jacob Preus has retired from the synodical presidency; he has been succeeded by Ralph Bohlmann, a conservative professor who had replaced John Tietjen as president of Concordia Seminary. In short, the history of the Lutheran Church—Missouri Synod since 1965 seems to validate the notion that its history as an immigrant institution, coupled with the unique character of its leadership from Stephan and the Saxons to Preus and the traditionalists, helps to explain its enduring conservatism.

NOTES

1. Oscar Handlin, *The Uprooted: The Epic Story of the Great Migrations that Made the American People* (New York: Grosset and Dunlap, 1951). See especially chapter 5, "Religion as a Way of Life."

2. Ibid., 117–43.

3. H. Richard Niebuhr, *The Social Sources of Denominationalism* (1929; reprint, New York: Meridian Books, 1957), 200–235.

4. Walter O. Forster, *Zion on the Mississippi* (St. Louis: Concordia, 1953), 540–63.

5. Ibid., 278–304, and 390–534; Carl S. Mundinger, *Government in the Missouri Synod* (St. Louis: Concordia, 1947), 163–219.

6. Fred W. Meuser, *The Formation of the American Lutheran Church* (Columbus, Ohio: Wartburg Press, 1958), 37.

7. August C. Stellhorn, *Schools of the Lutheran Church—Missouri Synod* (St. Louis: Concordia, 1963) offers much material on the early schools of the church.

8. Quoted in Otto F. Hattstaedt, *History of the Southern Wisconsin District of the Evangelical Lutheran Synod of Missouri, Ohio, and Other States* (Madison: Wisconsin Historical Record Survey, 1941), 74.

9. See Niebuhr, *Social Sources*, 211–12.

10. Stellhorn provides an account of the language problem in his *Schools of the Lutheran Church—Missouri Synod.*

11. Marcus Lee Hansen, *The Immigrant in American History* (1940; reprint, New York: Harper Torchbooks, 1964), 136–37.

12. Niebuhr, *Social Sources*, 221.

13. Meuser, *Formation of the American Lutheran Church*, 37.

14. Hattstaedt, *History of the Southern Wisconsin District*, 44.

15. Niebuhr, *Social Sources*, 222.

16. Forster, *Zion on the Mississippi*, 349–51. See pp. 267–77 for nativist hostility in St. Louis during the 1840s.

17. Hansen, *The Immigrant in American History*, 114. In general, see chapter 5, "Immigration and Puritanism."

18. "Thesen über das Halten und den Besuch von Trinkhallen Saloons von seiten der Glieder einer christlichen Gemeinde," Missouri Synod, Northwestern District, *Proceedings* (1875), 48–61; Hattstaedt, *History of the Southern Wisconsin District*, 37. In 1883 in the convention of the Eastern District of the Missouri Synod, C. Frincke, Jr., treated the topic: "Kann ein Christ mit gutem Gewissen einen Saloon halten?" He defined a saloon and then argued that operating a saloon belonged in the realm of adiaphora. God's Word did not forbid the drinking of liquor. However, he continued, even though operating a saloon is not sinful, it might become sinful through other concomitant circumstances. Missouri Synod, Eastern District, *Proceedings* (1883), 45–49.

19. Hansen, *The Immigrant in American History*, 115–16.

20. Arthur C. Repp, "Concordia Historical Institute and Its Educational Role in the Church," *Concordia Historical Institute Quarterly* 37 (July 1964): 39.

21. Hansen, *The Immigrant in American History*, 134–35.

The German-American Alliance in Nebraska, 1910–17

2

It is a curious fact that even though America is a nation of immigrants, the development and influence of non-English-speaking immigrant groups and their institutions have been largely ignored in our national and state histories. Through the decades, the number of newcomers has been immense and their political and sociocultural impact great. In Nebraska, for example, approximately forty percent of the total population in 1910 was of foreign stock.[1] Even though these people participated intelligently and extensively in the political and economic affairs of the state, their group goals, interests, and institutions remain unassessed and frequently misunderstood.

Ever since the frontier of settlement swept across the Great Plains, the largest single ethnic group in Nebraska has been German. In 1910 approximately 20 percent of the state's inhabitants, or about one-half of all the foreign-born and their children, were of German origin. Although the largest proportion of them lived in rural areas, especially in the northeastern part of the state, significant numbers were also found in Omaha, Lincoln, and in smaller cities such as Grand Island, Columbus, Norfolk, and Nebraska City.[2] In their adjustment to the new and unfamiliar American way of life, German immigrants, like other ethnic groups, were drawn together by their common language, heritage, and problems. Gradually they became aware of themselves as a cultural minority with a surprising measure of potential power in economic, political, and sociocultural matters.

Thus the immigrants went about building a society of their own within American society. Its strength was drawn largely from the number and effectiveness of the institutions, both formal and informal, that they created. In the rural areas, the churches were easily the most important. In the cities, however, the Germans successfully established a variety of social, cultural, economic, and political organizations.[3] One of the most important of these, one which effectively combined political and cultural goals, was the German-American Alliance of Nebraska, founded in 1910 as a branch of the National German-American Alliance. Representing as many as one hundred lodges, singing societies, and other organizations, the Nebraska Alliance sought valiantly to unify the German community in the state and to speak for it, particularly in politics.

It was not an easy task. Despite the centripetal force of language and culture, the Germans were not at all as solid a block as native Americans perceived them to be. Roman Catholics in particular formed a subgroup with their own loyalties, organizations, and publications. Moreover, the Lutherans and other Protestant groups each formed their separate camps. Taken together, these three elements, which were strongest in rural areas, became known as *Kirchendeutsche*. They were commonly hostile, not only to each other, but to a fourth group, the so-called *Vereinsdeutsche*, whose associations were primarily with societies and clubs. Usually urban dwellers, the latter customarily drew heavily on German immigrants who were culturally rather than religiously oriented.[4] "Possessed by an almost missionary eagerness to propagate and spread their particular Weltanschauung," Heinz Kloss has observed, "[they] looked upon Americans as spiritually dormant worshippers of the golden calf. They looked upon themselves and others of German stock as the leaven that would bring about the spiritual awakening and maturing of the Yankee loaf."[5] Each of the groups tended to be suspicious of the others and cooperation was rarely effected among them.

The founders of the German-American Alliance of Nebraska were largely from the liberal, more secularly minded segment of the German community. Prominent among them were Dr. Hermann Gerhard of Lincoln, a propagandist and founder of a German colony in Texas; Christian A. Sommer of Lincoln, advertising manager of the *Lincoln Freie Presse* and member of the Unitarian church; Fred Volpp of Scribner, a banker, Democratic state senator, and member of several lodges; John Mattes, Jr., of Nebraska City, a long-time Democratic member of the state legislature who was associated with both brewing interests and the German-language press; and Carl Rohde of Columbus, a Republican, a Lutheran, and a member of several lodges who was engaged in the liquor business.[6] But the organizing genius and guiding spirit of the Nebraska Alliance was its first and only president, Valentin J. Peter of Omaha.

Born in Bavaria in 1875, Val Peter came to America at fourteen years of age. Very early in life he became associated with the German-American newspaper business in Peoria and Rock Island, Illinois. In 1907 he moved to Nebraska, became the publisher and editor of the *Omaha Tribüne*, consolidated it with several other German-language newspapers of the state, and converted it into a widely circulated and influential daily. A member of the Elks and a variety of German social and benevolent organizations, Peter was also a devoted member of the Roman Catholic church.[7] The German-American Alliance of Nebraska, largely a product of his determined efforts, naturally was given extensive publicity in his newspaper.

The bond between the Nebraska organization and its parent, the National German-American Alliance, was close. Founded in 1901 in Philadelphia by Dr. Charles J. Hexamer, the *Nationalbund*, as it was often called, was originally established to further cultural objectives. It was part of a surge in organizational strength and expansion that characterized the German ethnic community in America during the two or three decades preceding World War I. Very quickly, however, the national organization acquired a reputation as being interested in little else than opposition to the prohibition movement. It was transformed into an ethnically based counterorganization to the Anti-Saloon League. When prohibition threatened a certain state or locality, the National Alliance would take steps to organize state and local branches, which in turn became politically active, attempting to form and lead public opinion, approving candidates for public offices, and marshalling "the German vote" in behalf of the antiprohibition cause.[8]

So it was also in Nebraska, where prohibition had a venerable history as a political issue. Throughout the 1880s and climaxing in the election of 1890 when a prohibition amendment to the state constitution appeared on the ballot, prohibition had been a divisive force, chiefly on an ethnoreligious basis.[9] The basic regulatory law was still the Slocumb Act, passed in 1881, which combined local option with high license fees. Although the enemies of prohibition had fought the Slocumb law bitterly when it was enacted, they were now its champions, even though more than half the state had voted itself dry by 1909.[10] Having lain dormant as a major political issue since its defeat in 1890, prohibition was reintroduced in 1907 during the progressive administration of Republican Governor George L. Sheldon, who unsuccessfully pushed for a county option law to replace the local option provision of the Slocumb Act. By shifting the option from incorporated cities and villages to the county, prohibition was presumably made easier because rural voters could participate in making the decision. Sheldon's support for county option unquestionably contributed to his defeat in 1908 by the Democratic candidate, Ashton C. Shallenberger, who enjoyed widespread support among German and Bohemian voters.[11]

During Shallenberger's administration, two developments served to complicate the situation for the Democrats. First, Governor Shallenberger chose to sign a bill that forbade the sale of alcoholic beverages after eight o'clock in the evening. Having thereby alienated his German support, he subsequently declared himself to be in favor of a county option bill.[12] The second major development was that prohibition gained an influential adherent in the person of William Jennings Bryan, who had just failed for the third time to win the presidency of the United States. For two decades

Bryan had benefited from German support even though he had always been personally dry. Now, however, he suddenly became "the arch enemy of *das Deutschtum.*"[13] In the past there had never been much question about where the Democratic party in Nebraska stood on the question of prohibition. But with the defection of Shallenberger and Bryan, the historic identification of the Democracy with "personal liberty" and as the friend of the immigrant was placed in jeopardy. By May 1910, it was obvious to the leaders of the German community that immediate and drastic steps had to be taken if their group interests were to be preserved. The result was a remarkable feat of organization, achieved in time for the primary election in August and the general election in November 1910. During those months, the Nebraska branch of the National German-American Alliance was conceived, born, and put to work.

Correspondence between Val Peter and Dr. Hexamer of the *National-bund* ensued. At Peter's request, Hexamer invited the Omaha Plattdeutscher Verein to assume leadership in the organization of a state branch.[14] The first step was to create an alliance of the German societies of Omaha and its vicinity. This was accomplished on May 29, 1910, when Peter was chosen president of the new Centralsverband of Omaha. This organization, in turn, passed a resolution calling for the founding of a statewide alliance during the great German music festival that was scheduled for the latter part of July.[15] Thus at each step the base for the state alliance was broadened. As thousands of German citizens of Nebraska converged upon Omaha for the *Sängerfest*, they would be exposed to the goals and objectives of the German-American Alliance. More than that, the plan permitted distinctly political goals to be cloaked in German culture.[16]

While the music festival dominated the scene in Omaha and won effusive praise in the English-language press,[17] the German-American Alliance of Nebraska was quietly organized on July 20, 1910. One hundred and fourteen delegates representing fifty-four organizations were present. Val Peter was duly elected president, although there was some sentiment in favor of Dr. Hermann Gerhard of Lincoln, who then became first vice president. John Mattes was chosen corresponding secretary, and Sen. Fred Volpp became treasurer.[18] With the exception of Gerhard, each held his office throughout the life of the Nebraska Alliance.

As an active churchman, Peter was interested in bringing the *Kirchendeutsche* also into the fold. Despite repeated invitations, however, the churches tended to keep their distance. No more than two or three church organizations participated. On the other hand, the presence of the Bier Brauer Unterstützungsverein[19] was perhaps more significant. Generally the membership of the Nebraska Alliance came from culturally oriented societies, singing groups, and farmer organizations. Approximately one-third of the membership came from German lodges affiliated with the Order of the Sons of Hermann. The close bond between the two is revealed by the fact that several of the new officers of the Nebraska Alliance were also leaders in the state organization of the Sons of Hermann.[20]

After adopting several resolutions, including one that severely condemned county option and prohibition generally, the Alliance swung into action.[21] A mere three weeks separated the organizational meeting from the primary election slated for August 16, 1910. Every effort had to be made to prevent Governor Shallenberger's renomination and to secure the election of Mayor James C. Dahlman of Omaha as the Democratic candidate for governor. Dahlman was as wet a candidate as the Democrats had ever had, and as the son of German immigrants, he was especially attractive to the Alliance.[22] United States Representative Gilbert Hitchcock, the publisher of the *Omaha World-Herald*, also received enthusiastic endorsement. As a candidate for the United States Senate, Hitchcock was much preferred over Bryan's candidate, Richard Metcalfe. Both Dahlman and Hitchcock wooed the German vote. While Dahlman declared himself to be "heart and soul against fanaticism and nativism (Fremdenhasz)," Hitchcock made much of his two years in Germany as a student and insisted that he had always opposed prohibition and county option.[23] Meanwhile, the Nebraska Alliance screened and approved other candidates for lesser offices on the basis of their stand on county option.

The open primary, which Nebraska had adopted in 1909, was another avenue for political action by the Alliance. Since the law permitted a voter to cast his ballot for any candidate of any party, the executive board explained to German voters in a widely distributed statement how it was possible for "liberal" Republicans to fight the fanatics in their own party by voting for Dahlman and Hitchcock.[24] A great migration of wet Republicans occurred on election day, especially in Omaha, with the result that Mayor Dahlman successfully, although narrowly, defeated Governor Shallenberger for the Democratic nomination.[25]

During the next three months, the Nebraska Alliance employed a variety of tactics to achieve its political goals. It exploited German Day festivities in Lincoln, set for October 6 and 7, 1910, by scheduling its first annual convention to meet at the same time and place. It supplied visitors at the festival with "foaming liquid refreshments" as well as badges picturing Abraham Lincoln and James C. Dahlman side by side. The resolutions passed by the convention were endlessly reprinted in the German-language press. The necessity of German unity and cooperation was repeatedly emphasized in order to advance the German spirit and German liberty and to frustrate xenophobic intolerance and puritanical fanaticism. A headquarters for political action was set up in Omaha.

Several prominent members of the organization, including John Mattes and Otto Leptin, the second vice president, worked full time as campaigners, agitators, and organizers of local alliances in the smaller cities of the state. German Day festivals were organized in other communities, including Falls City and Hastings. Circulars in both the German and English languages were printed and distributed which explained the position of the Alliance and which endorsed candidates of either party who were acceptable to the Alliance. Efforts were also made to enlist the support of other ethnic groups, notably the Czechs, by organizing separate branches for them in the Personal Liberty League. Participation in the Alliance's activities by the German churches and pastors was repeatedly encouraged. Val Peter even proposed the creation of German citizens' clubs in every German settlement, especially where the local churches refused to give official support to Alliance policies.[26]

The results of the election of 1910 provided a temporary respite for the German-American Alliance in Nebraska. A majority of Democrats and/or opponents of county option were elected to the state legislature. Gilbert Hitchcock won the preferential vote for United States senator. But "Mayor Jim" Dahlman went down in defeat, a victim, perhaps, of his opponents' efforts to identify him as the tool of the liquor interests.

To say that "the German vote floated on an ocean of beer," as some have observed, or to describe the Democratic campaign of 1910 as "an assault upon the very life of our state [by] a great debauching and o'erweening brewery trust," as the new Republican governor, Chester H. Aldrich, declared in his inaugural address, is to misunderstand the immigrant mind in politics.[27] Prohibition was more than an issue to most German voters. It was the political symbol of a general clash of cultures that confronted many immigrants as they adjusted to American society. Prohibition was cut from the same cloth as Sabbatarian legislation, governmental control of German parochial schools, objections to German-language instruction in public schools, women's suffrage, initiative, referendum, or any other device that promised to smooth the path for xenophobic legislation under the aegis of reform.[28] The native American had little understanding of the importance that the mother tongue and mother culture had for immigrant psychology. Thus Governor Aldrich could dismiss "personal liberty" as a "specious and deceptive" ploy of the beer barons. But it mattered little to a German Lutheran pastor, who was possibly an abstainer himself, how much of Dahlman's campaign fund came from the breweries. The important thing for him was that prohibition was a type of legislation that threatened the German life-style and value system. His parish school, he had ample reason to suspect, could be next on the nativistic reformer's list.

Shortly after the new legislature convened in January 1911, a bill was introduced by Rep. O. H. Moody of Ansley, a Republican, that specified that every child of school age was required to attend a public school at least three months of every year unless he attended a private or parochial school in which instruction was in English. At the same time, the bill required parochial and private schools to keep records of attendance and to supply monthly reports to the county superintendents of schools. Represented by John Mattes, the German-American Alliance lobbied effectively against the bill. Moreover, officials of the Lutheran and Catholic churches testified against it at an open hearing. In the end, the legislative committee to which the bill had been assigned voted almost unanimously to table it.[29] For the moment the threat had passed; but it reminded Germans of the unsuccessful attack on their schools in 1890, and it presaged the bitter fight of the post–World War I era when defenders of parochial school education went the full route to the United States Supreme Court to protect their rights.[30]

In 1912 the political activity of the German-American Alliance in Nebraska was relaxed compared to the contest of two years earlier. It gave full support to the gubernatorial candidacy of Democrat John Morehead, partially because his opponent, the Republican incumbent Chester H. Aldrich, was a leader of the "fanatical faction" of his party, as Val Peter described it. The initiative and referendum had been endorsed by both parties and therefore was sure to become law. The Germans were highly suspicious of these measures because they fully expected the prohibitionists to convert them into powerful weapons of intolerance.[31] According to Val Peter, the only recourse was a systematic program of political education. If local *Vereine* would conduct seminars for the discussion of issues and voting, he asserted, the threat posed by the initiative and referendum could be met.[32] When the ballots were counted in 1912, John Morehead was victorious. Moreover, friends of "personal liberty," mostly Democrats, were in control of both houses of the legislature.[33]

Although politics dominated the first years of the Nebraska Alliance, its founders had a much broader conception of what its activities ought to have been. They were aggressively conscious of their cultural heritage, and they wished to preserve it and promulgate it in dynamic ways. At the same time, they were totally loyal to America and its political institutions. They wished to assist and to lead their fellow German-Americans to higher levels of citizenship and civic responsibility.[34] Convinced that their maintenance of German language and culture was not incompatible with being thoroughly American in outlook, they epitomized their sentiments in the expression "Germania our Mother, Columbia our Bride."[35]

It was not necessary, they believed, for a man to forsake his mother in order to be loyal to his bride.

The Alliance pursued a variety of projects that were not directly related to politics. Among these was a sustained effort in behalf of forestation in the Sand Hills of Nebraska. Originally motivated by a desire to attract German immigrants to settle on unsold school lands, the project was sparked by Carl Rohde of Columbus. Rohde and his committee persuaded the legislature to pass a resolution authorizing the governor to appoint a commission to investigate the feasibility of forestation and to submit a comprehensive plan of action to the legislature.[36] Rohde was subsequently appointed chairman of the commission. Hampered by the legislature's failure to appropriate funds, the commission relied on the financial assistance of the Alliance. Finally, when the commission submitted its plan in 1917, the legislature was no longer interested. The exigencies of war caused the project to fade and die.[37]

Perhaps the most active arm of the Nebraska Alliance was its school committee, headed by Christian A. Sommer of Lincoln. During the years preceding American entry into World War I, Sommer worked ceaselessly for German language maintenance. He succeeded in having high-quality German literature placed in public libraries. He pressured the finance committee of the legislature to recommend a $1,000 increase in the appropriation for the State Traveling Library so that additional German and other foreign language books could be circulated. Sommer also propagandized the Alliance members to build their home libraries of German literature and got himself appointed as a member of the State Library Commission by Gov. John Morehead. Other activities of the school committee included efforts to initiate and improve German-language instruction in the public schools of the state. The introduction of new textbooks was encouraged, and stipends were offered for teachers attending a seminar in Milwaukee sponsored by the National German-American Alliance.[38]

But Sommer's most impressive accomplishment came with the passage of the Mockett law in 1913. This legislation, a mild reflection of similar laws enacted years earlier in Indiana, Kansas, and other states,[39] required authorities to inaugurate foreign language instruction on an elective basis in urban schools if the parents or guardians of fifty pupils above the fourth grade requested it. Not more than five hours each week and not less than one period per day was to be devoted to the language instruction.[40]

Sommer had planned his strategy with Teutonic thoroughness. First, he courted the support of J. E. Delzell, the state superintendent of public instruction, as well as several city and county superintendents of schools. Next, he persuaded the foreign language department of the University of Nebraska, along with a conference of German teachers, to lend their aid. After legal counsel had been secured to draft a law in proper form, a brochure entitled *Der deutsche Unterricht in den öffentliche Schulen Nebraskas*[41] was prepared and distributed. Similar materials in English outlined arguments in favor of the proposed legislation. Both were sent to pastors, teachers, and editors. Sommer then proceeded to line up the support of other ethnic groups, notably the Czechs, Swedes, and Danes. Anticipating nativist opposition in the legislature, he got one of the most distinguished Anglo-American members of the House of Representatives, John H. Mockett, Jr., of Lincoln to introduce his bill. These tactics, combined with discreet lobbying, led to an easy victory in both houses. The law went into effect on July 17, 1913.[42]

Although many communities instituted German-language instruction in conformance with the Mockett law, opposition was not unexpected. The Nebraska City school board, in particular, found technicalities to justify its failure to comply with parental requests. With the aid of the Alliance, the case eventually reached the Supreme Court of Nebraska, where in 1916 the Mockett law was upheld.[43]

The German-American Alliance continued vigorously to pursue its political goals in 1914. As in previous elections, attention centered on the races for the governorship and the legislative seats. This was because the success or failure of attempts to enact prohibition, women's suffrage, or compulsory school legislation depended largely on the attitudes of the men who held these offices.

German fears regarding the new initiative law were validated in 1914 when it was used to place women's suffrage on the ballot. Inevitably the Alliance worked against it. Strongly worded resolutions condemning it were adopted in the annual convention. Women's suffrage was a degrading thing, the Germans thought, and not at all a progressive measure. To them it was a menace to the home; it threatened to take wife and mother from her proper place and make her a contestant in the political arena.[44] On election day in 1914, women's suffrage was defeated by a relatively narrow margin of ten thousand votes and John Morehead was returned to the governor's mansion for another term.

From its very beginning, the tragedy of World War I cast a pall over the Nebraska Alliance. All parades and festivities were cancelled at the annual meeting in 1914, held in Columbus shortly after hostilities had begun. A deep sympathy for *das Vaterland* was apparent as speakers frequently made references to pledges of loyalty and financial assistance to Germany. Always sensitive to public opinion, the delegates resolved to do all in their power to correct the false impression they believed the

English-language press was giving the public regarding Germany and its part in the war. Meanwhile, contributions for the German Red Cross began to flow into the Alliance treasury. Eventually they totaled more than twenty thousand dollars. Fearing an Allied monopoly of the war news, the executive committee transmitted a letter to Pres. Woodrow Wilson and Secretary of State William Jennings Bryan protesting the closing of a German short-wave radio station in the United States.[45]

As publisher of the *Omaha Tribüne*, Val Peter fed his readers a steady diet of passionate partisanship for Germany. In this he was no different from the editors of hundreds of other German-language publications in America. Motivated by deeply felt bonds of culture and kinship and by what they conceived to be elements of justice and fair play, they sought to balance the prejudices that to their minds characterized the English-language press.[46] "Both here and abroad," Peter assured the Alliance delegates in 1915, "the enemy is the same! perfidious Albion! Over there England has pressed the sword into the hands of almost all the peoples of Europe against Germany. In this country it has a servile press at its command, which uses every foul means to slander everything German and to poison the public mind."[47]

By 1915 it was apparent that an easy German victory was not in the offing and that the European conflict had become a war of attrition. German Americans accordingly focused their ethnic intensities upon the hated war loans and the shipments of arms and munitions to the Allied powers. As they drifted away from the American consensus, the members of the Nebraska Alliance fervently expressed their emotions in a pack of resolutions, all the while asserting their loyalty to America, a sentiment that, indeed, was genuine. One of these resolutions is quoted at length:

As loyal American citizens, loving our adopted country and anxious for its future, we deprecate the enormous proportions attained by our trade in arms and ammunition. We believe that this hideous and wicked traffic should be stopped by law, and we commend both Nebraska senators, and those of our representatives in Congress who supported measures to that end in the last session. The trade in arms and ammunition is directly abhorrent to all believers in the Christian code of ethics, and to all human beings born with heavenly compassion in their hearts. It is building up in this peaceful country a military industry greater and more dangerous than any that has heretofore existed in any country of Europe. That industry, rich and powerful and greedy for continued profits, will prove a dangerous influence for fastening militarism upon us here in the United States. Because the arms and munitions which we export are used to kill the brothers, cousins, and other kin of millions of American citizens, the trade is creating bitter division along racial lines among our own people and threatening the homogeneity of citizenship which is essential to our nation's future greatness. Because it will be used to wipe out lives and property and to ruin the prosperity of our best customers, this commerce threatens our own future prosperity. Our profits lie in Europe's peace. Our security is linked with Europe's security. We feel it is our duty to God and to a Christian civilization to do nothing to prolong this frightful war and everything in our power to shorten it. In the presence of the awful tragedy in which the lands of our forefathers are plunged—a tragedy which can only mitigate—we brand as base and abhorrent the arguments that are urged to justify our active aid in prolonging and making more murderous and more destructive this appalling war.[48]

The position of the Nebraska Alliance on the European war remained largely unchanged during 1916. The partisanship of the *Omaha Tribüne* for the German cause continued unabated or, perhaps, more shrill than before. Val Peter regularly published chauvinistic editorials ground out by the erstwhile first vice president of the Alliance, Dr. Hermann Gerhard, who mercilessly castigated President Wilson for his allegedly pro-Allied policies. Insisting that American behavior was anything but neutral, the Alliance cleverly identified its position with that of the founding fathers of the Republic, who shunned all entangling alliances and presumably pursued a policy of strict neutrality. Demands were made for a policy that defended American lives and American interests with equal firmness and justice for both sides. Better protection was needed, the Alliance asserted, for American mail, for American commerce in noncontraband commodities, and for American merchants discriminated against by blacklists.[49]

As anti-German sentiment built up during 1916, the Alliance seemed to broaden its range of interest. Among the resolutions passed at the annual convention were several that were in no way related to traditional German-American interests. Motions favoring the construction of an adequate highway system, the erection of a new state capitol, improvement in the salaries of public school teachers, and the establishment of local lending libraries were all supported by the delegates.[50] Perhaps these resolutions were intended to screen the Alliance's unpopular stands on neutrality, war loans, munitions, and prohibition.

Perhaps the most significant development for the Alliance in 1916 was the new level of cooperation and participation that the *Kirchendeutsche* gave its activities and endeavors.[51] The impending crisis of war with the fatherland, together with portents of defeat in domestic political matters, served to unite the Nebraska Germans as never before. Val Peter had never relaxed his efforts to bring the church Germans into the Alliance. In 1916 he sent personal representatives to the conventions of the Evangelical Synod of North America and the Iowa Synod Lutherans. Both groups responded by sending official delegations to the 1916 convention of the Alliance. Other pastors also accepted special invitations to attend. All of them, ministers and priests, were made honorary members of the Alliance and were granted full rights of speaking and voting in the convention.[52]

The last great political effort of the Nebraska Alliance was made in 1916, when prohibition once more dominated state politics. Under Bryan's leadership, the dry faction within the Democratic party experienced continued growth. Keith Neville, a young, wealthy cattleman new to politics, was advanced as an acceptably wet candidate to head off the gubernatorial ambitions of Charles W. Bryan, the younger brother of the Great Commoner. Along with Senator Hitchcock and Edgar Howard, the candidate for lieutenant governor, Neville received strong backing from the German-American Alliance. Even though the Democrats won the governor's chair and swept both houses of the legislature in the November election, German hopes were dashed as the prohibition amendment won a surprisingly large majority of votes.[53]

The Nebraska Alliance endorsed no presidential candidate in 1916, disillusioned as it was with President Wilson's foreign policy. Dr. Hexamer of the national organization, however, came out for the Republican candidate, Charles Evans Hughes, as did Val Peter in the *Omaha Tribüne*. Not unexpectedly, the heavily German counties of northeastern Nebraska, traditionally Democratic strongholds, followed through with majorities for Hughes.[54]

The election of 1916 ushered in a series of events that was nothing less than traumatic for the German-American Alliance. All of the things it had fought for since 1910 were lost during the months that followed. Prohibition had been first. That it became law without the aid of women's suffrage was no comfort. Next came the declaration of war against *das Vaterland* on April 6, 1917. Its impact upon the spirit of the German community was incalculable. Yet within the month, the Nebraska legislature enacted the law to implement the prohibition amendment.[55] Shortly thereafter it created the Nebraska State Council of Defense.[56] Fortunately, the Germans could not know at that time the indignities that awaited them under that agency's authority.[57] Even the German books that Christian Sommer and his committee had placed in the State Traveling Library became the subject of an investigation by the legislature. Indeed, Sommer was forced to resign his post on the State Library Commission.[58]

And while an attack on the Mockett law was repulsed by the legislature of 1917,[59] Governor Neville requested its repeal in a special session called for March 26, 1918. In his message to the legislature, Neville branded it "vicious, undemocratic, and un-American."[60] The Senate, presided over by the Alliance's John Mattes, dutifully acquiesced in a unanimous vote, as the House also concurred, eighty-two to eleven.[61] All this, ironically enough, was at the hands of a governor whose election the German-American Alliance had supported and a legislature that was decidedly Democratic in composition.

In the wave of intolerance for all things German that swept across the land in the wake of war, it was inevitable that the German-American Alliance of Nebraska died quietly and unlamented. The loyalty of German citizens throughout the state naturally was questioned. It could not have been otherwise, considering the incessant defense of Germany by editors, clergymen, and other leaders of the ethnic community. Native-born Americans, government officials or members of the State Council of Defense could not be expected to have had a genuine understanding of the role of immigrant language and culture in our society. Yet for the majority of the members of the German-American Alliance, German ethnicity was of a traditional, nonideological character. It was a part of the countless, mindless acts of everyday life. It was emotional, not rational. Germany was a symbol of spiritual and cultural values, not of specific nationalist or ideological goals of the German imperial government.[62] Indeed, many of the Germans had emigrated to America in order to escape them. Thus American ethnic minority groups, Germans in particular, had historically been received with tolerance and good humor. Frictions and misunderstandings were both expected and overlooked. The German-American Alliance could be founded in Nebraska and be allowed to participate freely and effectively in the political affairs of the state. Many native Nebraskans did not like it, but there were few who were prepared to deny the Germans the right to so participate.

But with the outbreak of war in 1914, the circumstances began to change. Native Americans began to perceive an ideological character in the activities of the Alliance, the editors of the German-language press, or the Lutherans with their parish schools. The fact that this perception was largely in error made no difference. Emotional attachment for Germany increasingly seemed incompatible with loyalty to the United States of America. Inevitably the Alliance, essentially an institution for political action, met its demise. Whatever value it had had as an agency to mitigate the process whereby German immigrants could be absorbed into American society had disappeared, like water in sand.

NOTES

1. Nebraska State Planning Board, *Nebraska's Population: A Preliminary Report* (Nebraska State Planning Board, December 15, 1937), 16–18.

2. In Douglas County, which includes Omaha, 57.4 percent of all males of voting age were of foreign stock in 1910; in Lancaster County, which includes Lincoln and where native American influence was much more apparent, the figure dropped to 25.1 percent. See U.S. Bureau of the Census, *Thirteenth Census . . . 1910*, 3: 605–11.

3. Frederick C. Luebke, *Immigrants and Politics: The Germans of Nebraska, 1880–1900* (Lincoln: Univ. of Nebraska Press, 1969), chaps. 2 and 3.

4. Heinz Kloss, *Um die Einigung des Deutschamerikanertums* (Berlin: Volk und Reich Verlag, 1937), 31–35.

5. Heinz Kloss, "German-American Language Maintenance Efforts," in *Language Loyalty in the United States*, ed. Joshua Fishman (The Hague: Mouton, 1966), 227.

6. *Omaha Tribüne*, August 24, 1911; *Lincoln Star*, October 9, 1954; W. H. Buss and Thomas Osterman, *History of Dodge and Washington Counties, and Their People* (Chicago: The American Historical Society, 1921), 2: 490; *The Nebraska Blue Book and Historical Register, 1918* (Lincoln, 1918), 267; G. W. Phillips, ed., *Past and Present of Platte County, Nebraska* (Chicago: S. J. Clarke, 1915), 2: 208.

7. Ruth August, "Val J. Peter, Publisher," *American-German Review* 28 (October–November, 1960): 16–18; Arthur C. Wakeley, *Omaha: The Gate City and Douglas County, Nebraska* (Chicago: S. J. Clarke, 1917), 2: 860.

8. Clifton J. Child, *The German-Americans in Politics, 1914–1917* (Madison: Univ. of Wisconsin Press, 1939), 2–14; Kloss, "German-American Language Maintenance Efforts," 231.

9. Luebke, *Immigrants and Politics*, 141–50.

10. Addison E. Sheldon, *Nebraska, The Land and the People*, 3 vols. (Chicago: Lewis Publishing, 1931), 1: 843.

11. James C. Olson, *History of Nebraska* (Lincoln: Univ. of Nebraska Press, 1955), 253; Sheldon, *Nebraska*, 1: 844.

12. *Omaha Tribüne*, July 28, 1910.

13. Ibid., May 19, 1910. Wildly anti-Bryan articles became standard fare for the German readers of the *Tribüne* during May, June, and July 1910.

14. William H. Werkmeister, "Der deutsche Staatsverband" (unpublished typewritten Ms., Werkmeister Collection, Nebraska State Historical Society), 2; *Omaha Tribüne*, May 19, 1910. Werkmeister's account is based upon a publication by the executive committee in 1914. It includes a "Kurze Geschichte seiner Gründung und Entwicklung" as well as the reports of committees, resolutions, officers, and financial reports for the first four conventions of the organization. It was supplemented by a similar publication in December 1915. Both pamphlets are in the Werkmeister Collection.

15. *Omaha Tribüne*, May 26, 1910, and June 2, 1910.

16. There is no doubt that, in its inception, the political objectives of the

Alliance were paramount. Although there was much talk about cultural goals, the testimony of Peter and others is explicit (see *Omaha Tribüne*, May 26, 1910, and August 11, 1910; *Lincoln Star*, October 7, 1910.

17. *Morning World-Herald*, July 24, 1910; *Omaha Bee*, July 20 and 24, 1910.

18. *Omaha Tribüne*, July 28, 1910; *World-Herald*, July 22, 1910.

19. Brewers' Benefit Association.

20. *Omaha Tribüne*, July 28, 1910, and May 19 and 26, 1910. Mattes, Volpp, and Rohde were all officers of the Sons of Hermann.

21. *Omaha Tribüne*, July 28, 1910.

22. Ibid., September 29, 1910.

23. Ibid., August 4 and 11, 1910.

24. Ibid., August 11, 1910, see also July 28, 1910; *Lincoln Star*, October 7, 1910.

25. Sheldon, *Nebraska*, 1: 848.

26. *Omaha Tribüne*, September 8 and 15, 1910, and October 6, 13, 20, and 27, 1910; *Lincoln Star*, October 6 and 7, 1910; *World-Herald*, October 8, 1910. Meanwhile the state convention of the Baptist church, meeting in Omaha at the same time, passed a resolution condemning "Dahlmanism," which, the Baptists asserted, "opposes the most sacred interests of morality and public order. Its unconcealed friendliness for the elements of vice and crime renders Dahlmanism a menace to public morals" (*Omaha Bee*, October 8, 1910).

27. Carl Wittke, *The German-Language Press in America* (Lexington: Univ. of Kentucky Press, 1957), 164; Sheldon, *Nebraska*, 1: 852.

28. *Grand Island Daily Independent*, August 12, 1911; *Omaha Tribüne*, August 17, 1911.

29. *House Roll No. 116, Legislature of Nebraska, Thirty-Second Session, 1911; Omaha Tribüne*, February 2, 1911, and August 17, 1911; *Grand Island Daily Independent*, August 12, 1911; *Proceedings of the Thirty-Second Session of the Nebraska House of Representatives, 1911* (House Journal), 83, 90, and 200.

30. For the fight in 1890, see Luebke, *Immigrants and Politics*, 143; for the later struggle, see Jack W. Rodgers, "The Foreign Language Issue in Nebraska, 1918–1923," *Nebraska History* 39 (March 1958): 1–22.

31. Since women's suffrage, initiative, and referendum were ordinarily categorized as progressive measures and because German voters normally opposed them, the latter have frequently been identified as conservatives. This is at best a half-truth, for the Germans generally gave enthusiastic support to progressive legislation in social and economic matters that did not impinge upon cultural and religious concerns.

32. *Wöchentliche Omaha Tribüne*, August 12, 1912.

33. Sheldon, *Nebraska*, 1: 878–80.

34. Compare Val Peter's annual report in 1913. *Lincoln Star*, October 16, 1913.

35. *Omaha Bee*, October 2, 1913; Kloss, "German-American Language Maintenance Efforts," 229.

36. *Laws of Nebraska, 1913,* p. 138–39.

37. Werkmeister, "Der deutsche Staatsverband," 9–11; *Wöchentliche Omaha Tribüne,* October 14, 1915, and September 14, 1916; *Fremont Tri-Weekly Tribune,* August 27, 1912; *Columbus Telegram,* August 28, 1914.

38. Werkmeister, "Der deutsche Staatsverband," 14–16; *Omaha Tribüne,* August 24, 1911; *Wöchentliche Omaha Tribüne,* August 29, 1912, May 20, 1916, and September 21, 1916; *Omaha Bee,* October 7, 1915.

39. Kloss, "German-American Language Maintenance Efforts," 235–36.

40. *Laws of Nebraska, 1913,* 107.

41. *German Instruction in the Public Schools of Nebraska,* Werkmeister Collection.

42. *Wöchentliche Omaha Tribüne,* August 29, 1913, and October 23, 1913. The vote in the House of Representatives was 78 to 17; the Senate was unanimously in favor of the bill. Mockett had been Speaker of the House in 1903. A Mason and a Presbyterian, he had been a leader in the fight for county option (see *Nebraska Blue Book and Historical Register, 1915,* 432).

43. *State, ex. rel. Charles Thayer v. School District of Nebraska City, Reports of Cases in the Nebraska State Supreme Court,* XCIX (1916), 338–48.

44. *Columbus Telegram,* August 28, 1914; *Wöchentliche Omaha Tribüne,* August 27, 1914; see also *Lincoln Star,* October 15, 1913.

45. *Omaha Bee,* August 27, 1914; *Wöchentliche Omaha Tribüne,* August 27, 1914; *World-Herald,* October 7, 1915.

46. Wittke, *German-Language Press,* 238–42.

47. *Wöchentliche Omaha Tribüne,* October 7, 1915.

48. *Omaha Bee,* October 7, 1915; the *Bee's* transcription omitted a few sentences from the original resolution, which I have supplied and translated from German sources: *Wöchentliche Omaha Tribüne,* October 14, 1915; Werkmeister, "Der deutsche Staatsverband," 18 ff.

49. *Grand Island Daily Independent,* September 14, 1916: This issue contains English translations of all the resolutions passed at the seventh and last convention of the Alliance, which was held in Grand Island, September 13 and 14, 1916; see also *Omaha Bee,* September 15, 1916.

50. *Grand Island Daily Independent,* September 14, 1916; *Omaha World-Herald,* September 15, 1916; Werkmeister, "Der deutsche Staatsverband," 21 and 25.

51. This action paralleled similar efforts by the National German-American Alliance; see Child, *The German-Americans in Politics,* 122–28.

52. *Wöchentliche Omaha Tribüne,* September 14, 1916.

53. Among the victors was the secretary of the Nebraska Alliance, John Mattes of Nebraska City, who was reelected to his seat in the state senate. Despite his unpopular views on prohibition, women's suffrage, the war, and the Mockett Act, his peers returned him to the office of president *pro tem,* to which he had first been elected in 1915. The vote in favor of the prohibition amendment was 146,574 to 117,532 (Sheldon, *Nebraska,* 1: 913).

54. *Wöchentliche Omaha Tribüne,* September 14 and 21, 1916; Sheldon, *Nebraska,* 1: 910–11.

55. *Laws of Nebraska, 1917*, 425–51.

56. Ibid., 489–92.

57. Robert N. Manley, "The Nebraska State Council of Defense: Loyalty Programs and Politics during World War I" (M.A. thesis, University of Nebraska-Lincoln, 1959); Frederick C. Luebke, "Superpatriotism in World War I: The Experience of a Lutheran Pastor," *Concordia Historical Institute Quarterly* 41 (February 1968): 3–11.

58. Werkmeister, "Der deutsche Staatsverband," 16.

59. *Proceedings of the Thirty-Fifth Session of the Senate of the State of Nebraska, 1917* (Senate Journal), 852.

60. *Senate and House Journals of the Legislature of the State of Nebraska, Thirty-Sixth (Special) Session, 1918*, 38.

61. Ibid., 59 and 136.

62. Compare Joshua Fishman, "The Historical and Social Contexts of an Inquiry into Language Maintenance Efforts," in *Language Loyalty*, ed. Fishman, 27.

Legal Restrictions on Foreign Languages in the Great Plains States, 1917–23   3

A major effect of World War I on American social history was that it focused attention on the nation's apparent difficulty in assimilating the millions of immigrants and their children who had streamed to the United States during the preceding two decades. The national mood, darkened by fears and resentments of long standing and deepened by systematic wartime propaganda, favored the adoption of stringent laws limiting the use of foreign languages, especially in the schools. During the war itself, restrictions were usually extralegal and often the consequences of intense social pressure recklessly applied. After the war, however, many state legislatures enacted measures that were highly restrictive. The denouement of the movement came in 1923 when the United States Supreme Court declared one of these laws, Nebraska's Siman Act, to be unconstitutional.

Laws regulating the use of languages in the United States evolved in the latter half of the nineteenth century. Before then English was so preponderant in usage that its official adoption seemed superfluous in most states. Louisiana, which became a state in 1812, was an early exception because of its large French-speaking population. After the Civil War, when the number of non-English-speaking immigrants increased greatly, many states passed laws regulating the publication of legal notices in languages other than English. These were generally permissive rather than restrictive. Similarly, a few states legalized the practice of conducting public school in languages other than English. Such laws usually legitimized what was happening informally. When the population of a school district was solidly German, which was often the case in those years, the locally elected school board was likely to hire a German teacher who would instruct the children in the German language, or in both German and English, irrespective of what the statutory provision might have been. Thus a Kansas law of 1867 permitted instruction in the German language when "freeholders representing fifty pupils" demanded it. Although German was specified in some laws, the provisions usually applied to all foreign tongues, even though German Americans were nearly always responsible for the enactments and were their chief beneficiary.[1]

The mere passage of such laws invigorated opposition among guardians of Anglo-American traditions who insisted that English be the language of instruction in the public schools. California was the first to shift to this ground. Kansas followed in 1876, and three years later the Dakota territorial legislature directed that English be used exclusively in its schools. By 1890 the language issue dominated political debate in Wisconsin, where the famous Bennett law of 1889 made attendance in public or private schools compulsory for children and defined a school as one in which the common subjects were taught in the English language. Similar legislation was enacted in Illinois. Opposition in Catholic and German Lutheran quarters was massive and effective; in both states the restrictive laws were repealed in the early 1890s. Nevertheless, the trend continued elsewhere. In 1897 an Iowa law provided that all instruction in the public schools was to be in English, except in the teaching of foreign languages, and Louisiana specified in its constitution of 1898 that English was to be the language of its schools, save in its French districts.[2]

A fairly consistent pattern of legislation emerged during the decade before World War I, as European immigration reached its highest levels in the nation's history. At least seven states, including Texas (1905), Montana (1907), and Colorado (1908), obliged teachers to use English exclusively in their instruction. When Oklahoma and New Mexico were admitted as states in 1907 and 1912, English-language provisions were written into their constitutions, although in the latter case the needs of the large Spanish-speaking population were recognized. Other states again tied instruction in English to compulsory attendance and to textbook laws. None of these measures prohibited the teaching of foreign languages as subjects, since they were aimed primarily at the use of foreign languages as media of instruction.[3]

Support for laws specifying English as the language of instruction in the public schools often came from persons who lacked confidence in the nation's assimilative powers. They were eager to support any number of programs that promised to Americanize the immigrant. Too many immigrants had come in too short a time, they thought. In 1910, when the total population of the United States was 92 million, 23 percent of the nearly 13 million foreign-born persons ten years of age and over were unable to speak English.[4]

Additional support for restriction came from champions of public school education who saw private and parochial schools as obstacles to their improvement programs. Parents who objected to reform measures, they argued, could always withdraw their children and enroll them in private church schools. One-room parochial schools with pastors as teachers and with much instruction in a foreign language were not uncommon in the Great Plains states during the prewar years. Of all the ethnoreligious groups, the German Lutherans were most deeply committed to this kind of education and were therefore most frequently criticized for the inadequacies, such as they were, of their schools. Naturally, they felt threatened by the movement to specify English as the language of instruction, believing that laws restricting their own schools were next on the agenda, as they had been in Wisconsin and Illinois in 1889. They feared similar legislation in North Dakota, where in 1910 and 1920 bills were introduced to restrict instruction to English in all schools, public and private, and in all subjects except religion. Determined opposition from immigrant churches contributed to the defeat of both these bills. In Wisconsin in 1912 another bill, denounced as a "second Bennett law," which aimed to improve the quality of education in parochial schools, was also defeated.[5]

While the movement for restriction seemed to be the dominant theme during this period, counterpoint of a different spirit could also be heard. Several states enacted laws that specifically authorized public school instruction in a non-English tongue, usually at the behest of well-organized ethnic associations of nonreligious character. For example, Colorado in 1908 permitted German or Spanish to be taught when requested by the parents or guardians of twenty or more pupils. Similarly, a Nebraska statute of 1913 required the request by parents of fifty or more pupils for instruction to be given in any modern European language for one hour per day above the fourth grade. Unlike the Colorado measure, which served the needs of pupils deficient in English-language skills, the Nebraska law was partly intended to provide English-speaking pupils with an opportunity to study a foreign language. More importantly, however, it enabled a minority of German-American citizens in a given school district to secure formal instruction for their children in the mother tongue. Known as the Mockett Act, this measure had been lobbied through the state legislature by the Nebraska branch of the National German-American Alliance. No friend of ethnic parochial schools, the Alliance aggressively sought to broaden the influence of German language and culture in the public school system.[6]

Thus by the time World War I broke out in 1914, several separate trends in the regulation of foreign languages could be discerned. First, there were laws that provided a legal basis for instruction in foreign languages as a practical measure in communities dominated by non-English-speaking people; second, there was an opposite trend that favored laws to establish English as the language of the schools; and third, some states passed laws that made foreign-language instruction possible for English-speaking pupils.

The war in Europe placed severe strains on America's heterogeneous society during the period of United States neutrality, which extended from August 1914 to March 1917. There was a natural tendency for persons of Anglo-American heritage to sympathize with Britain and her allies, just as citizens with German antecedents often felt an emotional bond with their ancestral homeland. Inevitably the events of the war intensified loyalties and diminished tolerance for cultural diversity.[7]

Many German-American citizens, especially those who advocated programs of ethnic cultural maintenance, were tempted to indulge in extravagant partisanship for Germany. They staged rallies and bazaars for the German Red Cross; they bombarded their representatives in Washington with strongly worded letters and telegrams; German-language newspapers published intemperate editorials attacking the president for what were perceived as pro-Allied policies. While the opinions of these more vocal groups were not necessarily representative of the masses of German Americans, they were believed to be by dominant Anglo-American elements of the society. In the German-American view, it was in the interest of the United States to stay out of the conflict completely. That meant no loans to belligerents on either side, no shipments of war materiel, and no travel by American citizens on the ships of nations at war. In President Wilson's opinion, such policies would ultimately work to the advantage of Germany and therefore were unneutral and un-American. In a series of public statements, Wilson questioned the patriotism of German-American leaders whose understanding of the American interest differed from his own, although he never specified them by name or even by ethnicity.

Meanwhile, British propaganda had begun to portray Germany as a land of barbarians at war against western civilization, Kaiser Wilhelm as a merciless, grasping tyrant, and his soldiers as butchers of innocent women and children. By 1915 a "hate Germany" campaign was well under way in the United States. German Americans became resentful and fearful as their language and culture were disparaged and things German became objects of hatred.

When the United States declared war on Germany in April 1917, President Wilson emphasized that the enemy was the imperial government of Germany, not the German people, their language, or their culture. But in the frantic effort to mobilize the country's resources for war, such distinctions were lost to many minds. Rumors of German-American subversion flitted about, and many Americans succumbed to the fear that the country was swarming with spies.

A variety of government agencies and private organizations contributed to the growing anti-German hysteria. The Committee of Public

Information created a national mood of aggressive patriotism as it attacked dissent as disloyalty, extolled British culture, and fostered hatred for Germany. Meanwhile, the American Protective League organized a massive program to search out domestic espionage. The National Security League and its offshoot, the American Defense League, spread a virulent strain of superpatriotism and intensified the anti-German hysteria through indiscriminate attacks on German-American churches, schools, societies, and newspapers, describing them as inhibitors of assimilation and as agents of a worldwide Teutonic conspiracy.

Both organizations made special war on the German language. By eliminating German-language instruction from the elementary and secondary schools, the American Defense League proclaimed, the nation could destroy the means by which the kaiser and his henchmen were seeking to pervert American youth. One of its pamphlets, "Throw Out the German Language and All Disloyal Teachers," illustrates the logic of superpatriotism: "Any language which produces a people of ruthless conquestadors [*sic*] such as now exists in Germany, is not a fit language to teach clean and pure American boys and girls." The Germans, according to this tract, were "the most treacherous, brutal and loathsome nation on earth. . . . The sound of the German language . . . reminds us of the murder of a million helpless old men, unarmed men, women, and children; [and] the driving of about 100,000 young French, Belgian, and Polish women into compulsory prostitution."[8] The American Defense League also encouraged the public burning of German-language books.

Superpatriotic politicians and newspaper editors joined in the cry. In Lincoln, Nebraska, a newspaper began a campaign, ultimately successful, to remove a thousand German-language books from the collection of the State Library Commission. Richard Metcalfe, a political lieutenant of William Jennings Bryan, broadcast unconfirmed tales, soon repeated across the nation, about teachers in German Lutheran schools in Nebraska who whipped pupils who dared to speak English during recess periods.[9]

Many educators lent their authority to the war on German-language instruction in the schools. The most moderate argued that foreign-language instruction had to end because the heterogeneous mass of American society could be welded together only by means of English as the common national tongue.[10] In an address delivered to the National Education Association (NEA), the dean of the University of Minnesota College of Education asserted that subversive Germans expected to achieve their nefarious goals "by having German teachers teaching German ideals through the German language" in American schools.[11] Another educator announced that the German language was "lacking in euphony" and therefore "savors of the animalistic and does not induce a certain polish and refinement essential to civilized people." There should be no place for the German language in our schools, he insisted, because it upholds a philosophy that "prides itself in its inhumanity [that] murders children, rapes women, and mutilates the bodies of innocent men."[12] With comparable logic, a retired United States admiral insisted that German-language instruction be dropped because the textbooks glorify German things and German men who have shown themselves to be "arrogant, domineering, treacherous, dishonest, mendacious, scheming, unscrupulous, without honor, cruel, and murderous."[13]

The National Education Association also supported the campaign. Through one of its commissions the NEA condemned "the practice of giving instruction in a foreign tongue" as "un-American and unpatriotic." Although it was silent on classes in which students were taught to speak a foreign language, the NEA urged that "every legitimate means, both state and federal, be used" to make English the language of instruction in all public and private schools.[14]

The clamor was in fact much ado about very little. The campaign was directed chiefly against German-language instruction in the first eight grades. Yet few school systems offered instruction in any foreign language at that level. The United States Bureau of Education compiled statistics in autumn 1917 on the question. The data revealed that in only 19 of 163 cities of twenty-five thousand plus were such classes offered.[15]

In secondary schools, however, relatively few German-language classes had been dropped, although enrollments had decreased significantly. A *Literary Digest* poll of school superintendents conducted early in 1918 showed that only 149 of 1,017 respondents reported discontinuation of German-language classes. Many individual comments were published in the article, and most reflect the closed-mindedness and intolerance fostered by war propaganda. A superintendent in Grafton, North Dakota, offered a minority view when he replied that "to drop German as a language-study because we are at war with Germany would be indicative of that sort of stupidity and lack of vision that we believe is native in the Prussian intellectual atmosphere." Few of the educators quoted agreed with the calm assessment of Philander P. Claxton, the United States commissioner of education, who opposed the elimination of German-language instruction on the secondary school level. The United States is not at war with the German language, he wrote in a widely publicized letter, and "the fewer hatreds and antagonisms that get themselves embedded in our institutions and policies, the better it will be for us when the days of peace return."[16]

State councils of defense also shared in the fight to eliminate "the enemy language" from the public schools. Shortly after war had been declared, President Wilson urged each state government to form a commission to coordinate food and fuel production and conservation, mobilization of labor, sanitation, Americanization programs, and other aspects of the war effort on the state and local level. All states eventually complied, although the councils varied greatly in name, structure, and authority. Subordinate county councils of defense were also created and the various functions farmed out to committees of unpaid civilian appointees. In some states, especially in the West, state councils of defense were granted sweeping powers, sometimes of doubtful constitutionality. Public attention was most often attracted to the zealous manner in which some councils performed their duties relative to patriotism, Americanization, or disloyalty.

The councils of defense for the several Great Plains states each joined in the anti-German campaign. Most issued orders or requests in 1918 to eliminate German-language instruction in the schools. But in some states the councils of defense went much further, banning the use of the German language in church services, parochial schools, public meetings of all kinds, and even on the telephone. German-language newspapers were also attacked. The principal argument for suppressing the language was that the country, for the sake of unity, had to Americanize its foreign-born citizens and that continued use of the German language kept the immigrant "subservient to the Hohenzollern autocracy."[17]

The Nebraska State Council of Defense was one of the most active and influential of the several commissions established in the plains states. Its activities were guided by men who were thoroughly imbued with superpatriotic sentiments; it had the consistent support of influential newspapers, most notably the *Lincoln Star*, whose publisher himself became a member of the council. Bothered by the alleged failure of Nebraskans to support the war effort with appropriate enthusiasm, the state council in July 1917 conducted an investigation into the loyalty of the strong German element in the state. Leaders of the several German Lutheran synods were singled out for special attention and were broadly accused of disloyal behavior. Subsequent meetings of the council with Lutheran church officials moderated the antagonism a little, yet it is clear that the council deliberately sought to focus public indignation on the German Lutherans and their continued strong attachment to their ancestral language and culture.[18]

The Nebraska council took several steps in the development of its policy to curb foreign languages in the churches. On December 12, 1917, the council, relying on the force of public opinion rather than on law, banned the teaching or use of foreign languages in all private and denominational schools of the state. Church services in foreign languages, however, continued to be seen as a problem, and on June 8, 1918, the council issued a proclamation requesting that the ban on German be extended to all means of communication to the fullest possible extent. "All sermons and public speeches should be exclusively in the English language," the council ordered, "but where there are old people who cannot understand the English language and it is deemed necessary to give instruction in a foreign tongue, all publicity should be avoided in such instruction." Two months later the council clarified its ruling regarding religious instruction in German. Sunday schools were to be conducted in English, the council decreed, as should all religious services. The old people who could not understand English, according to this directive, could have the sermon briefly summarized for them in the foreign language shortly before or after the regular services. The regulation, still without force of law, applied equally to religious meetings in Swedish, Danish, Czech, and other languages in use in Nebraska, as well as to German.[19]

The records of the Nebraska council reveal that very few clergymen were willing to risk the wrath of adverse public opinion, which had been so effectively marshalled by the council. The Reverend John Gerike, a pastor of a rural Missouri Synod Lutheran congregation near Crete, Nebraska, was a courageous exception. He coolly informed the council that his congregation had voted to continue German services "until a law is passed forbidding the use of it."[20] But most church leaders, while objecting to the action as illegal and unfair, urged a willing conformance for the sake of harmonious public relations.

Other state councils pursued similar courses with similar results. In Montana, where the use of the German language in the pulpit was also forbidden, a few congregations fearfully suspended all public worship. In South Dakota, where the state council was empowered to act in any way "not inconsistent with the constitution and laws of South Dakota . . . which are necessary and proper for public safety," the ethnic conflict was as sharp as in Nebraska. On February 22, 1918, even before it had statutory authority to do so, the South Dakota council ordered the first statewide ban in the nation on German-language instruction in all public schools from the elementary grades through the universities. Its Order No. 4, which went into effect on June 1, 1918, prohibited the use of the German language at all public gatherings, including church meetings, and the ban on German-language instruction was extended to private and church-related schools. A subsequent order "prohibited the use of the enemy's language in public conversation except in cases of extreme emergency."[21]

In Kansas the state council acted with moderation and understanding, compared to its counterparts in most other Great Plains states. Although the Kansas council was thoroughly committed to its program to make the English language "universally understood and habitually used by all citizens," it carefully avoided the harsh and autocratic methods employed in neighboring states. This was due largely to the efforts of Martin Graebner, a clergyman and professor at Saint John's College, a Lutheran institution in Winfield, who had been placed in charge of the foreign-language problem in the state. A sensitive and knowledgeable man, Graebner successfully enlisted the voluntary support and cooperation of German-speaking organizations and communities in the state.[22]

On the local level, however, county councils of defense were often less circumspect than the state councils and tended to ignore the complexities of their tasks. A county council, for example, dictated in one instance which members of a German Lutheran church could attend German-language services and which could not. In Oklahoma, the Major County Council of Defense brusquely asserted that because "God Almighty understands the American language, address Him only in that tongue." In Nebraska, the Dixon County Council of Defense resolved on May 10, 1918, that all persons should abstain from the use of the German language at all times and in all places, including church and home, and "that the reading of German-language papers should immediately be discontinued by all who are to be considered loyal Americans." Two weeks later the Hall County, Nebraska, council resolved "that in this hour of our nation's greatest peril brought upon us by the murderous and ruthless Hun," all instruction in German in every school in the county, public and parochial, should stop and that all German schoolbooks be removed from every school. It requested further that the *Anzeiger-Herold* (Grand Island) cease publication at once; that the Liederkranz and the Plattdeutscher Vereen, two social organizations, change their names to English, rewrite their constitutions in English, and conduct all organizational activities in English; and that "the use of the German language in public and private conversation . . . be discontinued." The resolution was larded with such pornographic phrases as "brutal hordes of German ravishers and murderers." The council also declared its belief that Germany had "forfeited all claims to be classed among the civilized nations of the world."[23]

In their zeal to promote "a true spirit of patriotism," county councils of defense fostered disrespect for law. In South Dakota, when church officials protested an interpretation of the state council's Order No. 4, the Douglas County Council of Defense replied that it did not care what the state council or the state or federal judiciary had said; it simply would not tolerate preaching in the German language.[24]

A mob spirit took over in some communities. German Americans were subjected to threats, intimidations, beatings, tar-and-featherings, flag-kissing ceremonies, and star chamber proceedings in council of defense meetings. Their homes and buildings received liberal applications of yellow paint as a symbol of disloyalty.[25] In Texas a German Lutheran pastor was whipped after he allegedly continued to preach in German after having been requested not to by the Nueces County Council of Defense. In South Dakota a county council of defense itself became the object of mob threats when it met to consider the question of granting permits to pastors of German churches to give synopses of their sermons in German at the close of English-language services. In Nebraska a German Lutheran pastor of a church in Papillion was beaten by a mob; in Riverdale another was hanged in effigy and given three days to leave town. Schools and churches were ransacked for German-language books.[26] In South Dakota, Yankton high school students were praised for having dumped their German-language textbooks into the Missouri River as they sang the "Star-Spangled Banner." The burning of German-language books as parts of superpatriotic exercises occurred in Oakland, Hooper, and Grand Island, Nebraska. In Boulder, Colorado, a German-book-burning rally was sponsored by the University of Colorado preparatory school. Early in September 1918, the Lutheran parochial school in Herington, Kansas, was destroyed by fire by superpatriots.[27]

In both Kansas and South Dakota German-speaking Mennonite and Hutterite pacifists suffered grievous persecution. Superpatriots condemned them not merely because of their tenacious retention of the language, but also because of their refusal on religious grounds to accept military service or to buy war bonds. In Collinsville, Oklahoma, a Mennonite named Henry Reimer was strung up by a mob on April 19, 1918. Police persuaded the would-be executioners to cut him down before he died, on the promise that he would be given a trial by the county council of defense the next day. In Kansas vigilantes besieged rural families at night, firing pistol shots into the air and scattering written threats and warnings about the yard. In Newton a mob intimidated the students of the Mennonite Bethel College and displayed a sign that read, "Germans: speak the language of a civilized nation. The Hun language will be barred even in Hell." By the summer of 1918 some of the most conservative Mennonites of the Great Plains states decided that their status within the United States had become intolerable, and well over fifteen hundred persons resettled in the Canadian prairie provinces of Alberta, Saskatchewan, and Manitoba. The largest numbers came from Oklahoma and South Dakota, although others fled from Kansas, Nebraska, and Minnesota.[28] Many Hutterites from South Dakota also emigrated, starting in 1918. Within a few years all but one of their agricultural colonies in the state had been abandoned.

Most of the restrictions placed upon the usage of foreign languages during the war were extralegal. Even though the council of defense pronouncements were widely heeded, they were not legally binding. They were supported by the force of public opinion and by the threat of mob action. Some local governments passed city ordinances against speaking German in public places. Although unenforceable, such local measures were not often challenged. The attorney general of Nebraska gave it as his opinion that a proposed ordinance to forbid the speaking of a foreign language on the streets of Campbell, Nebraska, would be invalid because the legislature had never granted villages of the state such authority. He also implied that the ordinance would be unnecessary because "prudence and public policy" would soon prompt immigrants to desist from the use of the native tongue.[29] Had state legislatures generally been in session in 1918, many restrictive laws would have been passed. As it was, the governors of several states called special sessions to consider such legislation.

The most extreme of the wartime measures was enacted by the Louisiana legislature, which made it unlawful for any teacher or professor in any public or private institution at any level to teach the German language to any pupil or class.[30] A more moderate restriction was enacted in South Dakota. In this case the legislature forbade instruction by means of any foreign language in the public elementary schools of the state; it applied the same restrictions to public secondary schools and colleges, except for foreign languages as subjects; and finally, in the private schools and colleges of the states, the restrictions also applied, "except for foreign and ancient languages and religious subjects." In other words, South Dakota legislators, in contrast to the state's council of defense, made an explicit accommodation to its ethnoreligious minorities.[31]

In Nebraska the governor called a special session of the legislature to enact a sedition law and to repeal the Mockett language law of 1913, which he now denounced as "vicious, undemocratic, and un-American." By its repeal, the legislature removed the provision that school districts had to offer foreign-language instruction upon the request of the parents of fifty pupils. The legislature then approved the request by the Nebraska State Council of Defense that no foreign languages be taught in the elementary grades.[32] It also enacted a sedition law that enhanced the power of the state council of defense by requiring publishers of all materials in any foreign language to file copies with the council, along with English translations, as required by the federal Espionage Act. More significantly, enemy aliens were forbidden from acting "as lecturer, priest, preacher, minister, teacher, editor, publisher, or educator" without first filing an application and obtaining a permit from the Nebraska State

Council of Defense. One senator courageously but ineffectively denounced the act as "an insidious attack on the right of free speech and religious liberty." He was outraged by the provision that, as he said, made "our lawful and constitutional authorities subservient and subordinate to the council of defense, whose members are not elected, nor answerable to the people."[33]

The signing of the armistice on November 11, 1918 ended the war against Germany, but the war against German language and culture in the United States continued with scarcely any diminution. Just days before the fighting ceased, the voters elected new legislatures, which went into session in January 1919. Many of the new lawmakers were more determined than ever to impose linguistic uniformity upon the American people. Certain journalists and politicians continued to exploit popular fears. Gustavus Ohlinger, for example, continued to attack German-language instruction in American schools as he had during the war. In his view it was the keystone of subversion, just as the German-language press was the archenemy of Americanization. Before long twenty-one states enacted new laws relating to foreign languages in the elementary schools. Among them were the Great Plains states of Colorado, Kansas, Nebraska, New Mexico, Oklahoma, and South Dakota. All enactments specified English as the medium of instruction, and all except the New Mexico measure applied to all schools, public, private, and parochial.[34]

The passage of these new restrictive laws of 1919 was also due in part to proposed federal legislation known as the Smith-Towner bill, introduced in Congress in October 1918. One section of this bill specified that no state was to share in the apportionment of federal funds unless it "shall have enacted and enforced laws requiring that the basic language of instruction in the common-school branches in all schools, public and private, shall be the English language only." Yet many legislatures went beyond the requirement of the still-pending Smith-Towner bill and prohibited entirely the teaching of foreign language up to and including the eighth grade.[35]

The Kansas measure was forthright and unyielding: "All elementary schools in this state, whether public, private or parochial, shall use the English language exclusively as the medium of instruction." Oklahoma's law was nearly as blunt. South Dakota enacted a new law that listed the subjects that had to be taught in English; religion was not listed and therefore could be taught in German in parochial schools. Colorado used a similarly devious method to make English the language of instruction without touching religious education. New Mexico managed to specify English as the language of instruction in its public elementary schools, but made Spanish reading a mandatory subject for Spanish-speaking pupils.[36]

It was Nebraska's language law, however, that gained broader significance because it was ultimately declared unconstitutional by the United States Supreme Court in 1923. Sponsored by Sen. Harry Siman, it was one of several bills introduced early in the 1919 session to restrict the use of foreign languages in the state. Sentiment in favor of restriction was especially strong because of publicity given the recommendations of Nebraska's Americanization Committee, which had been appointed by Gov. Keith Neville to take the language issue out of the hands of the Nebraska State Council of Defense. Neville, in his address to the legislature as outgoing governor, had also called for a ban on foreign-language instruction in order, as he put it, to guarantee that Nebraska would be American in language, thought, and ideals. But Neville also favored a provision that would have specifically exempted religious instruction from the ban.[37]

By 1919 the ethnic churches, principally the body known today as the Lutheran Church—Missouri Synod, no longer objected to legislation requiring English in their schools, so long as the directive did not apply to religious instruction. Their acquiescence was partly an acceptance of political reality, but it was also a matter-of-fact recognition that in most parochial schools English was commonly used except in religion classes. The language laws of several neighboring states, including Iowa, South Dakota, and Colorado, explicitly applied to secular subjects only. Several lawmakers with Lutheran and Catholic connections tried in committee to amend the Siman bill similarly, but Siman and the majority were adamant despite editorials in leading state newspapers urging moderation.[38] One lawmaker's response distills the intolerance of the time: "If these people are Americans, let them speak our language. If they don't know it, let them learn it. If they don't like it, let them move. It is a good thing to learn. I would be ashamed to face my boy, when he returns from France, if I voted for this amendment [to authorize specifically the use of foreign languages for religious instruction in parochial schools] and had to tell him that I had done nothing to crush Kaiserism in this country."[39]

Other supporters of the Siman bill favored the closing of all parochial schools in the state. Some were motivated by a deeply rooted religious prejudice. For them the language bill was a ready and popular preliminary step toward the diminution of Catholic power in the United States. That the Siman bill would also work contrary to the interests of the German Lutheran synods was merely an unfortunate but unavoidable consequence of their commitment to parochial schools.[40]

Gov. Samuel McKelvie signed the Siman bill into law on April 9, 1919. Overwhelmingly approved in both houses of the legislature, the measure made it a misdemeanor "to teach any subject to any person in any language other than the English language . . . in any private, denominational, parochial or public school." The restriction applied only to the first eight grades.[41]

Shortly after the passage of the Siman law, officials of the Nebraska District of the Lutheran Church—Missouri Synod sought an injunction against the enforcement of the act on the ground that it was an unconstitutional infringement upon religious liberty. This action was guided by Arthur Mullen, a prominent Irish Catholic lawyer of Omaha, who arranged to have a Polish Catholic parish of South Omaha join the Lutherans as petitioner. The district court judge issued the injuction, but the attorney general immediately appealed to the Nebraska State Supreme Court.[42]

After much controversy and public debate, the Nebraska Supreme Court on December 26, 1919, denied the injunction and upheld the Siman Act. This tribunal understood the measure, not as an unconstitutional interference with religious liberty, but as an effort within the police power of the state to treat the language problem that had developed in the country because of the World War. Fearful perhaps of constitutional objections, the court added that the law did not prevent instruction of or in foreign languages outside regular school hours.[43]

This ruling by no means settled the matter. Some parochial schools, acting on the cue from the judiciary, arranged their daily schedules so that courses taught in foreign languages, chiefly religion, were offered before or after regular school hours.[44] Inevitably such steps were perceived as evasions of the law by the superpatriotic advocates of language uniformity and champions of public-school education; during the next two years they continued to push hard for new restrictive laws.

It was not until 1921 that state legislatures were again in session and able to respond to the continued agitation for language restriction. Five states, including South Dakota and Nebraska, thereupon enacted new laws. In Nebraska the Siman Act was replaced by the even more stringent Reed-Norval Act, signed into law on April 14, 1921. This measure forbade all instruction in foreign languages in public and private schools at all times, thereby closing the loophole noted earlier by the Nebraska Supreme Court. Ironically, the bill was originally introduced by Sen. Richard Norval of Seward to weaken the restrictions of the Siman Act. But in committee other senators, acting under strong pressure from the American Legion, wrote additional restrictions into the bill, leaving Norval no alternative but to disavow the legislation that bore his name.[45]

Shortly after the passage of the Reed-Norval Act, officials of the Lutheran Church—Missouri Synod sought an injuction against its enforcement just as they had in the case of the Siman Act. This suit was quickly appealed to the Nebraska Supreme Court, which on April 19, 1922, again upheld the constitutionality of the law forbidding the use of foreign languages in elementary schools.[46]

Meanwhile the famous *Nebraska v. Meyer* case was on its way to the United States Supreme Court. This litigation involved the teacher of a one-room parochial school maintained by Zion Lutheran Church of rural Hampton, in Hamilton County, the pastor of which was Carl F. Brommer, the president of the Nebraska District of the Lutheran Church—Missouri Synod. In January 1920, shortly after the Nebraska Supreme Court had observed in its decision of December 26, 1919, that the Siman Act did not prohibit foreign-language instruction outside regular school hours, Zion congregation declared its official schools hours to be from 9:00 to 12:00 in the morning and from 1:30 to 4:00 in the afternoon. It further directed the teacher, Robert Meyer, to conduct a class in religion in the German language from 1:00 to 1:30 P.M. each afternoon. Attendance was technically voluntary. On May 25, 1920, the county attorney appeared at the school while Raymond Parpart, a youngster in the fourth grade, was reading aloud in German the Old Testament story of Jacob's Ladder. Several days later Meyer was charged in the Hamilton County Court with having violated the Siman language law.[47]

Meyer's trial was conducted on December 13, 1920. The transcript reveals that the county attorney tried to blur the distinction between religious instruction in the German language and language instruction in which pedagogical materials happened to be religious. Meyer unquestionably was engaged in the former, but the jury was more likely to convict if the latter were the case. Further, the prosecution succeeded in convincing the jury that the announced starting time of 1:30 P.M., rather than 1:00 P.M. was a subterfuge to circumvent the law. Meyer was thereupon convicted and fined twenty-five dollars. With the support of church officials, he refused to pay and began his appeal.[48]

The Nebraska Supreme Court heard the case more than a year later, in February 1922. In the meantime the legislature had replaced the Siman Act with the Reed-Norval Act, although this did not alter the judicial proceedings. By a four-to-two vote the court decided against Meyer and upheld the constitutionality of the language law. Writing for the majority, Justice Leonard Flansburg asserted that permitting resident foreigners to educate their children in the language of their native land was inimical to the safety of the state. Justice Charles B. Letton, in a dissenting opinion, called the Siman Act a product of crowd psychology. He declared that foreign-language instruction was not harmful to the state and that the Siman Act was an arbitrary exercise of police power that interfered with the fundamental right of parents to control the education of their children.[49]

Another year passed before the United States Supreme Court heard the Meyer case. The Lutheran Church—Missouri Synod had decided to couple its suit (*Evangelical Lutheran Synod v. McKelvie*) with Meyer's and to place them both in the hands of Arthur Mullen. Meanwhile other litigation over Iowa and Ohio language laws (*Iowa v. Bartels* and *Ohio v. Pohl*), each of which involved teachers in Lutheran parochial schools, had been appealed to the Supreme Court and were heard during the fall session of 1922.[50]

Mullen's reading of legal precedent convinced him that to base his case on the First Amendment would be fruitless, since it applied to the federal government, but not to state governments. He decided instead to argue that the Fourteenth Amendment embraces religious liberty also when it prohibits state government from abridging privileges of United States citizens or depriving them of life, liberty, or property without due process of law. Mullen submitted a brief to the court in October 1922 and presented oral arguments in February 1923.[51]

The United States Supreme Court delivered its decision on June 4, 1923. The majority opinion, written by Justice James McReynolds, declared the Siman Act to be unconstitutional interference with Meyer's right "to teach and the right of parents to engage him so to instruct their children." Moreover, the court observed that no emergency had "arisen which renders knowledge by a child of some language other than English so clearly harmful as to justify its inhibition with the consequent infringement of rights long freely enjoyed." The Iowa and Ohio rulings were, of course, also reversed.[52]

Although the Meyer decision ended restrictive language laws among the states, the related issue of private and parochial school education continued until 1925, when the United States Supreme Court struck down an Oregon law requiring all children between the ages of eight and sixteen to attend public school. This act, championed by an alliance of the Ku Klux Klan and several Masonic bodies, was overturned in the *Pierce v. Society of Sisters of the Holy Names of Jesus and Mary* decision. Both the suit and the judicial ruling drew upon the precedents of the Meyer case.[53]

Thus the Supreme Court of the United States brought to an end the movement to impose legal restrictions on the use of foreign languages. Although the trend had originated in the prewar period, it had been strengthened greatly by war-born fears of German subversion in America and anxiety over the nation's capacity to absorb its millions of foreign-born citizens. The climax of the movement came in 1919 during the six months following the armistice. Drawing support from diverse elements in the population—superpatriots, xenophobes, champions of public-school education, and later such organizations as the American Legion and Masonic orders—the advocates of language restriction were especially strong in the states of the Great Plains. Every legislature in this region enacted some sort of restriction on foreign languages from 1918 to 1921. Ethnic churches, whose interests were most directly and most adversely affected by the movement, immediately turned to the courts for redress. Although state tribunals were unresponsive to their constitutional arguments, the federal judiciary ruled in their favor and thereby clarified and enlarged American freedom.

NOTES

The author acknowledges with gratitude the assistance of a fellowship in state and community history from the Newberry Library, Chicago, which enabled him to use its exceptional resources in the research and writing of this essay.

1. Heinz Kloss, "German-American Language Maintenance Efforts," in *Language Loyalty in the United States*, ed. Joshua A. Fishman (The Hague: Mouton, 1966), 233–35.

2. Ibid.; Cleata B. Thorpe, "Education in South Dakota, 1861–1961," *South Dakota Historical Collections* 34 (1972): 224; Paul Kleppner, *The Cross of Culture* (New York: Free Press, 1970), 158; Richard Jensen, *The Winning of the Midwest* (Chicago: Univ. of Chicago Press, 1971), 123, 134, and 219; J. C. Ruppenthal, "The Legal Status of the English Language in the American School System," *School and Society* 10 (December 6, 1919): 658–60.

3. Ruppenthal, "Legal Status of the English Language," 659–60.

4. I. N. Edwards, "The Legal Status of Foreign Languages in the Schools," *Elementary School Journal* 24 (December 8, 1923): 270; U.S. Bureau of the Census, *Thirteenth Census of the United States: 1910*, 1: 1266–67; Edward G. Hartmann, *The Movement to Americanize the Immigrant* (New York: Columbia Univ. Press, 1948).

5. Walter H. Beck, *Lutheran Elementary Schools in the United States*, 2d ed. (St. Louis: Concordia, 1965), 318–19.

6. Ruppenthal, "Legal Status of the English Language," 660.

7. This and following several paragraphs are summarized from my book *Bonds of Loyalty: German Americans and World War I* (De Kalb: Northern Illinois Univ. Press, 1974).

8. Quoted in Wallace Henry Moore, "The Conflict Concerning the German Language and German Propaganda in the Public Secondary Schools of the United States" (Ph.D. diss., Stanford University, 1937), 33–34.

9. Robert N. Manley, "The Nebraska State Council of Defense: Loyalty Programs and Policies during World War I" (M. A. thesis, University of Nebraska, 1959), 125–27.

10. "German Language," *School Review* 25 (October 1917): 598–600.

11. L. D. Coffman, "Competent Teachers for American Children," *National*

Education Association: Proceedings and Addresses (1918), 63. Coffman further charged that the National German-American Alliance was "responsible for the existence of 491 evangelical schools in this county, some of which were supported by state funds, in which German was the only language taught." In fact, the Alliance did not favor parochial schools, and none of them was supported by state funds. Moreover, German was usually not the sole language of instruction in them by the time of World War I.

12. H. Miles Gordy, "German Language in Our Schools," *Educational Review* 56 (October 1918): 257–63.

13. Caspar F. Goodrich, "Shall We Teach German in Our Public Schools," *Outlook* 119 (May 29, 1918): 192.

14. *Journal of Education* 87 (May 9, 1918): 514.

15. "Foreign Languages in the Elementary School," *School and Society* 6 (November 17, 1917): 583–84; *New York Times*, February 3, 1918.

16. "American Students Boycotting German," *Literary Digest* 56 (March 30, 1918): 29–31, 44–74; *New Republic* 14 (March 2, 1918): 146; *School and Society* 7 (March 30, 1918); *New York Times*, March 20, 1918.

17. Frank W. Blackmar, ed., *History of the Kansas State Council of Defense* (Topeka, Kans.: State Printer, 1921), 31, 68–74; *Report of South Dakota State Council of Defense* (n.p., n.d.), 43, 51–52, 74, 110; "Record of Proceedings of the State Council of Defense," ms. on file, Nebraska State Historical Society, Lincoln.

18. Robert N. Manley, "Language, Loyalty and Liberty: The Nebraska State Council of Defense and the Lutheran Churches, 1917–1918," *Concordia Historical Institute Quarterly* 37 (April 1964): 12–13.

19. Unidentified newspaper clipping, scrapbook, Werkmeister Collection, Nebraska State Historical Society, Lincoln; *Lutheran Witness* 37 (May 28, 1918): 185; Jack W. Rodgers, "The Foreign Language Issue in Nebraska, 1918–1923," *Nebraska History* 39 (March 1958): 7.

20. John Gerike to Nebraska State Council of Defense, Crete, Nebraska, March 12, 1918, Papers of the Nebraska State Council of Defense, Nebraska State Historical Society.

21. *Proceedings of the Thirteenth Convention of the Montana District of the Lutheran Church—Missouri Synod* (Glendive, Mont., August 24–26, 1964), 69; *Lutheran Witness* 37 (May 28, 1918): 164, and (June 11, 1918): 187. See also *School Review* 26 (June 1918): 458–59; *Report of the South Dakota Council of Defense*, 71; *New York Times*, February 23, 1918.

22. Blackmar, *Kansas State Council of Defense*, 70–71.

23. Alan N. Graebner, "The Acculturation of an Immigrant Lutheran Church: The Lutheran Church—Missouri Synod, 1917–1929" (Ph.D. diss., Columbia University, 1965), 27; Edda Bilger, "The 'Oklahoma Vorwarts': The Voice of German-Americans in Oklahoma during World War I," *Chronicles of Oklahoma* 54 (Summer 1976): 255; *Lutheran Witness* 37 (May 28, 1918): 164; unidentified newspaper clipping, scrapbook, Werkmeister Collection, Nebraska State Historical Society, Lincoln.

24. Graebner, "Acculturation of an Immigrant Church," 29.

25. See my *Bonds of Loyalty*, 1–24, 244–59, and my "Superpatriotism in World War I: The Experience of a Lutheran Pastor," *Concordia Historical Institute Quarterly* 41 (February 1968): 3–11; unidentified newspaper clippings, scrapbook, Werkmeister Collection, Nebraska State Historical Society, Lincoln.

26. *Lutheran Witness* 37 (December 10, 1918): 393; *Delmont* (South Dakota) *Record*, reprinted in ibid., 392; Manley, "Language, Loyalty and Liberty," 7; Clifford L. Nelson, *German-American Political Behavior in Nebraska and Wisconsin, 1916–1920*, Univ. of Nebraska–Lincoln Publication no. 217 (Lincoln, 1972), 31.

27. *Sioux Falls Argus Leader*, May 9, 1918; *Hooper* (Nebraska) *Sentinel*, July 18, 1918; Lyle W. Dorsett, "The Ordeal of Colorado's Germans during World War I," *Colorado Magazine* 51 (Fall 1974): 287; *Wichita Eagle*, September 6, 1918.

28. Arlyn John Parish, *Kansas Mennonites During World War I*, Fort Hays (Kansas State College) Studies, History Series, n.s. no. 4 (Hays, KS, 1968), 51–54; James C. Juhnke, *A People of Two Kingdoms: The Political Acculturation of the Kansas Mennonites* (Newton, KS: Faith and Life Press, 1975), 95–110; Norman Thomas, "The Hutterian Brethren," *South Dakota Historical Collections* 25 (1951): 276–80; *Report of South Dakota State Council of Defense*, 62–67; Allan Teichroew, "World War I and the Mennonite Migration to Canada to Avoid the Draft," *Mennonite Quarterly Review* 45 (July 1971): 219–49.

29. *Report of the Attorney General of Nebraska, 1918*, 220–21.

30. *Compilation of War Laws of the Various States and Insular Possessions* (Washington, D.C.: Government Printing Office, 1919), 47.

31. *South Dakota Session Laws, 1918*, chaps. 41, 42, pp. 47–48.

32. *Senate and House Journals, Special Session, 1918*, 38, 91, 180.

33. *Laws and Resolutions Passed by the* [Nebraska] *Legislature at the 36th (Extraordinary) Session, 1918*, chap. 9, pp. 50–51; unidentified newspaper clipping, scrapbook, Werkmeister Collection, Nebraska State Historical Society, Lincoln.

34. Gustavus Ohlinger, *The German Conspiracy in American Education* (New York: Doran, 1919); Edwards, "Legal Status of Foreign Languages," 272.

35. Moore, "Conflict Concerning the German Language," 91.

36. *Kansas Session Laws, 1919*, chap. 257, p. 352; *Oklahoma Session Laws, 1919*, chap. 141, p. 201; *South Dakota Session Laws, 1919*, chap. 168; *Colorado Session Laws, 1919*, chap. 179, p. 599; *New Mexico Session Laws, 1919*, chap. 146, p. 300.

37. Unidentified newspaper clipping, scrapbook, Werkmeister Collection, Nebraska State Historical Society, Lincoln.

38. *Lutheran Witness* 38 (February 4, 1919): 35; Edwards, "Legal Status of Foreign Languages," 274; *Senate Journal* (37th session) *1919*: 1046; *House Journal* (37th session) *1919*: 1007–8; unidentified newspaper clipping, scrapbook, Werkmeister Collection, Nebraska State Historical Society, Lincoln.

39. *Omaha World Herald*, February 25, 1919, quoted in Rodgers, "Foreign Language Issue," 13.

40. William H. Werkmeister, "Der Kampf um den Deutschunterricht in den öffentlichen Schulen Nebraskas," manuscript, Werkmeister Collection, Nebraska State Historical Society, Lincoln; Arthur Mullen, *Western Democrat* (New York: Wilfred Funk, 1940), 208, 212.

41. *Nebraska Session Laws, 1919*, chap. 249, p. 1019.

42. Werkmeister, "Der Kampf um den Deutschunterricht"; Mullen, *Western Democrat*, 215.

43. *Nebraska District of Evangelical Lutheran Synod v. McKelvie*, *Reports of Cases in the Nebraska Supreme Court* 104 (1919): 93.

44. Beck, *Lutheran Elementary Schools*, 331.

45. Edwards, "Legal Status of Foreign Languages," 272; *Nebraska Session Laws, 1921*, chap. 21, pp. 244–45; Beck, *Lutheran Elementary Schools*, 332; Werkmeister, "Der Kampf um den Deutschunterricht"; Mullen, *Western Democrat*, 219.

46. Mullen, *Western Democrat*, 219.

47. *State of Nebraska v. Robert T. Meyer*, Transcript of Testimony, District Court, Hamilton County, Nebraska, copy in the possession of the author. In his testimony Parpart incorrectly identified the Bible story as "Joseph's Ladder."

48. Ibid.

49. *Nebraska v. Meyer*, *Reports of Cases in the Nebraska Supreme Court* 107 (1922): 657.

50. Beck, *Lutheran Elementary Schools*, 333.

51. Mullen, *Western Democrat*, 220–26. Some account of Mullen's thinking is summarized in Thomas Hanley, "A Western Democrat's Quarrel with the Language Laws," *Nebraska History* 50 (Summer 1969): 151–71.

52. *Nebraska v. Meyer*, *U.S. Supreme Court Reports* 262 (1923): 390.

53. The *Society of Sisters* case is conveniently introduced in Lloyd P. Jorgenson, "The Oregon School of Law of 1922: Passage and Sequel," *Catholic Historical Review* 54 (October 1968): 455–66.

German-American Leadership
Strategies Between the World Wars 4

In 1928, midway between the two world wars, H. L. Mencken observed that with few exceptions the leaders of the Germans in America were an undistinguished and unintelligent lot, a collection of mediocrities, most of whom had something to sell. The few national German ethnic organizations still in existence, he noted, were led by entirely unimportant men. Moreover, the leaders of German immigrant churches were nonentities, unknown to the general public. The blame for this lamentable dearth of leadership, in Mencken's view, rested upon the German Americans themselves, who displayed an unfortunate tendency to follow inferior men. As Catholics they are slaves of their priests, he said; as Protestants they are slaves of their pastors; and when they leave the church they become slaves of the first political buffoon they encounter. During World War I, in Mencken's judgment, they had turned almost instinctively to fools for leadership.[1]

Mencken's surpassing skill in verbal hatchetry tends to overshadow the perceptive qualities of his analysis. Although he was a prisoner of his elitist prejudices, Mencken described circumstances that were typical of most immigrant groups in America. The vast majority of persons had emigrated in search of a better life. Coming from the lower classes of Europe, they were culturally backward persons who inevitably devoted their energies in America to material advancement. This worked against the emergence of wise and able leaders. When an educated and cultured person attempts to lead the apathetic masses of immigrants, Mencken wrote, he quickly becomes discouraged and succumbs to despair as his place is taken by demagogues, self-servers, and other third-rate noisemakers.

Yet, because of World War I, the experience of Germans in America was qualitatively different from that of any other immigrant group. The largest non-English-speaking group in the country, the Germans had already begun to arrive in the eighteenth century. They prospered in this country and were well received. They were proud of their language and culture; while many Germans assimilated with remarkable speed, others labored mightily to erect a complex of institutions that served to sustain ethnic culture. When German immigration dropped off sharply at the end of the nineteenth century, ethnic leaders sought to inhibit the inevitable disintegration of the group by espousing a new cultural chauvinism. Later, when Germany experienced its early successes in World War I, the leaders of German America were encouraged to exploit the kaiser as a symbol around which to rally the group, thereby bolstering a considerable financial investment in ethnic newspapers and a variety of other business establishments. An unprecedented measure of support seemed to unify the German Americans and to stimulate their leaders ever more boldly to flaunt partisanship for Germany. At the same time this behavior was infinitely offensive to persons whose emotional attachments were with the Allies. The advocates of the Allied cause, led by Pres. Woodrow Wilson and other champions of English culture, began to attack German-American leaders as disloyal and un-American. Unsure of the capacity of American society to assimilate ethnic diversities, they began a war on German culture in America as early as 1915. The German Americans, however, saw themselves as entirely loyal to the United States. In their view, strict neutrality was in the nation's best interest, whereas Wilson's policies would lead to war. That nonintervention worked to Germany's benefit was as incidental as the fact that Wilson's understanding of the national interest served to aid the Allies.[2]

The entry of the United States into the war in 1917 radically altered the circumstances of German Americans. Behavior that had been legal in the neutrality period was now tantamount to treason, and most persons of German birth or descent, regardless of citizenship, were suspected of nurturing some measure of loyalty for Germany. Although the spirit of oppression was not uniformly felt across the country, the German-American community generally experienced much persecution. Superpatriots delineated a new, narrowed conception of loyalty and demanded conformity from everyone. A fierce hatred for everything German pervaded the nation. German cultural symbols were debased; instruction in the language was practically eliminated in the schools; the use of the German language was restricted on the state and local levels; and German-language newspapers were harassed and censored. Gradually suspicion escalated to threats of violence, to forced sales of government war bonds, to liberal applications of yellow paint to churches, schools, and monuments, to vandalism, book-burnings, flag-kissing, tar-and-feather ceremonies, and, in one case, the lynching of an innocent German alien.

The German-American community was devastated by these events. For the majority of the seven million persons of German stock in the United States at that time, German ethnicity had become a source of social discomfort or deprivation. Countless families ceased conversing in the German language. Name changes were common among persons, businesses, and societies. Thousands stopped subscribing to German-language newspapers and periodicals. Memberships in ethnic organizations of all kinds plummeted. As a group, the German Americans were embittered, disillusioned, and demoralized, unsure of what appropriate behavior should be. For most of them, ethnicity had lost its savor. The injustices of World War I remained imprinted upon their memories, and they were eager to express their resentment in the polling booths. But above all they wanted to prevent a recurrence of the persecution. They were convinced that this could be accomplished best by avoiding obvious displays of German ethnicity. Few were ready to respond to a leader who promised to solve the problems of the Germans as an ethnic minority group. The majority were not interested in the promotion of ethnic consciousness or in the political defense of *das Deutschtum*.

At the core of the German ethnic group, however, were persons whose commitment to ethnicity was primary. They were convinced that the problems of the Germans in the United States were due to past failures of ethnic leadership. They believed that German Americans had been insufficiently aggressive during the prewar years, especially in politics, and that if German-American citizens would participate vigorously in political affairs at all levels their power would be such that no one would dare trample upon their rights. The most prominent of these ethnic chauvinists was George Sylvester Viereck, the notorious propagandist of Germany's cause during the neutrality period of 1914–17. In September 1919, a time when German Americans still suffered from sporadic superpatriotic violence, Viereck published an editorial on German ethnic leadership in his periodical, the *American Monthly*, as he had renamed the *Fatherland* of the prewar years. Noting that the Germans were a numerous and powerful force in American politics, he observed that they were now floundering for the want of a national leader. The need, he wrote, was for a new Carl Schurz, a man whose record of loyalty and service to the nation was impeccable, someone above envy and petty intrigue who could combine the wrangling and conflicting subgroups of German Americans and lead them by inspiring word and courageous deed out of the wilderness of war to a promised land of respect and honor. He should have financial independence and mastery of the English language, announced Viereck, and he must not be a recent immigrant or a newspaper man. As a possibility, Viereck mentioned Charles Nagel, who was well known among German Americans as the secretary of commerce in former President Taft's cabinet. But judging from his subsequent behavior, Viereck had himself in mind as the new leader of his ethnic group.[3]

Viereck's editorial evoked a variety of responses over the next several months. Most reveal how deeply German Americans were wounded by the humiliations of the war period and how earnestly they desired a restoration to their former status. Moreover, most respondents called for some form of political organization as the means to unite the group and to articulate its goals. The names of many persons were naively suggested as potential leaders in these letters, which collectively demonstrate a shallow understanding of the German ethnic group, its characteristics, and its relationships to the larger American society.[4]

The fact was that there was no possibility of a national leader arising who would fit the mold that Viereck described. The Germans in America never had had one in the past, not even the revered Schurz. This was because they were so diverse socially, economically, culturally, and politically that there was no common interest strong enough to bind them together. They were as heterogeneous as the nation itself, with its rich and poor, its educated and undereducated persons, its urban and rural divisions, its occupational range from unskilled laborers to mighty industrialists and financiers. The Germans included people who organized their lives around religious values and those who were secular-minded; there were pietists and ritualists, Catholics and Protestants, Democrats and Republicans.

Unlike blacks, Chicanos, or the Japanese, the Germans had no serious social or economic problems to unite them in a struggle against oppression. They had never been discriminated against in a serious way except during the World War I era, and even then it had not been universal or uniform. When the Germans had been persecuted it was chiefly because of the tenacity with which they clung to their language and culture. Even though German language and culture were not in fact as uniform as they appeared, their defense was the only foundation upon which a potential leader could base his appeal. Because it was in the economic interest of the press to emphasize ethnic unity and cultural maintenance and because leaders had no choice but to stress it in their speeches, sentiment in favor of nurturing the German language and culture appeared to be strong. Yet it was rarely capable of overcoming the centrifugal forces of personal or subgroup interest.

The inadequacy of ethnicity as a cohesive force was due also to the fact that the Germans, in their physical, linguistic, and cultural characteristics, were close to Anglo-American norms. Indistinguishable in appearance from dominant elements of American society, they were persons of Christian heritage who spoke a language closely related to English. It was possible for them to assimilate with astonishing ease if they so chose. When the retention of obviously German behavior became a source of discomfort or deprivation, as during World War I, the proportion of those who consciously abandoned ethnicity was dramatically enlarged.

In their long history in the United States, the Germans acted in concert only in response to external threats or events that impinged upon their culture. Prohibition, legislative threats to parochial schools, and anti-German propaganda are examples of issues that could temporarily stimulate German Americans to unity. When the threat disappeared, possibilities for strong leadership also vanished. If the defense of ethnic culture was the only basis for leadership, it was inevitable that when German-American voices were heard in the land, they sounded negative, harsh, and unattractive to old-stock Americans.

The alternative lay in the kind of leadership exemplified by Carl Schurz. As a politician, Schurz had not pursued specifically German-American interests. Even though he was willing enough to exploit German-American votes, he was essentially an American statesman who happened to have been born and educated in Germany. While his cultural heritage certainly influenced his goals and methods, his political appeal was rarely circumscribed by ethnicity. It was the quality of leadership in national affairs that gave him status and position. When he spoke on the issues, the nation as well as German Americans listened, even though they often did not agree with him. Thus Schurz's role as spokesman for his ethnic group was almost incidental—a by-product of his national leadership.

In the years following World War I, however, there was no one of German birth or descent of comparable stature on the national scene. Nagel probably came the closest. But he, like most men of modest fame in the political, business, or academic worlds, had no desire to be identified as the leader of the Germans. As for those persons who were closely tied to ethnic organizations, most were unknown to the public at large or were broken in spirit by the events of the World War—men such as Dr. Charles Hexamer, the former president of the defunct National German-American Alliance. There remained the vainglorious Viereck. Although his notoriety as a propagandist eliminated him from any substantial leadership role, Viereck saw himself in a different light.

The German immigrant churches in particular would have nothing to do with Viereck and his ilk. They had been the chief victims of superpatriotism, and superpatriotism had been stimulated by the verbal excesses of the German ethnic chauvinists. For the churches, ethnicity had been primarily a means to achieve religious ends; when it tended to hinder rather than to ease the attainment of their goals, they readily abandoned programs of language and culture maintenance. Most church leaders distrusted political activity as a way to accomplish their objectives, and they remained deeply suspicious of the ethnic political organizations, perceiving them as the heirs of the liberal, anticlerical traditions brought to America by the refugees of the revolutions of 1848.[5]

In most denominations there was a remarkably swift transition to English-language services in the first postwar decade, a mandatory step if the loyalty of the younger generation was to be retained. German-language church periodicals were gradually replaced by English equivalents. Most parochial schools converted to instruction in the English language. In the Evangelical Synod and in several Lutheran synods, notably the Iowa and Ohio synods, these alleged "nurseries of Kaiserism" virtually disappeared. Meanwhile, dozens of German Methodist congregations withdrew from German conferences and merged with parent organizations. Transition to English usage was especially dramatic in German Catholic parishes, and membership in the German Catholic Central-Verein, the national layman's organization, dropped to one-half of its prewar figure during the 1920s. Even the isolationist, pacifistic Mennonites, although slower to give up the use of German, developed extraordinary benevolence programs and voluntary relief work to demonstrate in positive ways their worth as American citizens.[6]

John Baltzer, president of the Evangelical Synod during the early 1920s, was typical of many German-American church leaders of the time. He repeatedly declared that his church, although German in origin, was thoroughly American in spirit and constitution. Yet he opposed the movement led by the great American theologian Reinhold Niebuhr, then a young parish pastor in Detroit, to merge the Evangelical Synod with other denominations. As a moderate, Baltzer admitted the inevitability and even the desirability of the transition to English, but he pleaded for a slowing of the process for the sake of clergymen and parishioners who could not accommodate themselves to an abrupt change. At the same time, some denominations, notably the Lutheran Church—Missouri Synod, inaugurated broad programs to equip the faithful for life in an English-speaking church. Sermons, instructional materials, religious literature, hymns, and prayers were published in English in the hope that orthodoxy could be sustained as linguistic barriers fell.[7]

In some respects the traditionally anticlerical Amerikanische Turnerbund acted much like the churches. Its leaders also believed survival depended upon transition to a nonethnic basis. By the 1920s, its political radicalism was only a memory, its name had been legally changed to the American Gymnastic Union, its periodical, the *Amerikanische Turnzeitung*, included many columns of English-language articles, and its adult male membership dwindled to about thirty thousand persons. Its national chairman, Theodore Stempfel, strongly objected to German ethnic politics and disapproved of mass protest meetings. The assimilationist drift of the *Turnerbund* was not unopposed, of course, and its leaders were bitterly attacked by the faithful, both within and without the organization.[8]

On the local level, thousands of ethnic clubs, societies, and associations of all kinds continued to exist, despite the corrosive effects of the anti-German hysteria. Some of their members advocated the conversion of their *Vereine* to "American" institutions, but most hoped to enjoy unobtrusively the pleasures of ethnic sociability, to celebrate their culture with drink and song, and to reap the economic rewards of ethnic contacts within the privacy of their organizational quarters.[9] A few societies experienced a resurgence of life after the war, as they were strengthened by persons whose ethnic consciousness had been awakened by wartime persecutions.[10] In many of the large cities, dozens of these societies were united into an umbrella organization, such as the influential United German Societies of New York and Vicinity.[11] Ordinarily not given to political activity, the umbrella organizations often coordinated charitable endeavors, such as relief programs for war sufferers in Germany, and promoted annual German Day cultural festivals, which by 1920 had begun to revive. Some members of the *Vereine* feared that organized political involvement was a senseless rocking of a leaky boat. But others attacked such attitudes as promoting self-indulgence, complacency, and a deceptive spirit of security. They urged participation in the activities of the two national organizations for German ethnic political action that had emerged in the immediate postwar period.[12]

The first of these was the Deutsch-Amerikanische Bürgerbund, or the German-American Citizen's League, which had its origin in Chicago under the leadership of Ferdinand Walther. It was deliberately patterned on the discredited National German-American Alliance, with state and local branches organized wherever sufficient interest could be generated. The Bürgerbund was dedicated to the revival of German language and culture and was motivated by a spirit of revenge. George Sylvester Viereck found such militancy to his liking and, for a time, served as its eastern regional director. Its leadership consisted largely of former National Alliance officers, but unlike that organization, it was openly and avowedly political. In August 1920, when it sponsored a national conference to support the presidential candidacy of Republican Warren G. Harding, it resolved "to sweep from office all miscreants, irrespective of party, who abused the authority conferred upon them by the people for the prosecution of the war, to make war upon their fellow citizens, who hounded and persecuted Americans of German descent, . . . who, contemptuous of any hyphen except the one which binds them to Great Britain, unmindful of the supreme sacrifice of Americans of German blood in the late war, attempt even now to deprive our children of the noble heritage of speech and song and prayer that has come down to us from our sires beyond the sea."[13]

The Bürgerbund was formally organized as a national body at a poorly attended meeting in Chicago in January 1921, when it adopted a series of resolutions defining its policies and commenting on current national and international issues.[14] Never very successful on the national level, the Bürgerbund was influential chiefly in Chicago and the Midwest, but even there it lacked the support of the German-language press. No German ethnic leaders of importance emerged from the organization. Its strategy was excessively chauvinistic; it spelled trouble in an intolerant age.[15]

The second national organization was the Steuben Society of America. Founded originally as a secret society in 1919, it was no less committed to political action than was the Bürgerbund. It also sought to protest against the treatment that Americans of German descent had suffered during the war, and it accepted the theory that if the Germans could unite they could hold the balance of political power in the United States. But this organization recognized that German Americans also had to establish their credentials for civic virtue and patriotism. Instead of screaming for its rights to be recognized, the Steuben Society hoped to demonstrate that it deserved respect. Hence, it constantly urged energetic participation by its members in the political life of America and, as its name suggests, publicized the contributions of Germans to the greatness of America from colonial times to the present. Its defense of Germany in international affairs was less strident than what was typical of the Bürgerbund, and to the disgust of the chauvinist radicals, it chose English as its official language. The Steubenites believed that this strategy would bring sufficient status and power to prevent the German Americans from being persecuted or ignored politically in the future.[16]

Although the Steuben Society became the best-known national German-American organization in the two decades between the wars, it also produced no significant leaders. Carl E. Schmidt of Detroit, an aging businessman of moderate wealth and culture who had played a minor role in Michigan politics, consented to serve as national chairman, but he never gave more than symbolic leadership to the society, which was centered in New York City. Thus leadership fell by default to Theodore H. Hoffmann, who was hobbled by acting chairman status until Schmidt's death in 1934.[17] As an instrument of German-American unity, the Steuben Society was also a failure. Throughout the interwar period it suffered from indecisive leadership, internal dissension, and severe criticism from German Americans outside the organization. Despite the respectability it enjoyed, its membership never exceeded 20,000.[18]

Even so, the Steuben Society's strategy was consonant with the advice of the historian Ferdinand Schevill, who had urged, in response to Viereck's 1919 editorial on the lack of German ethnic leadership, that any action the Germans took should be preceded by a self-examination "to discover the qualities . . . which have invited hostility and contempt." Such dispassionate reflection was difficult for the chauvinists; it was impossible for Viereck, who seemed to have learned nothing from the war. Eagerly seeking distinction as the leader of the German Americans, Viereck plunged into the political waters as the presidential election of 1920 approached. He exhorted his fellows to unified political activity in order to force decision makers in the national government to recognize German-American political power and to reward it when used to their advantage. He energetically supported the candidacy of Republican Warren G. Harding with every means at his disposal. First he tried to establish a German-American political action group, which he called the Committee of 96. When it failed to catch on, he shifted to the Bürgerbund, which, like almost all the German-language newspapers, endorsed Harding not because they regarded him highly, but rather as a means to defeat Democrat James Cox, whom they despised as the political heir of Woodrow Wilson. Everywhere Viereck preached boldness to the intimidated German Americans, and everywhere the press, to his delight, identified him as their leading spokesman. Indeed, as the campaign drew to a close, Cox singled out Viereck as his whipping-boy, as he denounced the return of hyphenism to American politics. But Viereck was not dismayed; such treatment was to be expected if he was to project himself successfully as the dauntless leader of all German Americans who were properly conscious of their ethnicity.[19]

Viereck's claim to ethnic leadership had little substance. The *New York Times* and other newspapers gave him much publicity because he was articulate and arrogant; apparently they assumed that he was also influential. But most German Americans, including the publishers of the German-language press, ignored or disputed his claims to leadership; many found his extremism appalling.[20] It is true that in the election of 1920 the majority voted overwhelmingly for Harding, as did the electorate generally, but they would have done so even if Viereck had remained silent.[21]

Viereck pressed on. Remembering Schurz's alleged delivery of the German-American vote to Abraham Lincoln in 1860 and his subsequent reward of the ministry to Spain, Viereck dispatched a congratulatory telegram to Harding with a reminder that six million Americans of German descent had voted Republican as he had predicted.[22] In January the Bürgerbund resolved to send a five-man delegation, including Viereck, to visit Harding before he took office and urge him to consider the great contributions of Germans to America when he made his cabinet appointments.[23]

Harding politely received the Bürgerbund delegation on February 16, 1921, while vacationing in Saint Augustine, Florida. The president-elect understood fully that he owed no debts to Viereck or, indeed, to the German-American voting population as a group. He assured the delegation that no candidate for high appointive office would be discriminated against because of German birth or descent. The effect of Viereck's well-publicized visit was to make it politically impossible for Harding to appoint a German American to any significant position, regardless of the candidate's qualifications. Ethnic politics, especially German, was simply repugnant to large numbers of native-stock voters. The Buffalo *Express*, for example, denounced the Viereck visitation as "ridiculously impudent," and in Kansas the Salina *Journal* called it "insolent stupidity." The American Legion protested against what it perceived as a German-American demand to receive an appointment to the cabinet. In Texas the state legislature adopted a resolution endorsing the stand taken by the Legion.[24]

Viereck and the chauvinists were disappointed with Harding's refusal to appoint a German American to high office. Even though it was apparent that their tactic was bound to be counterproductive, given the xenophobic tendencies of the times, they continued to pressure the president, especially in autumn 1921, when the position of ambassador to Austria fell vacant. Instead of agreeing on a single candidate, each of several activist elements within the German community, mainly in New York, lobbied for their own men. In the end Harding appointed a non-German.[25]

The whole affair resulted in laying bare a deep division within the ranks of Germans who were committed to united ethnic action. The Viereck clique believed in the open organization of raw political power; some even seemed to think that a frankly German political party would be ideal. They were opposed by persons, usually German-language newspaper editors and publishers, who were influential as leaders in local umbrella organizations. Fearful of renewed nativistic recriminations against the Germans, this group of leaders espoused a more covert strategy. They preferred to limit the public display of German ethnicity to cultural and social affairs such as German Day celebrations, bazaars, and benefit concerts. Meanwhile, they hoped to negotiate privately with leaders of the major political parties, trading German ethnic support for promises to pursue policies they favored. They wanted to bargain under circumstances where rationality and discretion could prevail, without the extremism of either Viereck and his followers or of latter-day superpatriots such as the leaders of the American Legion. No less committed to German ethnic goals than the extremists were, these moderates believed they could gain more for the Germans at less risk. Chief among them were the

Ridder brothers, Bernard and Victor, the owners and publishers of the *New Yorker Staats-Zeitung*, one of the largest and most influential of the German-language newspapers in the United States.[26]

Once it was apparent that no German American would get the Vienna post, Viereck began a sustained attack on the Ridders, Paul Mueller of the *Chicagoer Abendpost*, F. W. Elven of the *Cincinnati Freie Presse*, and the German-language press generally. Incensed by their refusal to publicize, much less support, the activities of the Bürgerbund and other chauvinist groups, Viereck denounced them in January 1922 as "renegade Judases" of "supine docility" and "bovine passivity" who meet "in secret conclave" with log-rolling politicians. In April he published his version of how the Ridder brothers, by their meddling, had prevented Bernard Heyn, a German-American attorney of New York, who had been a member of the delegation that had visited Harding, from getting the Austrian ambassadorship. The Ridders, charged Viereck, had inherited, not earned, their positions of leadership and were motivated solely by desire for financial gain. He complained that any potential leader who failed to concur in their dictation could expect to be punished by being denied publicity in the German-language press. Viereck pointed out that the Ridders' alleged manipulation had led to their banishment from the halls of the socially prestigious Liederkranz, whose president, William O. C. Kiene, had also become tangled in the Austrian imbroglio. Viereck dragged out what he considered to be dirty laundry from the war period to incriminate the Ridders. Finally, he reported that "throughout the country, Americans of German descent, desirous of bringing about harmony, are in open revolt against such individuals claiming leadership."[27]

Viereck's outbursts inevitably alienated intelligent men of good will among the German Americans. Frustrated by his failure to attract a substantial number of followers, Viereck next broadened his verbal attack to include his chief journalist rivals, the editors of *Issues of To-Day*, George Abel Schreiner and Frederick Franklin Schrader. Their periodical, closely tied to the Steuben Society of America, was strongly pro-German, like the *American Monthly*, but was better edited and more moderate in tone. In Viereck's indictment, Schreiner committed the crime of defending the French on one occasion, and Schrader had expressed some doubt about the truth of all the stories then circulating about forced prostitution of German women for black French soldiers then occupying the Rhineland.[28] But Viereck continued to suffer a steady erosion of support. Ultimately he was unable to command publicity in either the American or German-language press.

During the next two years the German ethnic group seemed to acquire a new sense of community. The storm-cellar mentality of the immediate postwar period faded as German-American leaders became more openly assertive of their rights and hopes. They made frequent references in their speeches and editorials to the wartime persecution their people had endured, and fresh voices were heard in favor of political organization. The Amerikanische Turnerbund, for example, received new, aggressive leadership in the person of George Seibel. He urged German Americans to ignore their differences, to unite in order to fight prohibition and other forms of cultural imperialism, and to denounce such international injustices to Germany as the French invasion of the Ruhr. Similarly, the United German Societies of New York acquired a Lutheran clergyman, Dr. William Popcke, as its president; he also espoused political organization to prevent the disintegration of Germany.[29] The German-language press also waxed more aggressive. The *New Yorker Staats-Zeitung*, for example, agreed that the time had come for all German Americans to develop a powerful, united political organization for their own self-protection and self-interest.[30] The Steuben Society of America emerged as the dominant political organization as the more radical Bürgerbund faded from the national scene. The *New York Times*, as well as the *Staats-Zeitung*, frequently publicized Steuben Society leaders and activity. Meanwhile, sympathy in the United States for Germany grew as the Weimar Republic struggled with inflation and the occupation of the Rhineland and the Ruhr. At the same time, revisionist historians and journalists, building on the widespread disillusionment with the Peace of Versailles, explained the origins of the Great War in terms much less favorable to Britain and France than given in the "official" version. Thus, as the election of 1924 approached, it appeared that German ethnic political action could succeed, even though the nation continued to be troubled by excesses of racism, xenophobia, and superpatriotism.

Most German Americans were disappointed with the major party candidates for president in 1924. Calvin Coolidge meant only a continuation of a Republicanism that had done little for them. Democrat John W. Davis was a hopeless compromise candidate who, to the Germans, symbolized Wall Street and the kind of financial manipulations that had dragged the United States into the war. Thus when Robert M. LaFollette, their battle-scarred hero from the days of the World War, ran as a third-party candidate, the majority of the German ethnic leaders rushed enthusiastically to his support. They loved him not so much for what he favored as for what he opposed. All they asked of any candidate was that he be against British and French dominance in international affairs, against the Versailles settlement and any arrangement, such as the Dawes Plan, that tended to perpetuate it, against the international bankers of Wall Street, and against the restrictive immigration legislation of 1924. If a candidate had a record of having opposed prohibition, women's suffrage, and American entry into the World War, so much the better. German ethnic politics thus rested on a foundation of negativism; positive goals were rarely defined. Because party loyalty did not exist, German ethnic leaders could shift easily from a conservative Harding in 1920 to a progressive LaFollette in 1924.

The Steuben Society of America (SSA) was especially active in the election of 1924. Its Political Committee sponsored a conference of German-American leaders in Chicago early in June to hammer out a platform for the edification of the major parties in their national conventions.[31] In August the SSA met to endorse LaFollette, and in September it staged a great rally in Yankee Stadium in New York. LaFollette himself addressed the assembly of 40,000 and told them with his usual eloquence what they wanted to hear—that Germans were hardworking, valuable citizens who had, by their intelligence, thrift, and endurance, contributed immeasurably to America's greatness. Crowds heard similar speeches at meetings staged in many other cities, including Philadelphia, Buffalo, Chicago, San Francisco, and Portland. By these means the German leaders hoped to demonstrate that their people were good patriotic Americans who happened to speak the German language and to value German culture; they were determined to revise the image of the German American as being more interested in Germany than in the United States.[32]

Still, memories of World War I remained vivid. No longer, announced the *New Yorker Staats-Zeitung*, will German Americans allow themselves to be muzzled, slandered, or harassed. The enemies of *Deutschtum* can be routed if German Americans will work together to present a united front.[33] "The German element," wrote Frederick Franklin Schrader, "knows when it is insulted, ignored, and impugned. It has a whole register of grievances, and since the policy is to dampen the smoldering fires of discontent rather than to put out the fire, the explosion will take place in due time, and it will not be to the liking of the powers that be."[34] Viereck reminded his readers that "no official rebuke was ever administered to the wretches who were guilty of . . . outrages [against Americans of German descent] except in a mild Presidential protest, utterly inefficient in checking the tendency to declare American citizens of German blood beyond the protection of the law."[35] Meanwhile, the national press gave extensive coverage to the activities of the Steuben Society and reported in considerable detail the political preferences of German leaders in the various states.[36]

But even with the LaFollette candidacy, the Germans could not achieve unity; it was impossible to define the group interest to everyone's satisfaction. It is true that the majority of the German-language news-papers condemned both the Democrats and the Republicans as they endorsed LaFollette, but the old divisions between the extremists and the more cautious editors and publishers had not disappeared.[37] Fearing a repetition of Viereck's strategy of 1920, F. W. Elven, the publisher of the *Cincinnati Freie Presse*, authored a lengthy editorial in which he reviewed the "flagrant tactlessness" of the Bürgerbund with its policy of ethnic separa-tism and of making demands in return for concessions. The appropriate leaders of the German ethnic group, insisted Elven, were the publishers of the German-language press; it was their duty to prevent "persons who lack every qualification of leadership to force themselves into prominent po-sitions and by their blunders compromise the cause of the German element." Elven argued that circumstances made ethnic political activity unwise. "We have our hands full at present to make amends for the sins of men of German blood who do not take their oath of allegiance too seriously and refuse to recognize the fact that we are not living in a German colony."[38] While Elven did not mention Viereck by name, it is clear whom he had in mind when he upbraided incompetent and impertinent political amateurs who "immured themselves with their itching vanity and monumental self-esteem." Others shared Elven's view. Schrader, for example, urged that the *Steubenfest* in Yankee Stadium be divested of all suggestions of "hyphenism" that were so susceptible to exploitation by "Anglomaniacs, Ku Kluxers, and the New York Morgan Gazettes." Nothing, he said, must be done "to suggest that our citizens of German origin expect either privileges or rewards in return for the solidarity they will manifest" on election day.[39] The *German American World* agreed with Elven that the Viereck visit to Harding was stupid and that German ethnic political segregation was the greatest of follies. Yet it adhered to the notion that if the German element was "to reassert its claim to that position of influence to which it is his-torically and economically entitled," it must remain neutral in the political contest until partisan lines are distinctly defined and then assign its weight to the candidate or party that is compatible with the German interest.[40]

Viereck was outraged by Elven's attack and published a lengthy defense of his own behavior. Later he countered with charges that German-language newspapers that supported Coolidge, such as Elven's *Freie Presse*, did so because they had been bribed with lucrative advertising contracts arranged by the Republican campaign committee. Viereck associated such corruption with the tragic suicide of Hans Hackel of the St. Louis *Westliche Post*; but he reserved special scorn for Val J. Peter, publisher of the Omaha *Tribüne*, who, according to testimony given before a congressional investigating committee, had flipped to Coolidge late in the campaign in return for $12,500.[41]

Any prominent German who disagreed with the dominant pro-LaFollette position was severely criticized in the German-American press. When Charles Nagel, whose loyalty to the Republican party was above reproach, announced that he intended to vote for Coolidge on the basis of nonethnic issues, the Steuben Society prepared a long rebuttal. The society charged that Nagel, although proud of his German heritage, chose Coolidge because he was the St. Louis representative of the Republican powers of Wall Street.[42]

The failure of LaFollette to win election in 1924 underscores the inability of the German-American leaders to marshal the ethnic vote. They obviously had not wielded the balance of political power, even though a substantial portion of LaFollette's five million votes was cast by persons of German birth or descent. Many thousands had also voted for the major party candidates, especially Coolidge. It was apparent that either major party could ignore the Germans if such a course were otherwise in their interest. Nevertheless, the German ethnic leaders continued to delude themselves. Carl Schmidt wrote that his Steuben Society had finally shed the party yolk. "If we continue to throw our vote whichever way our conscience may dictate, we will compel the respect of all parties, and will henceforth receive consideration by whatever party may be in power." Viereck insisted that support for LaFollette had cut across all German ethnic classes and group divisions; he even toyed with the idea of a third party "recruited largely from the German element."[43] Viereck, Schmidt, and other leaders knew that German Americans generally were still bitter about their wartime treatment; they erroneously assumed that the masses would translate their resentment into unified political action. This capacity to misinterpret experience and to believe only that which conformed to preconceptions gives substance to Mencken's observation that the Germans in America were led by mediocrities. Yet the actual voting behavior of German American citizens belies his charge that they almost instinctively followed fools.

There was no way that the strategy urged by the Steuben Society of America could produce strong political leadership among the Germans. In this view, party loyalty was an evil; support was to go to the party that would cater to the ethnic group interest. Such a policy precluded the possibility of a German ethnic leader achieving prominence in one of the major parties.[44] Election to important political office was therefore impossible. The only remaining avenue to a leadership position was to work through ethnic organizations such as the Steuben Society. But this alternative offered no long-term promise, for the Germans constituted a disintegrating constituency—a melting iceberg, in the words of one observer. Moreover, the Steuben Society as a matter of policy played down the leadership of its officers. Despite his many years of service at the head of the Steuben Society, Theodore Hoffmann was not even well known among German Americans.

The bankruptcy of the idea that the Germans held the balance of political power in the United States, provided they could unite, was made manifest by the presidential election of 1928, when they were hopelessly split by the candidacies of Herbert Hoover and Al Smith. One group insisted that Smith's Democratic party was still the party of Woodrow Wilson, William McAdoo, and A. Mitchell Palmer and that the hated prohibition amendment had been foisted upon the American people by Southern Democrats. Hoover, they said, was of German descent and proud of it; besides, he had saved thousands of Germans from starvation in his relief work after the war. But others saw Hoover as a pro-British conservative and a prohibitionist. They much preferred the Irish-Catholic Smith, with his open record of opposition to prohibition, his distrust of England, and his support for liberal, progressive measures. Capitalizing on this sentiment, the Democratic National Committee flaunted the names of persons who endorsed Smith, including the well-known former Republican congressman Richard Bartholdt of Missouri, Theodore Hoffmann of the Steuben Society, Charles Korz of the Catholic Central-Verein, Val Peter of the Omaha *Tribüne*, baseball players Babe Ruth and Lou Gehrig, and even the disdainful H. L. Mencken.[45] But there were still other Americans of German descent, chiefly pietistic Protestants, who favored Hoover precisely because he was "dry." After the election, the usually apolitical *Christliche Apologete*, a Methodist periodical, hailed the new chief with a full-page portrait. Meanwhile Lutherans rejected Smith simply because he was Catholic.[46]

The German-American press was similarly divided. A few newspapers, including Elven's *Cincinnati Freie Presse*, endorsed Hoover. A few more, such as Paul Mueller's *Chicagoer Abendpost*, supported Smith. But the great majority, the *New Yorker Staats-Zeitung* among them, were reluctant to offend any significant number of their subscribers and remained independent or even ignored the election entirely.[47]

The Steuben Society of America was incapable of providing leadership under these conditions. At first its organ, the *Progressive*, edited by Frederick Franklin Schrader, dismissed Hoover as pro-British and praised Smith as the champion of all that was dear to German Americans. In August, however, Schrader made a sudden switch, offered apologies to Hoover, and recommended his election. Certain local branches of the SSA also publicly announced for Hoover, but the national organization, wracked by internal dissension, finally endorsed Smith in mid-October. It severed its ties to the *Progressive* and declared the *Steuben News*, the publication of the New York council, to be its official voice in the future.[48]

After the fiasco of 1928, German Americans spoke less of what could be accomplished through political unity. References to World War I became less frequent. Viereck abandoned all pretense of ethnic leadership as he surrendered the editorship of the *American Monthly* to others. The Steuben Society of America continued to exist, of course, but its effectiveness was scorned in many quarters. Unable to agree on presidential candidates, it unintentionally abdicated a national leadership role as it concentrated on state and local politics. Meanwhile, the *Steuben News* larded its pages with glowing accounts of the heroic deeds of the ethnic fathers. Sanitized tales of Steuben, Schurz, De Kalb, Lieber, Sigel, and many others were repeated ad nauseam, as ever more obscure Americans of German origins were discovered and publicized in this effort to lay claim to authentic Americanness.

But the number of German Americans who were attracted by such unrelieved filiopietism diminished steadily. By the end of the 1920s the Americanizers were firmly in control of most German immigrant churches. The number of German-language publications, including church periodicals and trade journals, dwindled to 172, only a fourth of the prewar figure, and the multifarious *Vereine* continued to atrophy and die. In 1930 Oscar Illing, editor of *Die Neue Zeit* of Chicago and an old-time German-American journalist in the Viereck mold, delivered an extended lamentation on the impending fate of German America. Illing saw betrayal everywhere. No ethnic institutions, least of all the German-language press, escaped his jeremiads: all were led by fearful, self-serving cowards who avoided controversy and gave lip service only to the maintenance of language and culture. In his view, singing societies, for example, had degenerated into English-speaking businessmen's clubs where German songs could sometimes be heard, but were sung by hired singers. Illing could offer no remedy for the dissolution of ethnicity; he repeated the threadbare lines about political unity, but admitted it was impossible of attainment. He refused to understand that for the ethnic masses, immigrant language and culture could not be perpetuated beyond the point of their social or psychological utility. Illing wanted German Americans to organize in order "to cultivate the imponderable properties of German culture," and he resented it fiercely when ordinary people could not share his elitist values. The only bright spot in Illing's ethnic world was the new Carl Schurz Memorial Foundation, which he understood to be a great German-American cultural institute of imposing character and financial power sure to compel respect.[49]

Although the Schurz Foundation never became quite what Illing imagined, it was symbolic of a new emphasis in German ethnic life at the beginning of the 1930s. The futility of the political strategy having finally become obvious, leadership fell increasingly to the moderates, led by the editors and publishers who stressed the importance of cultural education programs.[50] Still, new efforts were made to create national organizations capable of serving the interests of Germans in America. One of these, the German-American Federation of the U.S.A., embodied all the cultural goals of the Steuben Society but specifically rejected politics as a means to achieve them. Merely a revival of the old prewar National German-American Alliance, it had difficulty attracting supporters, partly because of the interest shown in it by several American proto-Nazi organizations.[51] More important was the National Congress of Americans of German Descent, an informal conference that met in New York in October 1932 under the auspices of the German-American Conference of Greater New York and Vicinity. The guidance of the Ridder brothers was much in evidence at this meeting. Cynically interpreted, the congress was an attempt by the German-language press to sustain and revive the ethnic community in a time of economic distress, just as the officers of participating ethnic organizations hoped thereby to preserve their positions of authority and respect.

The United States was approaching the depth of the Great Depression at the time of the first National Congress of Americans of German Descent. It was surprisingly well attended. Most delegates represented national, regional, and city organizations and alliances, but ethnic craft unions, socialist workers groups, and church bodies had no interest in such an affair. At the core of the congress were cultural chauvinists whose prosperity and education permitted them the luxury of cherishing ethnic heritage for its own sake. Many speakers urged the assembly to lead the German element to its rightful place in American society. Their repeated use of such words as "recognition" and "respect" demonstrate that they were still troubled by the status deprivation engendered by World War I. The congress seemed to flounder about in search of some device or some institution that promised to preserve ethnic culture. It supported proposals to create an institute for research in ethnic language and culture, and to establish German houses at universities, German-language instruction programs, information bureaus, and cultural exchanges with Germany. The least realistic was a proposal to create a German-American university.[52]

Meanwhile, the Schurz Foundation had been established in Philadelphia. Supported by substantial contributions from several wealthy German-American businessmen and industrialists, it made no pretense to ethnic leadership per se. Instead, the foundation promoted cultural exchange programs and sought to acquaint Americans with German cultural achievements through its beautifully edited magazine, *American-German Review,* which started in 1934.[53]

Philadelphia was also the scene of the second National Congress of Americans of German Descent, held in October 1933 in commemoration of the 250th anniversary of the first German settlement in America in 1683 at Germantown. Devoid of new ideas and unable to overcome the constrictions of economic depression, the congress movement died thereafter. Quite sensibly, neither the first nor the second congress had shown any concern for Germany, possibly out of fear of being identified with Nazism. But both congresses also tended to ignore the problems of the approximately four hundred thousand immigrants from Germany who entered the United States during the 1920s.[54]

When the older generation of immigrants (or "Grays," as they were traditionally called) commented at all on the postwar arrivals from Germany ("Greens"), it was usually in uncomplimentary terms. They were distressed chiefly because the latter showed little interest in the preservation of *Deutschtum* and often formed organizations of their own rather than supporting older, established institutions, most of which desperately needed the backing of the newcomers. In one instance, the Greens were even criticized for joining the liberal Evangelical Synod, which was presumably less committed to German-language maintenance, rather than the conservative, orthodox Missouri and Wisconsin Lutheran synods. Observers in Germany also disparaged the postwar emigrants as having an unprecedented proportion of complainers and renegades who, after one year in America, preferred to speak bad English rather than good German.[55]

The Greens themselves saw their circumstances differently. One of their most eloquent spokesmen was Dr. Fritz Schlesinger of New York, who addressed the first National Congress of Americans of German Descent in 1932. He reminded the assembled Grays that the postwar immigrants had come seeking a new life, believing that America offered them more opportunities and better security than did Germany. Unlike the earlier immigrants, most of whom were farmers and workers who had arrived before 1895, the Greens were representative of all levels of German society, including a disproportionate number of intellectuals. The majority, said Schlesinger, were interested in a rapid acculturation and hence tended to regard the use of the German language as a necessary evil during the transition period. They had not pursued *Deutschtum* in America and generally considered it a hindrance to a successful adjustment. Schlesinger explained that soon after their arrival these immigrants discovered that most ethnic associations were interested in perpetuating an outmoded form of German culture. Moreover, the *Vereine* seemed both unprepared and unwilling to serve the needs of the newcomers. Forced to be self-reliant, the Greens therefore used the societies for the only thing they were good for—convenient social contacts. The idea that the immigrant had a duty of some kind to preserve *Deutschtum* in America never occurred to them. Schlesinger further pointed out that most of the agencies for cultural preservation, such as the Carl Schurz Memorial Foundation, the Goethe Society of America, the many singing societies, and the great umbrella organizations like the United German Societies and the German-American Conference, were almost exclusively run by second- and third-generation German Americans.[56]

The problem of German-American unity, according to Schlesinger, concerned social class much more than people were willing to believe. Americans of German descent completely overlooked the fact that Germany was a land sharply divided into social strata and that in their private social relationships Germans rarely crossed the traditional lines. Upon his arrival in America, the newcomer found persons of all classes and occupations mixed together in the *Vereine;* furthermore, the leaders seemed chiefly to be "self-made" men, economically successful but culturally deficient. Thus the immigrant intellectuals—academics and professional people, many with language problems that forced them to accept work beneath their educational level—felt economically inferior but culturally superior to most of the German Americans. Made uncomfortable by this anomaly, they often preferred to seek admission to American circles rather than to ethnic organizations. Yet these persons were precisely the ones who were expected to be the new champions of German *Geistesgüte.* Even the simpler people among the Greens, Schlesinger observed, sensed a provincialism or the lack of progressive or modern spirit among the German-American leaders. Finally, Schlesinger pleaded for a deeper involvement in American political affairs, not in terms of the German ethnic group interest, but in the service of the entire American society. Ties to German political parties must be severed, he said, and preoccupation with daily political events in Germany must end, if German American unity was to be achieved.

Schlesinger, a Jew, was obviously thinking of the Nazi party and the advent of Adolf Hitler, who came to power in Germany three months later. Other postwar immigrants were also thinking of Hitler, but in rather more favorable terms. American Nazi organizations were formed as early as 1924. Their memberships consisted almost exclusively of urban workers or proletarianized members of the German middle class who found few of their American dreams fulfilled. In their frustration, they consciously rejected assimilation, disparaged American life, and embraced fascism. At no time did the Nazi organizations attract a collective membership of more than a few thousand persons.[57] But because of their ideology of authoritarianism, racism, and extreme nationalism, they crowded the staid, bourgeois German-American societies from the stage of public attention, beginning with Hitler's rise to power in 1933. From then until the American entry into World War II, the activities of the Friends of the New Germany and its successor, the so-called German-American Bund, were daily fare in the *New York Times* and other major metropolitan newspapers. By the end of the decade, Fritz Kuhn, the leader of the Bund, was the best-known German in America.[58]

American Nazi organizations, like the older ethnic societies, were also concerned with German-American unity and leadership. But instead of basing their appeal on culture, the Nazis used race. In their view, all Germans everywhere were united by blood and were thereby bound in loyalty to the Fatherland. Anti-Semitic and anti-Communist propaganda was spread to attract popular support; brutal methods and threats of violence were employed in a series of efforts, most of them unsuccessful, to take over or to discredit the old umbrella organizations and the Steuben Society.

The leaders of the German-American Bund repeatedly demonstrated ignorance of American society and of the place of German immigrants in it. They understood nothing of American ideals and values or of the extent to which the masses of German Americans shared them. The efforts of Kuhn and his coterie to assume the leadership of German America on dictatorship principles must be written off as an abject failure. Even the German foreign ministry was frequently embarrassed by Bundist blunders and took all steps short of outright repudiation to control the organization.

Yet the American Nazis succeeded in keeping the established leaders of the ethnic group off balance. This was partly due, of course, to the apparent success of the Hitler government in both domestic and foreign affairs during the 1930s. Few prominent old-line German-American leaders were willing to speak out forcefully and consistently against Nazi outrages, so proud were they of the positive accomplishments of the new regime. They took delight in the way Hitler violated the detested Treaty of Versailles. The leaders of the Americanized German churches likewise refrained from condemning Hitlerism.[59] Indeed, some of the churchmen seem to have been encouraged to indulge in their own versions of anti-Semitism.[60] Unlike secular societies, the churches did not count Jews among their members. Thus only German-Jewish and Socialist organizations fought vigorously and relentlessly against American Nazism from 1933 to World War II.[61]

As a matter of policy, the leaders of the old organizations generally avoided commenting on Nazi excesses. In the cases of the churchmen, silence was partly the consequence of their *Weltanschauung;* disposed to divide human affairs into two separate worlds of the sacred and the profane, they rarely discussed contemporary issues of any kind. But the leaders of the secular organizations were fearful of losing their positions of prestige. Their societies had already been enervated by depression and assimilation, and they were reluctant to risk alienating even small parts of their constituencies. Some leaders were practically driven to take strong anti-Nazi stands by the Bundists, whose bully tactics left them no choice. Their moral perceptions dulled by ethnocentrism, the leaders of the German-American Conference of New York and the Steuben Society of America refrained from taking a forthright anti-Nazi stand until 1938, when the insolence and contempt of the Nazi challenge to their leadership was so general it could no longer be ignored.[62]

Two other events in 1938 stimulated a somewhat more general and open criticism among German Americans of Hitler and National Socialism. One was the imprisonment in a concentration camp of Pastor Martin Niemöller, a special hero of German Protestants who had been a commander of a German submarine in World War I. The other was the *Kristallnacht* pogrom of November 1938, touched off by the assassination in Paris of a German diplomat by a young Polish Jew. These acts finally goaded both the *Kirchendeutsche* and the *Vereinsdeutsche* into condemning Nazism.[63] But even thereafter, muted pride in Hitler's deeds was more common in the German-language press than was consistent condemnation.[64] Some small-town newspapers, such as the *Fredericksburg* [Texas] *Wochenblatt,* concentrated on local news and ignored the world crisis generally; a great many papers, among them the *Sheboygan* [Wisconsin] *Amerika,* tried to present a neutral or objective reporting of the news; a few, such as the *Iowa Reform* [Davenport] and the *Dakota Freie Presse* [Bismarck], were clearly pro-German, anti-Semitic, isolationist, and intensely anti-Roosevelt.

Just before World War II began in 1939, Carl Wittke, the eminent historian of German America, who was then a dean at Oberlin College, encapsulated the moral problem faced by the leadership in his own ethnic group. It was apparent, Wittke wrote, that newspaper accounts of Nazi atrocities against the Jews were not exaggerated and that there were millions of persons in Germany who were appalled by the policies of the Hitler regime. But instead of giving moral support to honorable men who were fighting against fearful odds for decency, humanity, and brotherhood, the leaders of the German element preferred to extol the glories of the "Forty-eighters" and their flaming liberalism while excusing Nazi excesses as a passing phase or characterizing "the noble fuehrer" as an unfortunate "victim of an ignorant or brutal minority of his party."[65]

Whereas H. L. Mencken had been disdainful of German ethnic group leadership, Wittke was simply disgusted. He was offended by their moral obtuseness and narrow chauvinism. It is clear, moreover, that their record over the two decades of the interwar period is distinguished by neither insight nor foresight. Most spokesmen for the group, self-appointed or otherwise, were deficient in understanding their constituencies and how they, as leaders, might relate to the great masses of Americans of German origins or descent. Remarkably various in economic status, religious belief, and even in language and culture, most German Americans, unlike the core of leaders, were not moved primarily by ethnic considerations. Hundreds of thousands of persons who were technically counted as German Americans had no significant measure of identification with the ethnic group. Indeed, some were antagonistic to programs for the preservation of ethnic identity. Others perceived ethnicity as inhibiting the attainment of other goals deemed more important. Church Germans, for example, abandoned ethnicity at an accelerated pace during the 1920s and 1930s.

But even those leaders who shared the desire for ethnic unity could not agree on how it should be attained. Some persisted in strategies that were inevitably counterproductive, given the character of the times, and thus stimulated further fragmentation of the ethnic group. Filled with bitterness and resentment over their treatment in World War I and perturbed by an enduring sense of having lost status, they first hoped to regain respect through united ethnic political action. Some advocated the use of raw political power; others preferred persuasion. After the political strategy had failed repeatedly during the 1920s, they shifted to an emphasis on culture. But their programs were based upon elitist values at variance with those of the masses. The leaders refused to believe that immigrant language and culture could not be effectively perpetuated beyond the period of social or psychological utility. Vitiated by the Great Depression, cultural programs faded as the American Nazis, ever bold and arrogant, captured public attention with their strategy of blood. This racist quest for German-American unity, appealing chiefly to recent, postwar immigrants, was so antipathetic to American ideals and habits of thought and attitude that it eventually drove most traditional German-American leaders into opposition. This meant that, except on the local or personal levels, the attainment of ethnic group goals by means of organized activity was abandoned with the advent of World War II.

One may scarcely speak of German ethnic leadership in the United States since World War II. The Steuben Society of America, the Catholic

Central-Verein, the Carl Schurz Memorial Foundation, the American Turners, and more than a dozen other national organizations continued to exist, sustained by large numbers of German-speaking refugees from central and eastern Europe who arrived during the 1940s and 1950s.[66] Old patterns persist. The attitudes of the old Bürgerbund are presently reincarnated in the Deutsche-Americanische National Kongress and in the Federation of American Citizens of German Descent. Their rhetoric and strategies often seem unchanged from what they were in the 1920s.[67] But no one listens; these organizations, united chiefly by a hatred of Communism, are unknown to the general public and ignored by most German Americans who may have heard of them. Meanwhile, German ethnicity thrives in many hundreds of local *Vereine* throughout the land, but especially in major centers of German population, such as New York, Cleveland, and Chicago, plus Florida and California. They gather together persons whose attachment to the German language and culture is more emotional than intellectual, more social than political, who are interested chiefly in maintaining an associational environment in which they may converse, dine, play, sing, and dance with others who share their values and attitudes.[68] Ironically, it is this dimension of German life in America that the chauvinists of half a century ago predicted could not survive without their leadership.

NOTES

1. H. L. Mencken, "Die Deutschamerikaner," *Die Neue Rundschau* 39 (Band 2, November 1928): 486–95.
2. This and the following several paragraphs are summarized from my book *Bonds of Loyalty: German-Americans and World War I* (DeKalb: Northern Illinois Univ. Press, 1974).
3. *Viereck's The American Monthly* 11 (September 1919): 5. Compare George Seibel, "German-Americanism," *American Monthly* 25 (March 1932): 9.
4. *Viereck's The American Monthly* 11 (October, November, December 1919): 42, 76, 107.
5. *German American World* 7 (February 15, 1924): 224; Rudolf Cronau, *Drei Jahrhunderte Deutschen Lebens in Amerika*, 2d rev. ed. (Berlin: Dietrich Reimer, 1924), 661; J. Eiselmeier, *Das Deutschtum in Angloamerika* (Berlin: Deutschen Schutzbund Verlag, n.d.), 30; Heinz Kloss, "Deutschamerikanische Querschnitt: Vereinsdeutsche, Nationalsozialisten, Kirchendeutsche," *Die evangelische Diaspora* 16 (1934): 170–71.
6. See my more extended treatment of this development in *Bonds of Loyalty*, 314–18. See also James C. Juhnke, *A People of Two Kingdoms: The Political Acculturation of the Kansas Mennonites* (Newton, KS: Faith and Life Press, 1975), 113–16; H. Kamphausen, *Geschichte des religiosen Lebens in der*

Deutschen Evangelischen Synode von Nordamerika (St. Louis: Eden Publishing House, 1924), 300–333; Heinz Kloss, *Um die Einigung des Deutschamerikanertums: Die Geschichte einer unvollendeten Volksgruppe* (Berlin: Volk und Reich Verlag, 1937), 164–66.

7. Kamphausen, *Geschichte des religiosen Lebens*, 313; Alan N. Graebner, "The Acculturation of an Immigrant Church: The Lutheran Church-Missouri Synod, 1917–1929" (Ph.D. diss., Columbia University, 1965), 83–161.

8. *Amerikanische Turnzeitung* (New Ulm, Minnesota), May 1, 1921, January 14, 1923, and May 27, 1923; *American Monthly* 13 (March–May 1922): 15, 85; Kloss, *Um die Einigung*, 302–3. See also Noel Iverson, *Germania, U.S.A.* (Minneapolis: Univ. of Minnesota Press, 1966), 32–35, 91–120.

9. *New Yorker Staats-Zeitung*, September 22, 1924.

10. Ibid., December 21, 1920, and September 6, 1920; [Paul G. Kreutz], *Ein Gedenkwerk zum Goldenen Jubiläum des Plattdeutschen Volksfest-Verein von New York und Umgebung* (New York: Plattdeutsche Volksfest-Verein, 1925), 174–76.

11. *New Yorker Staats-Zeitung*, November 10, 1920. In the early 1920s, the Plattdeutsche Volksfest-Verein listed eighty-three member organizations (Kreutz, *Gedenkwerk*, 275–80).

12. For examples, see Kreutz, *Gedenkwerk*, 171–80; *History of the Liederkranz of the City of New York, 1847–1947* (New York: Drechsel Printing, 1948), 48–53.

13. *Viereck's The American Monthly* 12 (September 1920): 199; *American Monthly* 13 (August 1921): 169, 175, and 14 (September 1922): 205; Niel M. Johnson, *George Sylvester Viereck: German-American Propagandist* (Urbana: Univ. of Illinois Press, 1972), 82; Kloss, *Um die Einigung*, 295–300.

14. *New York Times*, January 11 and 12, 1921; *American Monthly* 12 (February 1921): 359–60.

15. See the scathing editorial from the *Cincinnati Freie Presse*, reprinted in English in *German American World* 7 (March 15, 1924): 281–82.

16. *Steuben News* 11 (May 1939): 2–4; Cronau, *Drei Jahrhunderte*, 661; "The German-American Element and the Next Election," *Issues of To-Day* 6 (September 29, 1923); "The German-American in Politics," *Issues of To-Day* 5 (October 21, 1922): 4–5.

17. Dr. Franz Koempel, "On the Twentieth Anniversary of the Steuben Society of America," *Steuben News* 11 (May 1939).

18. In addition to numerous articles in *American Monthly, Issues of To-Day,* and *German American World*, see the *Steuben News*, which began in 1929. Compare Kloss, *Um die Einigung*, 287.

19. *Viereck's The American Monthly* 11 (October 1919, February 1920): 42, 181; *American Monthly* 12 (March, April, July, August 1920): 4, 46, 133, 165; *New York Times*, September 5, and October 17, 1920; *Literary Digest* 66 (September 18, 1920): 11–12; Johnson, *Viereck*, 82–87.

20. Johnson, *Viereck*, 82.

21. Luebke, *Bonds of Loyalty*, 325–28.

22. Johnson, *Viereck*, 88.
23. *New York Times*, January 11 and 12, 1921.
24. *American Monthly* 12 (February 1921): 359–60; 13 (March 1921): 9; Johnson, *Viereck*, 89; *New York Times*, January 15, and February 17, 1921. Viereck later published a lengthy article defending his role in the affair and included lengthy excerpts from his correspondence with President Harding (see Alexander Harvey, "German-American Unity and the President," *American Monthly* 16 (July 1924): 136–43).
25. See the convenient summary of this affair in Johnson, *Viereck*, 90–91. Viereck's version appears in *American Monthly* 16 (July 1924): 141–43.
26. Viereck assailed the German-language press as early as February 1921, when it became clear that the editors refused to support the Harding visitation (see *American Monthly* 12: 357).
27. *American Monthly* 13 (January 1922): 344, and 14 (April 1922): 40–42. Viereck continued his "exposure" of the Ridders in the May issue of *American Monthly* 14: 74–76. An extraordinary display of hypocrisy, this article accused the Ridders of being "professional German Americans" who "aim to build up their own prestige and the power of their newspaper at the expense of their fellows" by "shrewdly utilizing every political break, every personal spite and every personal vanity." No one was more intimately acquainted with such behavior than Viereck himself.
28. *American Monthly* 14 (June 1922): 104–5.
29. *Amerikanische Turnzeitung*, September 16, 1923; *New York Times*, October 22, 1923. Viereck applauded the selection of Seibel, whom he described as "just the man to lead the Turnerbund back to its true ideals which had been deserted so ignominiously by its former president, the unspeakable Stempfel" (*American Monthly* 15 [September 1923]: 213). See also ibid., 15 (August 1923): 183.
30. *New Yorker Staats-Zeitung*, September 16, 1924.
31. *German American World* 7 (July 1, 1924): 440.
32. *New Yorker Staats-Zeitung*, September 16 and 22, and October 9, 14, and 15, 1924.
33. Ibid., September 16, 1924.
34. "The Potentiality of 'the German Vote,' " *German American World* 7 (February 1, 1924): 199–200.
35. *American Monthly* 16 (September 1924): 225. See also ibid., 16 (October 1924): 250.
36. *New York Times*, August 15, 30, and 31; September 11, 21, and 22; and October 1, 5, 9, 10, 13, 22, 23, 25, and 26, 1924.
37. "Voice of the German Language Press," *German American World* 7 (1924): 442–43, 473, 495–96, 547.
38. Reprinted in translation in *German American World* 7 (March 15, 1924): 280–81.
39. *American Monthly* 16 (October 1924): 255.
40. *German American World* 7 (April 1, 1924): 298.

41. *American Monthly* 16 (June, July, August, December 1924): 105, 136–43, 158, 311.

42. *New Yorker Staats-Zeitung,* October 17 and 24, 1924.

43. *American Monthly* 16 (December 1924): 312, 318. See also Alexander Harvey, "The German-Americans and the LaFollette Vote," *American Monthly* 16 (December 1924): 318–19, 330.

44. Sen. Robert Wagner of New York, who was born in Germany, never ran as a German-American candidate and carefully avoided identification with German-American political organizations, save the German-American Roland Society, which was staunchly loyal to the Democratic party.

45. *New York Times,* October 22, 1928; *New Yorker Staats-Zeitung,* October 23 and 25, 1928; Richard Bartholdt, *From Steerage to Congress* (Philadelphia: Dorrance, 1930), 422.

46. *Der Christliche Apologete* 90 (November 14, 1928): 1083; Douglas C. Stange, "Al Smith and the Republican Party at Prayer: The Lutheran Vote— 1928," *Review of Politics* 32 (July 1970): 347–64.

47. *New Yorker Staats-Zeitung,* October 26, 1928; *New York Times,* October 25, 1928.

48. Mencken, "Die Deutsch-Amerikaner," 490; Kloss, *Um die Einigung,* 288; *New York Times,* October 8, 14, 17, 19, and 20, 1928; *Steuben News* 1 (November 1928): 4.

49. *American Monthly* 23 (May, June, July 1930).

50. For an impassioned plea for the cultural strategy and a rejection of ethnic political action by a distinguished German-American academician, see Kuno Francke, *Deutsche Arbeit in Amerika* (Leipzig: Felix Meiner, 1930), 91.

51. Deutschamerikanischen Bürgerbund von Nebraska, *Protokoll der fünften Jahres-Versammlung* (Omaha: December 1931), 17–19; Kloss, "Deutschamerikanische Querschnitt," 167; *Steuben News* 4 (November 1931): 1, 4, and 4 (December 1931): 2.

52. *Erster National-Kongress der Amerikaner Deutschen Stammes. Sitzungsberichte und Erläuterungen. New York City, October 27–30, 1932* (New York: Deutsch-Amerikanische Konferenz von Gross-New York und Umgebung, n.d.). See also *New York Times,* October 28, 29, and 30, 1932.

53. Eugene E. Doll, *Twenty-five Years of Service, 1930–1955* (Philadelphia: Carl Schurz Memorial Foundation, n.d.), 3–9; *American Monthly* 23 (November 1930): 34–35; *American-German Review* 1 (September 1934): 56.

54. *Steuben News* 6 (November 1933): 2; Kloss, "Deutschamerikanische Querschnitt," 168.

55. George Seibel, "German-Americanism," *American Monthly* 25 (March 1932): 10, 14; Oscar Illing, "The Americans of German Blood," *American Monthly* 23 (June 1930): 44; Kloss, "Deutschamerikanische Querschnitt," 173.

56. *Erster National-Kongress,* 50.

57. Diamond, *Nazi Movement,* 146, 169; Klaus Kipphan, *Deutsche Propaganda in den Vereinigten Staaten, 1933–1941* (Heidelberg: Carl Winter Univer-

sitätsverlag, 1971), 51–55; O. John Rogge, *The Official German Report* (New York and London: Thomas Yoseloff, 1961), 129.

58. In addition to the books by Diamond and Kipphan, see Leland B. Bell, *In Hitler's Shadow: The Anatomy of American Nazism* (Port Washington, NY: Kennikat, 1973); Alton Frye, *Nazi Germany and the American Hemisphere, 1933–1941* (New Haven: Yale Univ. Press, 1967); and Arthur L. Smith, Jr., *The Deutschtum of Nazi Germany and the United States* (The Hague: Martinus Nijhoff, 1965).

59. *Steuben News* 6 (July 1934): 3; *Die Abendschule* (St. Louis) 79 (May 4, 1933): 709, and 80 (June 14, 1934): 796–97.

60. See several articles in *Der Christliche Apologete* (Methodist) 101 (1939), but especially "Verfolgung und Ausweisung der Juden" by John C. Guenther, 57–58. For other examples, see *Kirchenzeitung* (Reformed) 103 (January 11, 1933): 6, and 108 (May 17, 1938): 16; *Kirchenblatt* (American Lutheran), August 12, 1939, 9, and August 26, 1939, 3; *Die Abendschule* 80 (September 21, 1933): 167, and (December 14, 1933): 371.

61. *New York Times*, April 4 and 8–11, 1938; *New Yorker Staats-Zeitung*, September 16, 1939; *Sonntagsblatt* [New York] *Staats-Zeitung und Herold*, September 15, 1940; Robert E. Cazden, *German Exile Literature in America 1933–1950* (Chicago: American Library Association, 1970), 42, 44.

62. Kipphan, *Deutsche Propaganda*, 93. A detailed account of the fight is given in *Steuben News* 11 (October 1938): 3, 5, 7; see also *Steuben News* 11 (June 1938): 8, (August 1938): 3, and (September 1938): 3.

63. *Kirchenzeitung* 108 (February 22, 1938): 11, (April 12, 1938): 14–15, (May 3, 1938): 14, (December 6, 1938): 15; *Kirchenblatt* 81 (March 19, 1938): 6, and (April 16, 1938): 11; *Der Christliche Apologete* 101 (January 4, 1939); *New York Times*, October 3 and 9, and November 23, 1938; Dieter Cunz, *The Maryland Germans, A History* (Princeton: Princeton Univ. Press, 1948), 414, 437; Johnson, *Veireck*, 193; Diamond, *Nazi Movement*, 276–77.

64. "Foreign-language Press: 1047 Immigrant Newspapers," *Fortune* 22 (November 1940): 92–93. Even after *Kristallnacht*, the Ridders' *New Yorker Staats-Zeitung* refrained from strong criticism of Hitlerism.

65. *Cleveland Plain Dealer*, reprinted in *American Turner*, August 13, 1939: 6.

66. *Die Vereinswelt: Wegweiser der Deutschamerikaner, Sonderbeilage New Yorker Staats-Zeitung und Herold*, May 13, 1973. See especially the article by the publisher Erwin Single, "Aus der Werkstatt der Verlager," 3.

67. *Die Vereinswelt*, 1954: 3; *Der Deutsch-Amerikaner: D.A.N.K. Mitteilungen* 8 (January 1966): 2, (April 1966): 9, (August 1966): 6, and (October 1966): 3.

68. *Die Vereinswelt, 1973; Deutsch-Amerikanische Jahreskalender des Staates Ohio, 1963* (Cleveland: Ernst Printing and Calendar Co., [1962]); 78. *Jahres-Bericht und Mitglieder-Verzeichnis, Schwaben-Verein Chicago* (1956); *20. Jahre-Vereinigung der Donauschwaben von Chicago* (1973), especially the article by Christ N. Herr, "Die Vereinigung der Donauschwaben in Chicago: Entstehung und Werdegung," 17–35.

For a hundred years, from the age of Jackson to the era of Franklin Roosevelt, German Americans complained about the political apathy they perceived to be characteristic of their ethnic group. As they saw it, German immigrants tended to be phlegmatic or lethargic when it came to political matters, at least in contrast to the vigor and industry they displayed in their economic pursuits. The Germans also appeared to be politically backward and ineffective, at least in comparison to the Irish. In this view, apathy explained why the number of German Americans nominated and elected to political office was rarely commensurate with the proportion of German Americans in the electorate. The frequently voiced complaint went still further: American politicians paid insufficient attention to the needs and desires of their German constituents, and they rarely seemed to appreciate the magnificent contributions Germans had made to American greatness.

There was, of course, a substantial factual basis for these charges, depending upon one's definition of political behavior and the role of politics in a multiethnic, democratic society. Most of the critics took a narrow view of politics; for them, it was primarily a matter of voting and holding office. But a meaningful assessment of political behavior encompasses much more, such as becoming a citizen, paying taxes, assuming jury duty, and serving in the armed forces. It takes in any discussion of political issues and the relationships of an ethnic group to governmental and political processes, in newspapers, editorials, public addresses, or sermons, and it also includes the influence such activity may have on the formation of public policy. Thus, for a German-American clergyman to take a stand on the compelling issues of the day—slavery, prohibition, compulsory public school education, neutrality in world wars—or to refuse on theological grounds to take a stand on such issues, is also to behave politically. One cannot easily separate political behavior from other activities. It is woven into the fabric of life, with all its complexities and contradictions; it reflects relationships with work, play, beliefs, values, and aspirations.

Although such a comprehensive view of political behavior is not new, few recent studies of German-American political history have placed ethnic leaders in such an enlarged social and cultural context. Officeholding, for example, has not been studied systematically or with appropriate comparisons. There is good evidence that many German-born persons held minor political office already in the pre–Civil War era, but we do not know how their activity compares to that of either the native-born or other immigrant groups. We know also that only five persons of German birth have ever been elected to the United States Senate. But that fact has little meaning unless it is compared statistically to the record of other groups.

Another important aspect of ethnic officeholding concerns pre-emigration experience. The Irish, for example, had acquired crucial political skills in their long struggle against English dominance in Ireland. Accustomed to questioning the legitimacy of formal government, they felt comfortable in America with the extralegal arrangements developed by nineteenth-century urban political machines. In addition, the Irish had no language barrier to impede their political acculturation. By contrast, German immigrants, speaking a foreign tongue and accustomed to authoritarian regimes buttressed by the church, brought little political experience to America. Moreover, Germans were much more likely than the Irish to settle on farms, where isolation from political activity was more or less inevitable in the nineteenth century. In the cities, however, Germans generally enjoyed better economic prospects because of their crafts, education, and wealth than did the Irish, whose poverty and lack of skills forced them to pursue any means of survival, including the political. Thus the Irish immigrant as policeman and ward politician became a fixture in our national mythology, but we can hardly imagine a German equivalent.

Political involvement was discouraged by some of the German immigrant churches. The Mennonites in particular were commited to the doctrine of the two kingdoms—the sacred and the secular—and taught that, while the Christian was in the world, he was not of it. Politics was a worldly snare, according to this view, and was to be avoided except in those cases when the defense of the faith demanded it. Certain German Lutheran theologians, especially of the Missouri Synod, held similar views. Insisting upon a total separation of church and state, they explicitly encouraged a spirit of separatism as a means of preserving their "pure doctrine" and shielding the young from the allurements of a sinful world. Politics in America, these theologians believed, was hopelessly corrupt; as a group, politicians were greedy, ignorant hacks given to bribery and demagoguery. Such attitudes naturally precluded any encouragement to political officeholding by the laity.

Another important question regarding officeholding by immigrants concerns the relationship between the official and his ethnic group. Did a German-born holder of high political office see himself as a representative of his own ethnic group, or did he rise above such considerations in order to serve broader constituencies? It seems clear that an ethnic politician could successfully adopt the former role only under special conditions, such as when his group comprised the majority (or its functional equivalent) in his electoral unit or when ethnic group interest happened to coincide with the majority view. In the nineteenth century, Irish-American politicians in such cities as New York, Boston, and Chicago often enjoyed these circumstances, but the electoral constituencies of German-American politicians were usually less highly concentrated. More important, German-American voters were frequently spread across the socioeconomic spectrum and hence rarely held uniform views on the political issues of the day. In other words, the German ethnic community, unlike the Irish, was ordinarily so diverse, with its rich and poor, its educated and uneducated, its skilled and unskilled workers, its urban as well as rural residents, its Catholics and Protestants, that unity in support of anything or anyone was rarely possible to achieve. Hence, the numerous lamentations about the lack of German unity by the most idealistic of German-American leaders, who, it is worth noting, were usually journalists, not practicing politicians.

Such leaders understood, of course, that the Germans in America were a remarkably diverse and divided group. They hoped, however, that unity could be achieved through an appeal to German idealism, whatever its relationship may have been to the issues of the day. But such a notion was fundamentally elitist in character and ignored the fact that ordinary voters were more likely to be moved by practical "bread-and-butter" considerations. This is not to suggest that the common folk lacked idealism, but rather that the things they valued were ordered differently. Thus we have the familiar rhetoric of the Forty-eighters—that grand generation of political refugees—who were outraged by slavery in a republic and whose idealism usually led them to strong support for Abraham Lincoln and the newly founded Republican party. Yet the common people among the Germans in America noticed that in many states Republican leaders were often persons who just a few years earlier had been prominently associated with the nativist, anti-Catholic Know Nothing party. Moreover, ordinary German Americans, who often had close ties to religious institutions, also observed that the prominent German-American leaders were usually anticlerical freethinkers or atheists, some of whom regularly castigated the churches and their clergy. It should not surprise us, therefore, that a large proportion of German-American voters marched to different drummers and voted Democratic.

The vocal German idealists were also highly critical of the American political system and its apparent pragmatic qualities. Despite their intelligence and erudition, they failed to understand that pragmatism was a necessary ingredient in the American political recipe and they were too impatient or disdainful to discover this truth through experience. Nor did they understand that the Constitution of the United States, through its provisions for an electoral college, indirectly and unintentionally dictated a two-party system. Thus, from the 1850s to the 1920s, from Karl Heinzen to George Sylvester Viereck, we have examples of German-American leaders who were advocates of a German-American political party—a third party united on the basis of German idealism that would hold the balance of power. By positioning itself between the two major parties, such an organization presumably could force one or the other major party to do its bidding. Ironically, the bald pragmatism inherent in this approach was espoused in the name of idealism.

The advocates of this strategy, believing in the superiority of German idealism and in the power of their logic, naively hoped to transcend German-American heterogeneity to forge an ethnic unity and thus an effective voting bloc. But they failed to see that their efforts could generate only resentment and disdain among non-German political leaders. An ethnic politician who tried to force one or the other party to support the interests or ideals of his group could never expect to attain a position of power or influence in a major party. Such a strategy would inevitably narrow the base of his support. The most that could be expected was that a major party would temporarily bend to support the minority interest, but the long-range effect would be to remove ethnic leaders from genuine political power within the major party structures.

In the American system, especially in the nineteenth century, advancement in political officeholding was a concomitant of loyalty to party and not to the ideals of a minority ethnic group. If a politician worked faithfully and consistently for his party, he could expect to move gradually to higher levels of leadership, authority, and power. This system, however, placed a considerable strain on the typical German-American politician. If advancement is linked to party loyalty, it is incumbent upon the politician to support his party even in those instances when it pursues a course contrary to ethnic group interest or to ethnically defined ideals. Faced with this dilemma, those German-American politicians who chose loyalty to party over idealism were forced to abandon strong identification with their ethnic group; those who chose loyalty to idealism over party could not win reelection.

An example of the latter is the revered Carl Schurz. Schurz was truly a man of extraordinary talents—a brilliant journalist and orator, minister to Spain, Civil War general, senator from Missouri, secretary of the interior, and, at least by his own account, a confidant of most presidents from Lincoln to Theodore Roosevelt. Americans generally paid attention to Carl Schurz only when he transcended ethnic politics to speak and act on issues that were important to the entire nation. His idealism led him to oppose slavery, to support Lincoln, to advocate Radical Republicanism in the Reconstruction era, and later to lead the Liberal Republican movement. In those instances his views were shared by countless Americans of reformist tendencies; the fact that they were rooted in his German culture was incidental to his success. But when Schurz tried to function as an ethnic politician, he was less successful. He was elected to only one office—by the Missouri legislature, not by the voters of Missouri directly—and he had no chance of reelection. It is true that Lincoln and other political leaders perceived him as being exceptionally influential with German voters and that they sometimes fashioned their strategies accordingly; yet there is no convincing evidence that Schurz was actually able "to deliver the German vote," especially among the thousands of Catholics, Lutherans, and other church people who distrusted him. Ultimately, Schurz's real eminence was as an *American* statesman, not as a German American. His effectiveness emerged from his eloquent exposition of national issues, not those that preoccupied the attention of the German-American ethnic group.

Sen. Robert Wagner of New York typifies those German-born politicians who chose loyalty to party over ethnic idealism. Invariably loyal to the Democratic party, Wagner pragmatically pursued policies that were framed by the interests of his multiethnic constituency. Throughout his career as a Democratic politician, from urban wards in New York to the U.S. Senate, Wagner always played down his German birth. Although he was interested in the affairs of the Roland Society (a German Democratic political organization in New York City), he never gave it publicity. In the end, his record of legislative accomplishment as the champion of the interests of the common, laboring people in New York and the nation easily exceeded the achievements attained by Schurz. One specialized in words, the other in deeds.

Wagner's long political career, which spanned four decades, was thus largely independent of the Germans as a special interest group and therefore of the vagaries of ethnic politics. Unlike the Irish or the blacks, who were united by economic deprivation, social ostracism, and religious discrimination, the generally more prosperous Germans had no reason to act in concert except to defend their culture. Issues capable of stimulating the Germans to unite politically, such as prohibition and attacks on parochial schools, were usually temporary. When the threat faded, so did opportunities for political leadership based on German group interest. Moreover, the defense of German ethnic culture was essentially a negative enterprise. It was usually a question of what the Germans were *against* rather than what they were *for*. If a German-American political leader had no reason for existence other than the defense of ethnic culture, he inevitably sounded strident, uncompromising, and unattractive to nonimmigrant voters.

Still, ethnocultural clashes were endemic in the nineteenth century, and the political conflict they generated flared from time to time and from place to place, sometimes with remarkable intensity. An early controversy concerned questions of citizenship and the right to vote and hold office. Nativist fears of immigrant voters were greatly augmented in the 1830s and 1840s as huge numbers of Irish and Germans arrived in the United States. Because most of the former and probably half of the latter were Roman Catholics, they imported a value system that sometimes contrasted sharply with the pietistic Protestantism characteristic of American society at that time. Eager to limit the influence of such immigrants in the political process, many old-stock Americans used the Whig party to attack the status of the foreign-born as equal citizens.

Nativism took on a variety of forms and goaded many thousands of ordinary German immigrants to act politically on the local level, where they usually affiliated with the Democratic party. The Democrats, inspired by Jeffersonian concepts of the negative state and spurred by the Jacksonian rhetoric of egalitarianism, were pleased to have immigrant voters add to their strength. In the 1850s, as immigration soared to new heights and as the old Whig party foundered on the rocks of slavery, nativism and anti-Catholicism became the driving force behind the short-lived Know Nothing party. In some states, this organization was quickly superseded or displaced by the new Republican party. Determined to halt the extension of slavery into the territories, if not to abolish it, the party of Abraham Lincoln rested on an ideology attractive to the articulate, educated political refugees of the 1848 Revolution. Many common folk among the German immigrants also rallied behind this new banner, most dramatically in Missouri, where Republicanism was free of the taint of Know Nothingism. But elsewhere, especially in districts distant from slave states where German workers feared the competition of free blacks, many German voters remained true to the Democracy as a bulwark against nativism. Nevertheless, the essentially erroneous idea that German voters had provided the margin of victory for Lincoln in 1860 became fixed in the minds of many political leaders.

In the decades following the Civil War, the majority of German-

American voters in most states drifted back to the Democratic party. This was generally true of Catholic Germans and, less consistently, of Lutherans. Other German Protestants, especially those of pietistic tendencies, continued to find Republicanism congenial.

This division of the German vote along religious lines rested partly in differing views about the role of government in questions of morality. Old-stock Americans, overwhelmingly Protestant, tended to believe that religion was a matter of the heart, not the head—that it was more emotional than intellectual—a matter of "right behavior" more than "right belief." Emphasis was accordingly placed on the conversion experience and a pious life as marks of God's having chosen a person for eternal salvation. According to this view, the Christian life was a constant struggle against Satan and sin, and as the sincere Christian did battle with the forces of evil, he was expected to use all legitimate weapons to vanquish the foe, including the power and authority of the government. Thus slavery should be rendered unconstitutional; the slavery of alcohol should be legislated out of existence; pious, God-fearing women should be enlisted in the battle through women's suffrage; Sabbath-day proprieties should be preserved by means of a multitude of so-called blue laws; and by various regulatory measures, the schools of the immigrants should be hindered so that public schools could socialize the children to proper Protestant values. Many German Evangelicals, Baptists, and Methodists were in basic agreement with this view and therefore in varying degrees supported the Republican party, which generally supported these measures.

But programs of coercive reform were offensive to large numbers of German Catholics and Lutherans, especially of the more theologically orthodox or conservative synods. For them, religion was more creedal, more formal, more authoritarian. In their view, the central role of government was to guarantee the fullest measure of personal liberty consonant with law and order. For the government to legislate morality by means of prohibition or Sabbatarian legislation was to invade the authority of the church. They argued, for example, that a bottle of whiskey, by itself, was neither good nor evil. Sin lay in its abuse: it was not wrong to drink, but it was a sin to get drunk. Similarly, many Germans were appalled at the effect that Sabbath laws could have on their traditions of "continental Sundays"—amiable conversation, convivial drinking, and innocent dancing in beer gardens or, for that matter, at church picnics. From their standpoint, women's suffrage was merely a political trick to double the prohibitionist vote. Worse, it threatened the role of women as wives and mothers and thereby the centrality of the family. As for restrictive school legislation, both Catholic and Lutheran Germans could unite against it, as they did in Wisconsin and Illinois *circa* 1890, to shatter the dominance of the Republican party when it supported the regulation of parochial schools. After all, they thought, the public schools were little more than tax-supported institutions for pietistic Protestants.

As a result, ethnocultural issues were capable of producing remarkable majorities among German voters for the Democratic party in state and local elections late in the nineteenth century. It is important, however, not to overstate the case. Pietistic Germans, of course, tended to remain Republican. Furthermore, Christian religious polarities had little relevance for the anticlerical intelligentsia and none at all for the German Jews, while urban workers attracted by socialist doctrines rejected such notions as detractions from the struggle against economic oppression in an industrializing America.

In general, the pattern of German voting behavior underwent a transformation in the 1890s. The symbolic politics of the 1870s and '80s continued to be important in those states, counties, or cities where ethnocultural issues were raised, but in other respects German-American voters responded more strongly as constituents of other collectivities— that is, as farmers, factory workers, merchants, mechanics, teamsters, teachers, saloon keepers, or as rich men or poor, as young persons or old, as veterans of the nation's wars, or as opponents of imperialistic foreign policies. This became especially clear during the Populist era of the 1890s, when urgent economic issues, including currency reform, railroad regulation, and tariff questions, reduced the salience of ethnocultural conflicts. In some states distinctive German voting almost disappeared. Nevertheless, historic attachments of certain German subgroups continued for many more decades, even though they were less firm than formerly. Catholic Germans, for example, tended to remain loyal to the Democratic party, but it became easier for them to be dislodged from that adherence, at least temporarily. Independent voting among Germans, as among Americans generally, increased significantly in the early decades of the twentieth century.

At the same time, foreign policy issues increased in importance for many German Americans. In earlier decades, before the creation of the German Empire in 1871, few German immigrants regarded the governments of their home states in Europe with affection. Most German states had been authoritarian, repressive, intolerant of religious diversity, and unresponsive to the needs of the common people. But many German-American hearts swelled with pride as Bismarck whipped the French in 1871 and placed his Prussian king on an imperial German throne. Although thousands of Germans had emigrated to escape military service, their pulses quickened at the news of German victories on European battlefields. A new sense of German-American ethnicity developed as the number of immigrants from rapidly industrializing Germany declined, and ethnocentric publicists deliberately cultivated a new pride in things German to halt the erosion of the German-American community caused by assimilation. This movement was institutionalized on a national level in the creation of the National German-American Alliance, which during the early years of the twentieth century claimed an inflated membership in the millions.

Such activity came to an abrupt end during World War I. Throughout the neutrality period of 1914–17, the German ethnic leaders and associations such as the National German-American Alliance worked tirelessly for American neutrality, hoping thereby to prevent the United States from joining the Allied powers against Germany. Countless speeches and editorials were written in support of neutrality, against Britain and France, and in defense of Germany; many hundreds of churches, *Vereine*, and other organizations conducted fund-raising campaigns, rallies, and bazaars for the German Red Cross. The effect was to create an illusory image of strength and unity among German Americans. Most prominent German-American leaders perceived Pres. Woodrow Wilson as a partisan of the Allied cause and therefore opposed his reelection in 1916. Among the masses of German-American voters, however, there was no such unanimity, even though they displayed a slight shift toward the Republican candidate.

In April 1917, only a few months after the election of 1916, the United States Congress, at President Wilson's request, declared war on Germany. Suddenly, behavior that had been perfectly legal (though indiscreet) in the neutrality period became unpatriotic, if not treasonable. Thousands of superpatriotic Americans now believed it to be their duty to wage a war on German culture on the domestic front. German-language newspapers were subjected to crippling censorship, German-language instruction in the schools was nearly eliminated, and all manifestations of German culture—from the performance of Beethoven's symphonies to the presentation of Schiller's plays—were discouraged, if not expressly forbidden. Innumerable acts of oppression were committed against innocent German-American citizens, whose loyalty to their adopted country was now under suspicion. In varying degrees, national, state, and especially local governments supported the anti-German hysteria. For many German Americans, Wilson became the symbolic source of their persecution, and many thousands sullenly awaited the day when they could punish Wilson's party in the privacy of a voting booth.

Already in the off-year election of 1918, the Germans, especially in the midwestern states, registered a sharp drop in Democratic voting. Two years later, when Democratic governor James Cox of Ohio ran for president as a Wilson surrogate, the Germans had their revenge. Even though there were nagging domestic problems of inflation, labor unrest, and agricultural discontent, German voters tended to ignore them as they turned to the Republican candidate, Warren Harding, in dramatic numbers. It was not that they were *for* Harding; it was that they were *against* Wilsonism as represented by Cox. Once again, negativism characterized German-American voting.

Scores of German-American precincts recorded enormous margins for the Republican candidate, sometimes at a ratio of 100 to 1, especially in German Protestant communities. Even in German Catholic precincts in rural Wisconsin, Minnesota, and North Dakota, Democratic voting dropped to a third of what it had been four years earlier. In Milwaukee, where German voters found both the Democrats and Republicans wanting, they turned in huge numbers to Eugene Debs, the Socialist candidate, who at that moment remained in a federal prison, a victim of the wartime Espionage Act. Similarly, in Minnesota, thousands of Germans supported the Farmer-Labor party.

The politics of revenge continued through the 1920s. By 1924 German-American spokesmen became more assertive as they endorsed the futile third-party presidential candidacy of Robert M. LaFollette, the senator from Wisconsin, who had come to symbolize resistance to American participation in World War I. That LaFollette's Progressive ideology was in sharp contrast to the Republican conservatism the Germans had supported four years earlier mattered little. They loved him for what he had opposed, not for what he favored. Party loyalty meant nothing to them; what mattered most was that a candidate oppose British and French dominance in world affairs and any arrangements that perpetuated the prescriptions of the Treaty of Versailles.

The majority of the German-language newspapers backed LaFollette, and German Americans supplied a substantial part of his vote. Still, careful analysis reveals that old divisions among the Germans remained, both in leadership and voting behavior. This was laid bare in 1928, when the Democratic party candidacy of New York governor Al Smith, the very symbol of urban ethnic politics, was simply too much for Protestant German voters. The pietists rejected Smith because he was "wet"; the Lutherans, because he was Catholic. But Herbert Hoover was also controversial. Some German Americans insisted that because Hoover was allegedly of German descent and because he had saved many thousands of Germans from starvation in Europe after World War I he deserved their support. Others dismissed him as a prohibitionist conservative who would surely follow a pro-British foreign policy.

So hopeless had the effort to unify the German-American vote become that thereafter most German ethnic publicists abandoned the concept and concentrated instead on cultural goals. This was not true, however, of the notorious German-American Nazis. Their strategy of blood and strong-arm tactics was repugnant to all but a tiny minority and revealed that they understood nothing about either American politics or the essential character of the German ethnic group in the United States. Still, many leaders of the German-American churches, the German-language press, and the old established societies were reluctant to repudiate Nazism, either in Germany or America, so earnestly did they desire a strong place for Germany in international affairs and so deeply did their affection for things German run.

Since the mid-1930s, German-American political behavior has taken on a substantially different character. In earlier decades there had been open and vocal attempts to organize the German Americans into a bloc of voters unified by ethnic group concerns. The German-language press had taken strong positions and had argued them forcefully and sometimes stridently; organizations had been created to marshal the German-American vote on a national scale. But as the assimilation process took its toll of ethnic consciousness, Hitlerian brutality and Nazi excess transformed German ethnicity in America into a source of social and psychological discomfort, if not distress. The overt expression of German-American opinion consequently declined and, in more recent years, virtually disappeared as a reliable index of the political attitudes of those Americans for whom German ethnicity continues as a significant part of their lives. In other words, German-American leadership has disappeared even though distinctive German-American voting has continued in some quarters.

This change became apparent in the 1930s and '40s when German-American opposition to Franklin Roosevelt and his foreign policies accounted for much of what was described as midwestern isolationism. German-American voters simply wanted no involvement in another war with Germany. The domestic concomitants of fighting against one's ancestral homeland remained etched in their memories. Thus, in the presidential election of 1936, midwestern German Catholics gave strong support to William Lemke of the Union party, supported as he was by the vehemently anti-Roosevelt rhetoric of the "radio priest," Father Charles E. Coughlin of Michigan. Four years later, many thousands of other German-American voters deserted Roosevelt for Republican Wendell Willkie, whose obviously German name and whose criticism of the drift toward war they found comforting.

Such German-American voting without the benefit of articulate leadership has continued through the decades since World War II. At the same time, the Germans have disappeared as an ethnic group in cities such as New York; the German-language press had continued its long decline into obscurity; and no politician would ever think of addressing his German ethnic constituency directly or explicitly. It is even likely that many voters of German descent are themselves unaware of the extent to which German ethnic feeling still influences their political behavior. Yet careful analysis suggests that, for example, Harry Truman's surprising victory in 1948 may be partially explained by the return of many midwestern German Catholic farmers to the Democratic fold following their defection from Roosevelt in 1940 and '44.

Sensitivity to foreign policy issues has usually explained the extent to which German-American voting can be distinguished from that of other definable collectivities, especially in the Midwest. In the 1950s, Dwight Eisenhower benefited from Republican gains in German Catholic precincts, where resentment over the Korean War was strong. Likewise, other German-American voters bought the argument of Republican senator Joseph McCarthy and others that the Democratic party was "soft on Communism," firmly believing that the cold war demonstrated that the Soviet Union, not Germany, had always been America's most formidable enemy. As political analyst Kevin Phillips has observed, such a view conveniently transformed the German-American discomfort of 1935–45 into patriotic perception.

The election of 1960, which pitted the cold warrior Richard Nixon against the Irish Catholic John Kennedy, carried overtones of 1928. German Catholics returned strongly to the Democratic party while Republican voting was reinforced in German Protestant precincts. In 1968, however, when Nixon's Democratic opponent was a Protestant, many German Catholics once again voted Republican. In fact, Nixon's greatest gains over his 1960 performance came in German Catholic districts in midwestern states.

Such analysis only skims the surface and tests only the most obvious issues and the most prominent candidates. It is largely based on fragmentary rather than systematic analysis of data. Although historians have studied German-American political behavior in the nineteenth and early twentieth centuries in great detail and with much sophistication, they have ignored the last three decades. Similarly, political scientists have been preoccupied in their analyses, not with white ethnic political behavior, but with more pressing questions concerning blacks, Spanish-speaking ethnic groups, and women; with basic economic and social variables; and with foreign policy issues.

Nevertheless, the cumulative record of historical scholarship during the last twenty years has revealed much about the successive concerns of

German Americans as a group. In the nineteenth century German immigrants were moved first by questions of their status in the American democracy and then by issues of ethnocultural clash. Still later, as immigration declined and assimilation accelerated in the twentieth century, foreign policy issues became transcendent. Historical analysis also explains why strong leadership never could have emerged from the diversity of German America and how, in recent decades, German ethnic leadership has disappeared entirely, even though distinctive voting can still be discerned among certain elements within the ethnic community. A summary view of German-American political behavior thus demonstrates how strongly political developments have been conditioned by cultural influences and how intricately they are woven into the fabric of our national history.

BIBLIOGRAPHICAL NOTE

The bibliography of books and articles that explicitly treat the involvement of the German ethnic group in American political history is not extensive. Earlier works tended to concentrate on the achievements of prominent leaders; more recent efforts focus on the voting behavior of large numbers of ordinary people of German birth or descent. My own publications are in the latter category.

General treatments that are especially useful include the essays by Kathleen N. Conzen, "Germans," and Edward R. Kantowicz, "Politics," in *Harvard Encyclopedia of American Ethnic Groups*, ed. Stephan Thernstrom (Cambridge, MA: Harvard Univ. Press, 1980), 405–25 and 803–13. See also Joseph S. Roucek, "The Germans," in *America's Ethnic Politics*, ed. Joseph S. Roucek and Bernard Eisenberg (Westport, CT: Greenwood, 1982), 155–69. For the general context of German-American editorial opinion, see Carl F. Wittke, *The German-Language Press in America* (Lexington: Univ. of Kentucky Press, 1957).

Numerous works have been published on prominent German-American political leaders. Among the best are Hans Trefousse, *Carl Schurz: A Biography* (Knoxville: Univ. of Tennessee Press, 1982), and J. Joseph Huthmacher, *Senator Robert F. Wagner and the Rise of Urban Liberalism* (New York: Atheneum, 1968).

German-American political behavior is an essential ingredient in a group of books treating nineteenth-century American political history on the state or regional level. I have relied especially on Lee Benson, *The Concept of Jacksonian Democracy: New York as a Test Case* (Princeton: Princeton Univ. Press, 1961); Ronald R. Formisano, *The Birth of Mass Political Parties: Michigan, 1827–1861* (Princeton: Princeton Univ. Press, 1971); Paul Kleppner, *The Cross of Culture: A Social Analysis of Midwestern Politics, 1850–1900* (New York: Free Press, 1970), and *The Third Electoral System, 1853–1892: Parties, Voters, and Political Cultures* (Chapel Hill: Univ. of North Carolina Press, 1979); Richard J. Jensen, *The Winning of the Midwest: Social and Political Conflict, 1888–96* (Chicago:

Univ. of Chicago Press, 1971); and Samuel P. McSeveney, *The Politics of Depression: Political Behavior in the Northwest, 1893–1896* (New York: Oxford Univ. Press, 1972).

Particularly useful for an understanding of the political behavior of German-American religious groups are Philip Gleason, *The Conservative Reformers: German-American Catholics and the Social Order* (Notre Dame, IN: Univ. of Notre Dame Press, 1968), which is a study of the Central-Verein; James C. Juhnke, *A People of Two Kingdoms: The Political Acculturation of the Kansas Mennonites* (N. Newton, KS: Faith and Life Press, 1975); and Norman Graebner, "Lutherans and Politics," in *The Lutheran Church in North American Life*, ed. John E. Groh and Robert H. Smith (St. Louis: Clayton Publishing House, 1979), 12–30.

Scholars have tended to neglect the study of German-American political behavior in the twentieth century. Clifton Child, *The German-Americans in Politics, 1914–1917* (Madison: Univ. of Wisconsin Press, 1939) is an old-style analysis of the National German-American Alliance. Clifford Lee Nelson, *The Impact of War: German-American Political Behavior in Nebraska and Wisconsin, 1916–1920* (Lincoln: Univ. of Nebraska Publication No. 217, 1971) illustrates the use of more systematic concepts and methods. Ronald H. Bayor, *Neighbors in Conflict: The Irish, Germans, Jews, and Italians of New York City, 1929–1941* (Baltimore: Johns Hopkins Univ. Press, 1978) illuminates political rivalries among different ethnic groups in an urban setting. Sander Diamond, *The Nazi Movement in the United States, 1924–1941* (Ithaca, NY: Cornell Univ. Press, 1974) is an excellent analysis of that unfortunate phenomenon.

Historians have virtually ignored German-American political behavior since 1940. In their influential book, *Beyond the Melting Pot* (Cambridge, MA: MIT Press, 1970), Nathan Glazer and Daniel P. Moynihan declared that the Germans had ceased to exist as an identifiable group in New York City. Nevertheless, much data indicate that German ethnicity continues to be an important correlate of voting behavior, especially in the Midwest. In this respect, Kevin Phillips, *The Emerging Republican Majority* (New Rochelle, NY: Arlington House, 1969) is especially helpful.

Patterns of German Settlement in the United States and Brazil, 1830–1930

6

To understand the successful development of the United States, there is nothing like the study of the development of the colonies of Rio Grande do Sul.

— Vianna Moog[1]

Comparisons between the United States of America and the United States of Brazil, as the southern giant was known following the promulgation of the constitution of 1891, are common, if not commonplace. If the former has been characterized properly as the Colossus of the North, the latter may well be called the Colossus of the South. Both countries are huge, populous, and rich in resources; both occupy vast portions of their respective continents. Although the United States lies within the temperate zone and Brazil mostly in the tropical, both imported enormous numbers of Africans to feed the voracious appetites of their respective plantation systems. Both, seduced and bedeviled by slavery, rid themselves of that iniquitous institution in the latter half of the nineteenth century, one earlier and violently, the other later and peacefully. Both countries, moreover, received streams of European immigrants in the same century, large in proportion to their respective populations, in Brazil partly as a substitute for slave labor, in the United States despite slavery and its legacies.[2]

Immigrants from the German-speaking states of Europe were enormously important for both countries. In the United States German immigration was exceeded only by the Irish and, in the century from 1830 to 1930, amounted to nearly six million persons, less an undetermined number of returnees or remigrants. In Brazil, where the size of both the receiving population and the immigration was generally much smaller, the Germans were the fourth largest group, ranking behind the Portuguese, Italians, and Spanish. Easily the most important of the northern European groups to go to Brazil, the Germans were the only large group with a majority of Protestants to go to that Catholic and Latin country. Official data indicate that approximately two hundred thousand persons arrived from German-speaking countries during the century in question, a mere 3.5 percent of the volume of German emigration to the United States (table 1).[3]

The context of immigration was radically different in Brazil compared to that which pertained in the United States, despite certain superficial similarities. A fundamental difference arises from the fact that many thousands of German-speaking immigrants settled in the American colonies during the colonial period. Often called Palatines, they were especially numerous in Pennsylvania. They began to arrive in the 1680s, increasing gradually until the 1750s. Many assimilated rapidly into colonial society so that when the enormous German immigration of the nineteenth century commenced, the newcomers were able to build upon the social and cultural foundations laid by their predecessors a century earlier.[4] Nothing comparable occurred in Brazil during its colonial period.

Neither country experienced significant immigration from any source during the half century from 1775 to 1825, an era of war, revolution, and domestic turmoil for most of Europe. Unlike the newly independent United States, Brazil during this period became the refuge of royalty as the Portuguese king and his government fled before Napoleon's armies. Both the Portuguese and their Brazilian successors were aware of the deep divisions between the landed elite and the impoverished workers and slaves. Early in the nineteenth century they developed policies to encourage the immigration of non-Portuguese persons for the purpose of creating a middle class in Brazilian society, especially in the subtropical south, where there were no slave-dependent plantations. Such an infusion, some leaders argued, would counter the deeply rooted abhorrence of the Brazilian upper class for manual labor and their disdain for commercial enterprise. Had the Brazilian government failed to sponsor its program of recruitment and subsidy early in the nineteenth century, it is likely that later and larger patterns of chain migration and formal colonization would not have occurred and that the German component in the population of Brazil would never have attained significant levels. In contrast to the Brazilian, American society, from its beginnings in the seventeenth century, consisted largely of independent farmers, artisans, and petty merchants—the very kinds of persons the Portuguese government had hoped to attract to Brazil. Hence the government of the United States felt no need to develop strategies to recruit European settlers or to subsidize colonization ventures, as did the Brazilians.[5]

Thus even before the establishment of independence in 1822, the Brazilian government deliberately and actively sought immigrants from Europe and offered a variety of inducements to lure them to the New World, including at different times free passage, animals, seeds, and implements, plus loans and grants to colonization companies. Germans were especially recruited in the 1820s to populate Brazil's southernmost

Table 1. German Immigration to the United States and Brazil

Decade	Total immigration to U.S.	German immigration to U.S.	German % total immigration to U.S.
1820–29	128,502	5,753	14.5
1830–39	538,381	124,726	23.2
1840–49	1,427,337	385,434	27.0
1850–59	2,814,554	976,072	34.7
1860–69	2,081,261	723,734	34.8
1870–79	2,742,137	751,769	27.4
1880–89	5,248,568	1,445,181	27.5
1890–99	3,694,294	579,072	15.7
1900–09	8,202,388	328,722	4.0
1910–19	6,347,380	174,227	2.7
1920–29	4,295,510	386,634	9.0
Total	37,520,312	5,881,324	15.7

Decade	Total immigration to Brazil	German immigration to Brazil	German % total immigration to Brazil
1820–29	7,765	2,236[a]	30.0
1830–39	2,669	207	7.8
1840–49	7,303	4,450	60.9
1850–59	117,592	15,815	13.4
1860–69	110,093	16,514	15.0
1870–79	193,931	14,627	7.5
1880–89	527,869	19,201	3.6
1890–99	1,205,803	15,992	1.3
1900–09	649,898	13,848	2.1
1910–19	821,458	25,902	3.2
1920–29	846,522	75,839	9.0
Total	4,490,903	204,721	4.6

[a]Recent research indicates that this figure, based on official sources, seriously underestimates the size of the German emigration to Brazil (see note 6).

Sources: U.S. Bureau of the Census, *Historical Statistics of the United States: Colonial Times to 1970* (Washington, D.C., 1975), 105; José-Fernando Carneiro, *Imigração e colonização no Brasil* (Rio de Janeiro, 1950), facing p. 60. Other sources offer variant data for Brazil; compare B.R. Mitchell, *International Historical Statistics: The Americas and Australia* (Detroit, 1983), 141–43, and Thomas W. Merrick and Douglas H. Graham, *Population and Economic Development in Brazil: 1800 to the Present* (Baltimore, 1979), 91.

province of Rio Grande do Sul and to strengthen the defense of that area. German farmers were seen as especially desirable. In 1824 a colony was founded at São Leopoldo, located twenty miles north of Porto Alegre in the eastern part of the *serra*, a hilly, forested region between the flood plain of the Rio Jaquí on the south and the grass-covered plateau to the north. In some respects the colony at São Leopoldo was a Brazilian equivalent to the Germantown settlement established near Philadelphia in 1683; in other respects it resembled Ebenezer, the Salzburger colony in Georgia, founded in 1734 to help anchor the southern frontier of the English colonies.

Statistically, the German immigration of the 1820s was similar in both countries—usually less than a thousand persons per year—although it is likely that the Brazilian total for the decade surpassed that for the United States.[6] Then, whereas the numbers of persons headed for the United States spiraled upward dramatically to the climactic year of 1854 (when 215,000 persons arrived from the German states), the emigration to Brazil ended altogether. In the 1840s, annual immigration from all sources rarely exceeded a few hundred persons, of whom almost all were from either Portugal or Germany. A decade later the Brazilian totals gradually increased to ten or fifteen thousand per year, of whom approximately a fifth were German. Still, the huge numbers of Germans that descended upon the United States in the 1880s had no counterpart in Brazil, where they seldom exceeded five thousand per year until 1891, following the final abolition of slavery in 1888 and the overthrow of the empire in 1889. Thereafter German immigration again dropped off and exceeded five thousand only in the years immediately preceding World War I. Not until the 1920s, when the total for the decade surpassed 75,000, did Brazil experience its heaviest influx from Germany. In the immediate postwar years from 1919 to 1921, the German immigration to Brazil actually exceeded that to the United States. This increase, which was substantial in relation to the prewar Teuto-Brazilian population, had the natural effect of slowing the process of assimilation at a time when, in the United States, it had accelerated because of the legacies of World War I. During the century following the 1820s, the Brazilian pattern paralleled the American only in the first decades of the twentieth century, although usually at a lower rate.[7]

Germans emigrated to both countries from approximately the same regions and for approximately the same reasons. In the early decades they came from the western and southern German states; later northern and eastern parts of Germany were more important. Most came because of interrelationships in inheritance customs, demographic behaviors, economic well-being, and cultural concerns.[8]

In general, the social and cultural characteristics of the German emigrants to both the United States and Brazil were also much the same.[9] They were persons mostly of the lower and lower middle classes seeking a better life in the New World. Political and religious concerns, while not absent, were not often primary considerations. Data on Germans in the United States are much more comprehensive than for Brazil, although the Germans of Rio Grande do Sul have been studied in exquisite detail by Jean Roche, a French scholar.[10] Impressionistic evidence suggests that both migrations consisted of similar proportions of unskilled workers, farmers, artisans, craftsmen, storekeepers or petty merchants, and professionals, although late in the nineteenth century the major Brazilian cities attracted many highly trained technicians and businessmen, many of whom saw their Brazilian residence as temporary.

There is no reason to believe that, at the time of emigration, literacy rates were different between the two contingents. Religious divisions were also similar, but few German Jews appear to have gone to Brazil. Catholics formed a strong minority in both groups, although they were probably a little stronger among the Brazilians because of the virtual absence of Protestantism in that country. According to one estimate made in the early 1920s, 54 percent of the Germans in Rio Grande do Sul were of Protestant origins, the remainder Catholic. No doubt similar proportions were characteristic of other major concentrations of Germans in Brazil.[11] After their arrival in the New World, however, the German Protestant denominations evolved differently in the two countries. In the United States the several Lutheran synods were highly successful in shepherding German immigrants into their folds. Other churches, such as the Reformed, Evangelical, Methodist, and Mennonite, were less important. In Brazil the predominant Protestant church was the Evangelical, with the Lutheran ranking second. Moreover, the Brazilian Evangelical synods maintained close administrative and financial ties with the Prussian state church, a relationship that had no parallel in the United States.[12]

Germans generally were much less attracted to Brazil as a new home than to the United States. Some of the reasons are obvious: Brazil offered an unfamiliar climate with strange, tropical diseases; uncertainty of land titles; undeveloped transportation systems; and a virtually nonexistent school system.[13] Although German emigrants had no experience with political democracy as practiced in the United States, most were favorably disposed toward it. Certainly they were not drawn to the elitist, imperial regime of Dom Pedro II, nor was the apparent instability of the later republican government perceived as much of an improvement. The United States was considered to be progressive and dynamic, a world leader in industrial and technological development; Brazil was often seen as backward and undeveloped.

In addition, Brazil suffered from much negative publicity in the German press, which regularly described Brazil as unattractive for Germans.[14] Problems emerging from religious differences were especially difficult. For example, Brazil, one of the most Catholic countries in the world, held Protestant marriages to lack legality and treated them as concubinage, thereby clouding inheritance rights of Protestant immigrant children. Moreover, Protestant houses of worship were not allowed to display the standard insignia of churches, such as crosses and spires. But there were other problems as well. Unfortunate publicity attended problems connected with immigrant recruitment efforts of the Brazilians and from controversy over the use of German sharecroppers in the coffee-producing areas of São Paulo. These circumstances prompted the Prussian government in 1859 to issue a directive that curtailed the recruitment of immigrants in its domain. Although Brazil responded by moderating some of its offending laws in the early 1860s, Prussia did not rescind its *Heydt'sche Reskript*, as it was called, until 1895.[15]

The Brazilian census of 1920 provides a statistical summary of a century of German emigration. It reveals that Germany ranked a distant fourth behind Portugal, Italy, and Spain as a source and that German immigrants and their descendants were highly concentrated in the southernmost states of Rio Grande do Sul, Santa Catarina, and Paraná, where the majority lived in agricultural areas.[16] Other significant colonies were to be found in the major cities, especially Porto Alegre, São Paulo, and Rio de Janeiro. By 1930, approximately two hundred thousand persons had entered the country from Germany and, in addition, many thousands more of German-speaking immigrants had arrived from other countries, notably Russia. From this undetermined total must be subtracted remigrants, but they were matched many times over by the Brazilian-born children of the immigrants. According to one generous estimate made by a German-Brazilian, the number of persons of German birth and descent in 1920 in Rio Grande do Sul alone had grown through immigration and natural increase to between 360,000 and 400,000 persons in a total population of 2,142,000.[17]

But the German flow to Brazil was a mere trickle compared to the flood of newcomers who sought jobs and homes in the United States, where, during the century from 1830 to 1930, at least one of every six immigrants was German-speaking. In most years late in the nineteenth century, immigrants from Germany outnumbered those from any other country. By 1900 they and their children constituted a tenth of the total population of the entire nation.[18] Like the Teuto-Brazilians, German Americans tended to concentrate in specific regions. About 85 percent resided in the middle Atlantic states and in the Midwest. Moreover, about two-thirds lived in cities, a vastly greater proportion than in Brazil. Huge concentrations developed, especially in New York City and Chicago, that dwarfed the largest German-Brazilian urban enclaves, which were located in Porto Alegre and São Paulo. The proportions of German Americans who were unskilled workers and servants (roughly 40 percent at the end of the nineteenth century) apparently was much greater than the comparable Brazilian share, just as the percentage of farmers (about 35 percent) was much smaller.[19]

In both the United States and Brazil, however, there was great diversity in the German immigrant population that was largely unnoticed by the receiving population, which tended to think of the Germans in their midst as a unified group with common characteristics. Thus important distinctions within the German immigrant society with respect to place of origin, variations in regional speech or dialect, religious divisions, and social and political differences were lost on both Anglo-Americans and Luso-Brazilians, who tended to lump them all together on the basis of their presumably common language.

But careful study reveals striking differences in the provincial origins of Germans in the United States. For example, Württembergers were heavily concentrated in Philadelphia but were comparatively rare in Milwaukee. Mecklenburgers flocked to Milwaukee but not to Philadelphia. Hanoverians were common in Cincinnati and St. Louis, but relatively uncommon in Wisconsin and Michigan.[20] Even within German enclaves, both urban and rural, distinct provincial concentrations developed. For example, in New York's *Kleindeutschland* of 1860, Bavarians dominated the Eleventh and Seventeenth wards, Prussians the Tenth, and Hessians the Thirteenth.[21] Settlement patterns in rural districts were much the same. In Warren County, Missouri, 17 percent of all the many Germans resident there in 1860 were from the tiny German principality of Lippe-Detmold; at the same time, Lippe-Detmolders were virtually absent in St. Charles County, another heavily German county located immediately to the east.[22]

Such concentrations also developed in Brazil. In Rio Grande do Sul many of the early settlers of the 1820s were from Holstein, Hanover, and Mecklenburg; later many arrived from the Rhineland, especially the Hunsrück district south of the Mosel River.[23] Similarly, Pomeranians were especially numerous in the state of Espírito Santo, where even today Teuto-Brazilians are known as *pomeranos*, regardless of origin.[24] Many other provincial clusters developed, especially in Rio Grande do Sul and Santa Catarina, where one valley might be inhabited almost entirely by Germans from one state or region and the next by Germans from another.

Thus Westphalians were numerous in Estrela, Pomeranians in Santa Cruz, and Swabians in Panambí.[25]

But there were profound differences between the two countries in the nineteenth century patterns of settlement in rural areas. In the United States, countless thousands of Germans, intent upon preserving an agricultural way of life in the New World, streamed through the ports of entry such as New Orleans and New York, seeking land in the states and territories of the North and West. Sometimes the immigrants, lacking the means to settle on farmland directly, would practice a trade or labor as an unskilled worker for a year or more before they could settle on the land. The farms the immigrants acquired, whether by purchase from the government, a previous owner, or a railroad that had received a government grant, by preemption, or by homesteading, usually were shaped by the rectilinear surveys established by the Land Law of 1785 and subsequent amendatory legislation. The land passed into the hands of individual farmers in small parcels, usually consisting of 160 acres. There were notable instances of colonization companies or associations that acquired large tracts for division among their members, thereby permitting one ethnic group to settle an area exclusively, but the predominant pattern required the farmer, whether native or immigrant, to compete individually for land ownership. Thus a small number of successful German immigrants on the land would attract others—often relatives or acquaintances from their home town in Europe—and slowly a rural cluster would develop, usually intermixed with native-born Americans or other immigrants, but sometimes almost exclusively German and Catholic or Lutheran or some other denomination.[26]

In Brazil a rather different pattern emerged. Government policy and land laws unintentionally encouraged the development of exclusive ethnic enclaves, a circumstance the Teuto-Brazilians readily perceived as an advantage.[27] They were attracted especially to the hilly, forested, and still uninhabited land in the subtropical southern provinces that lay between the coastal plains (often very narrow) and the cattle country of the interior uplands. They liked the abundance of wood, the reasonably fertile soil, and the more than adequate rainfall. Moreover, the landscape was somewhat reminiscent of certain parts of Germany.[28]

Typically the German agricultural settlement was organized around what they called a *Schneiss* or *Pikade*. The founders of a colony would decree a long, straight cut through the forest that could later become a road. Individual settlers would then receive long, narrow plots of land of one or two hundred acres that stretched out at right angles to the road. Farmhouses were built at the side of the road, thereby creating a strung-out rural village similar to the *Waldhufendorf* or *Strassendorf* of central

Germany. Several such *Pikaden* would constitute a colony. At the center of the colony would be the *Stadtplatz*, which would consist of a cluster of buildings, including the church, school, civil offices, stores, workshops, and a mill. Sometimes the farms would adjoin a river instead of a *Pikade*, and elongated properties would stretch in from the river bank. But the essential spatial organization remained the same.[29] Of course, not all Teuto-Brazilian pioneer farmers lived in such agricultural settlements; others struggled to survive in even more primitive and isolated conditions. The line-village pattern, rarely found in the United States because land laws and custom worked against it, allowed the rural Teuto-Brazilians to live as they pleased in virtual isolation from other social and cultural groups. In such a setting they did not have to conform to preexisting standards. Linguistic acculturation was unnecessary. Their situation required only minimal adaptation to the social environment.[30]

The physical environment was another matter. Some of the rural colonies, such as Blumenau and Joinville, were organized by entrepreneurs who had the forests partially cleared and roads built before placing German *colonos* on the land, thereby enhancing the chances for individual success. But as the land was taken up and as settlers spread out into new areas, they often encountered formidable environmental obstacles. If a settler came into a frontier area and devoted all his energy to clearing the forest so that he could farm as he had in Europe, he was almost sure to fail. By the time he could accomplish the task of clearing the land of trees, crucial planting seasons would have passed. Instead, the German pioneers typically adapted the primitive slash-and-burn techniques that they had learned from the *caboclos*, who were poor and despised natives of mixed Indian and Portuguese blood. Lacking capital and credit, as well as effective means of transportation, many Teuto-Brazilian farmers also turned to indigenous crops of manioc and maize, which they planted among the partially carbonized tree trunks. When the fertility of a given clearing was exhausted after several years, the pioneer would move to another spot and start the process over again. Such primitive, subsistence agriculture often became a more or less permanent part of the German-Brazilian way of life in some areas and sometimes continued long after improvements in transportation and access to credit and world markets rendered such methods obsolete.[31]

As a result of these environmental influences, the rural Teuto-Brazilians do not fare well in comparison to their German-American counterparts, even though they were commonly perceived as highly successful by their countrymen. Many remained in poverty and extreme isolation for generations, well into the twentieth century.[32] Because their settlements tended to be exclusive of other ethnic groups, they were able to achieve the critical mass necessary, despite a relatively low population density, to create the various institutions and associations that naturally perpetuate ethnocultural forms. Churches were the easiest to create, but the Teuto-Brazilians also established all the familiar ethnic organizations and societies, as well as a German-language press. Because Brazilian public schools were not well developed in the nineteenth century, the Germans created their own, which were often taught by the parish pastor.[33] All these agencies combined to maintain the use of the German language, to preserve German cultural forms, and thereby to slow the assimilation process. For example, data from the Brazilian census of 1940 show that in Rio Grande do Sul, 97.6 percent of the German-Brazilian families habitually spoke German in their homes. Even in São Paulo, where Germans were well dispersed within the metropolis, the proportion still exceeded 50 percent.[34] In all these respects, the Teuto-Brazilians were not much different from German-Americans; the variation lay in degree, not in kind. Few German communities in the United States had resisted assimilation as effectively as the typical German community in rural southern Brazil.

Such rural societies were a world apart from the ethnic communities that developed in the large towns where Germans constituted a majority, such as São Leopoldo, Blumenau, Joinville, Brusque, and São Bento. In such places they were able to evolve self-contained socioeconomic structures that included all the strata—rich entrepreneurs and professional persons at the top, supported by small merchants, clerks, skilled industrial workers, and at the lower levels, unskilled laborers and the farming population of the surrounding countryside. In such a society there was little economic interdependence with other groups and few incentives to develop social intercourse with Luso-Brazilian society.[35] These communities were not unlike the German-American enclave in nineteenth-century Milwaukee described by Kathleen Conzen.[36] Still, there were few small cities in the United States that were so dominated by the German element as were those Brazilian places.

In some of the large coastal cities, most notably Porto Alegre, São Paulo, and Rio de Janeiro, where the Germans constituted a small fraction of the total population, they were still numerous enough to develop the complex of supporting voluntary organizations that gave coherence to their immigrant society. Inevitably, however, as they went about their daily tasks as industrialists, professional people, merchants, craftsmen, and laborers, they had many more interpersonal contacts with members of the dominant Luso-Brazilian society than did their isolated rural cousins. Naturally they learned Portuguese much more rapidly. Assimilation in such a setting was relatively easy for persons so inclined.

Urban occupational structures within the German communities of both countries were similar. In the United States, data from the census of 1890 show that German immigrants were strongly represented in the food industries, such as baking and meat packing. Brewers were eight times as common among the German-born than among the white population at large; bartenders were twice as frequent. German Americans engaged in retailing of all kinds; they were also attracted to domestic and personal services, such as barbering and hairdressing. Inevitably it was difficult for them to find employment in occupations that required a good knowledge of the English language, but they were proportionately numerous among musicians, chemists, artists, and architects.[37] Comparable data for Brazil are not readily available, but Jean Roche has shown that in Rio Grande do Sul Teuto-Brazilian manufacturers dominated the manufacture of leather and glass, and were leading producers in brewing, metallurgy, furniture, tobacco processing, and soap—industries also frequently associated with Germans in the United States.[38] Other members of the Teuto-Brazilian elite made fortunes from trade with Germany. The social environment of Brazil, conditioned in part by the reluctance of Luso-Brazilians from engaging in materialistic business pursuits, strongly encouraged the rapid economic advancement of Teuto-Brazilian businessmen. In the United States, German-American businessmen had no comparable advantage, except perhaps in New York, which was the major port of entry for goods from Germany.

The urban Teuto-Brazilians were significantly different from their American counterparts in that a substantial proportion were *Reichsdeutsche* —subjects of the German kaiser—who looked upon their residence in Brazil as temporary and who had no interest in acquiring Brazilian citizenship. Many were educated, middle-class persons employed by German firms with offices in Brazil; they looked forward to the day when they could return to their mother country. Often disdainful of Luso-Brazilian culture, they involved themselves in Brazilian affairs only insofar as such matters impinged upon their immediate business interests. Many such persons knew little and cared less about the rural colonies. Yet the impressions that members of the Luso-Brazilian elite gathered about the Germans in their country were often derived from their contacts with the city people, unrepresentative though they may have been. Of course, persons with such attitudes could also be found in German-American communities, but there they were on the whole less influential and less often thrust into leadership positions. In the United States, the German immigrant population was rather more diverse in character and distribution, and hence less subject to dominance by *Reichsdeutsche*.

Such comparisons between German immigrants in the United States and in Brazil reveal many similarities in origin, occupation, education, socioeconomic status, religious affiliations, demographic patterns, and cultural concerns. Similar social structures were erected in both countries. Many parallels in their respective histories of adaptation and assimilation might also be drawn. But the differences between them may be the more instructive. The two streams of German immigrants flowed to dramatically different environments, both physical and social, as well as economic, political, and cultural.

In contrast to the German Americans, many Teuto-Brazilians came to the New World in response to government recruitment efforts and subsidies. In their settlement patterns, they were more highly concentrated regionally, displayed sharper distinctions in the characteristics of their urban and rural communities, and tended toward greater rural isolation. The physical environment of Brazil forced more dramatic adaptations in rural settlement patterns and agricultural practices, while imposing more persistent rural poverty. The social environment required the Germans independently to maintain their levels of literacy (which were much higher than those of the receiving Brazilian society) through the establishment of private educational systems that were generally superior to government schools. These circumstances often combined to produce among Teuto-Brazilians attitudes of cultural superiority and disdain for Luso-Brazilian culture, at least among their leaders. The process of assimilation was thus slowed, compared to the rate generally experienced in the United States. This tendency in turn was augmented by the fact that the language, culture, and often the religion of the Germans, as northern Europeans, were significantly different from what prevailed among the majority of Brazilians.

In other words, the cultural differences between the German immigrants and their hosts were noticeably greater in Brazil than in the United States. The potential for conflict was therefore accordingly increased, as the destructive anti-German riots of 1917 in Porto Alegre, São Paulo, Rio de Janeiro, and other cities demonstrate. In response to the presumed threat posed by an "enemy" ethnic group that seemed to resist assimilation, the Brazilian government enacted repressive legislation during World War I and later, especially in the Vargas era.[39] These laws were intended to accelerate the assimilation and integration of the German immigrants and their descendants into Brazilian life. Nothing approaching their severity was ever enacted in the United States.

The German ethnic group thus played a rather different role in the history of Brazil than in the United States. Comparisons between the two countries, as Vianna Moog claimed, help to explain why.

NOTES

1. Vianna Moog, *Bandeirantes and Pioneers*, trans. L. L. Barrett (New York: George Braziller, 1964), 173.

2. Frank Tannenbaum, *Slave and Citizen* (New York: Knopf, 1946) and, more fully, Carl Degler, *Neither Black nor White: Slavery and Race Relations in Brazil and the United States* (New York: Macmillan, 1971).

3. *Historical Statistics of the United States to 1970* (Washington, D.C.: Government Printing Office, 1975), 105; José Fernando Carneiro, *Imigração e colonização no Brasil* (Rio de Janeiro: Universidade do Brasil, 1950), facing p. 60; T. Lynn Smith, *Brazil: People and Institutions* (Baton Rouge: Louisiana State Univ. Press, 1963), 118–43.

4. For a perceptive discussion of the process of acculturation among Pennsylvania Germans, see Stephanie Grauman Wolf, *Urban Village: Population, Community, and Family Structure in Germantown, Pennsylvania, 1683–1800* (Princeton: Princeton Univ. Press, 1976), 127–53. The best general survey of German immigration to the United States is the extended essay by Kathleen N. Conzen, "Germans," in *Harvard Encyclopedia of American Ethnic Groups*, ed. Stephan Thernstrom et al. (Cambridge, MA: Harvard Univ. Press, 1980), 405–25. LaVern J. Rippley, *The German-Americans* (Boston: Twayne, 1976) is also excellent. Most other studies of the history of Germans in America are more limited in scope, but see my *Bonds of Loyalty: German Americans and World War I* (DeKalb: Northern Illinois Univ. Press, 1974), chaps. 2 and 3.

5. There are no general studies of German immigration to Brazil in the English language, but there are some in German. The best brief treatment is Karl Heinrich Oberacker, Jr., "Die Deutschen in Brasilien," in *Die Deutschen in Lateinamerika*, ed. Hartmut Fröschle (Tübingen, West Germany: Erdmann, 1979), 169–300. See also Carlos Fouquet, *Der deutsche Einwanderer und seine Nachkommen in Brasilien: 1808–1824–1974* (São Paulo: Instituto Hans Staden, 1974). For the Brazilian portions of this essay I have drawn extensively upon my book, *Germans in Brazil: A Comparative History of Cultural Conflict during World War I* (Baton Rouge: Louisiana State Univ. Press, 1987), especially chapter 1, "A Century of German Settlement in Brazil, 1818–1918."

6. It is likely that the official data recorded on table 1 seriously underenumerate the German immigrants who settled in Brazil in the 1820s. Mack Walker, *Germany and the Emigration, 1816–1885* (Cambridge, MA: Harvard Univ. Press, 1961) estimates that the total for the decade was between 7,000 and 10,000 instead of the 2,326 shown. George P. Browne, "Government Immigration Policy in Imperial Brazil, 1822–1870" (Ph.D. diss., Catholic Univ. of America, 1972), 95 and 105, suggests that 10,000 is closer to the actual figure. Personal correspondence with Browne (July 30, 1986) affirms this estimate and suggests that it may have actually exceeded 10,000. In that case, German immigration to Brazil significantly exceeded that which flowed to the United States in the 1820s.

7. Immigration generally contributed approximately the same proportion to the population increases of both the United States and Brazil. In the century from 1840 to 1940, immigrants accounted for 9.4 percent in Brazil and

9.8 percent in the United States. When the children of immigrants are added, the proportions rise to 19 and 21.7 percent respectively. In the neighboring countries of Canada and Argentina, immigration accounted for great population increases. By this mode of calculation, first- and second-generation immigrants provided 40.8 percent of the population incɾease in Canada and 58 percent in Argentina (see Thomas W. Merrick and Douglas E. Graham, *Population and Economic Development in Brazil, 1800 to the Present* [Baltimore: Johns Hopkins Univ. Press, 1979], 39).

   8. Walter D. Kamphoefner, *Westfalen in der neuen Welt* (Münster, West Germany: Coppenrath, 1982). The best general treatment of German emigration in the English language is Wolfgang Köllmann and Peter Marschalck, "German Emigration to the United States," *Perspectives in American History* 7 (1973), 499–554. Walker, *Germany and the Emigration*, is also excellent. In the German language the most useful book is Peter Marschalck, *Deutsche Überseewanderung im 19. Jahrhundert* (Stuttgart: Ernst Klett, 1973). For the historiography of German emigration, see David Luebke, "German Exodus: Historical Perspectives on the Nineteenth-Century Emigration," *Yearbook of German-American Studies* 20 (1985): 1–17. There has been no systematic study of the German sources of emigration to Brazil, but see the comparative data for the post–World War I period gathered and interpreted by Hartmut Bickelmann in *Deutsche Überseewanderung in der Weimarer Zeit* (Weisbaden: Franz Steiner, 1980) 14–15, 49, 149, 150, and 165.

   9. This generalization, which is based entirely on impressionistic evidence, may be proved wrong by systematic research. For example, the excellent study by Wolfgang von Hippel demonstrates that there were sometimes startling differences in property ownership among emigrants from Württemberg, 1856–62, depending upon destination. But Hippel does not distinguish between Brazil and the United States. Instead, his New World categories are reduced to North America and South America. His data show that for this span of seven years, Germans headed for South America were somewhat wealthier than those going to North America. The differences for some years, notably 1858, 1861, and 1862, were dramatic. Although Hippel makes no note of it, the differences for these years may be related, first, to the Panic of 1857 in the United States and, second, to the onset of the American Civil War (Wolfgang von Hippel, *Auswanderung aus Südwestdeutschland: Studien zur württembergischen Auswanderung und Auswanderungspolitik im 18. und 19. Jahrhundert* [Stuttgart: Klett-Cotta, 1984], 267, but see also 254–66).

   10. Jean Roche, *La colonisation allemande et le Rio Grande do Sul* (Paris: Institut des Hautes Études de l'Amérique Latine, 1959). Nothing quite so comprehensive exists for the Germans of any state in the United States.

   11. *Hundert Jahre Deutschtum in Rio Grande do Sul, 1824–1924* (Porto Alegre: Typographia do Centro, 1924), 448 and 496. See also João Guilherme Correa de Souza, "Uma comunidade Teuto-Brasileira: Aspectos de sua estrutura e organização sociais," in *I. Colóquio de Estudos Teuto-Brasileiros* (Porto Alegre: Univ. Federal do Rio Grande do Sul, 1963), 196–99.

12. I have attempted to describe the distinguishing characteristics of the several German immigrant churches in my *Bonds of Loyalty*, 35–42. An extensive literature on the Teuto-Brazilian churches exists. Among the most useful books are Ferdinand Schröder, *Brasilien und Wittenberg: Ursprung und Gestaltung deutschen evangelischen Kirchentums in Brasilien* (Berlin and Leipzig: Walter de Gruyter, 1936) and Joachim Fischer and Christoph Jahn, eds., *Es begann am Rio dos Sinos: Geschichte und Gegenwart der Ev. Kirche Lutherischen Bekenntnisses in Brasilien* (Erlangen, West Germany: Verlag der Ev.-Lutherischen Mission, 1970).

13. Moog, *Bandeirantes and Pioneers*, has treated environmental and cultural comparisons between the United States and Brazil at length (e.g., see pp. 17–25).

14. Walker, *Germany and the Emigration*, 127–29 and 177–81. See also Luebke, *Germans in Brazil*, chap. 3, "The German Ethnic Group in Brazilian Society, 1890–1917."

15. George Browne, "Secularization and Modernization in Imperial Brazil: The Question of Non-Catholic Marriage," *Revista de Historia de America* 83 (1977): 121–33; Gerhard Brunn, *Deutschland und Brasilien (1889–1924)* (Cologne and Vienna: Böhlau, 1971), 127–54; Fritz Sudhaus, *Deutschland und die Auswanderung nach Brasilien im 19. Jahrhundert* (Hamburg: Hans Christian, 1940), 99; personal correspondence with George P. Browne, July 30, 1986.

16. Vianna Moog has pointed out that Rio Grande do Sul, the state with the highest concentration of Teuto-Brazilians, is *least* like the rest of Brazil and *most* like the United States, with its ideal of family settlement on farms in rural areas. See *Bandeirantes and Pioneers*, 172.

17. Karl Heinrich Oberacker, [Sr.], *Die volkspolitische Lage des Deutschtums in Rio Grande do Sul* (Jena: Gustav Fischer, 1936), 92–95. See also Heinz Kloss, *Statistische Handbuch der Volksdeutschen in Übersee* (Stuttgart: Publikationstelle Stuttgart-Hamburg, 1943), 61–67.

18. Conzen, "Germans," 406.

19. Data for the German-Brazilian occupational structure are not readily available, even for Rio Grande do Sul, and hence these comparisons must remain impressionistic.

20. Kamphoefner, *Westfalen in der neuen Welt*, 82–122, especially the tables on pp. 91 and 100. See also Stanley Nadel, "Kleindeutschland: New York City's Germans, 1845–1880" (Ph.D. diss., Columbia University, 1981), which strongly emphasizes the regional or particularistic variations in the social and cultural characteristics of the Germans in that city. Many other historians recognize the importance of this variable, but none has incorporated it in his or her research design as effectively as Nadel, who associates it with residence, occupation, religious affiliation, marriage patterns, and household structures.

21. Nadel, "Kleindeustchland," 73–75 and 299.

22. Kamphoefner, *Westfalen in der neuen Welt*, 108–9.

23. Roche, *La colonisation allemande*, 124; compare Ferdinand Schröder, *Die deutsche Einwanderung nach Südbrasilien bis zum Jahre 1859* (Berlin: Ev. Hauptverein für deutsche Ansiedler und Auswanderer, 1931), 81–92.

24. Ernst Wagemann, *Die deutschen Kolonisten in brasilianischen Staate Espírito Santo*, Schriften des Vereins für Sozialpolitik, vol. 147, pt. 5 (Munich and Leipzig: Duncker und Humblot, 1915).

25. Roche, *La colonisation allemande*, 124.

26. This theme has been developed in many books, dissertations, and articles. I cite the one most familiar to me: the second chapter of my *Immigrants and Politics: The Germans of Nebraska, 1880–1900* (Lincoln: Univ. of Nebraska Press, 1969), 16–32.

27. Brazilian land law was both complicated and inconsistent, as T. Lynn Smith has pointed out. For an informative summary of this topic, which in itself is eminently worthy of careful comparison to the United States, see his *Brazil: People and Institutions*, 257–317, in which he treats land division, surveys, titles, and land tenure.

28. Preston James, "The Expanding Settlements of Southern Brazil," *Geographical Review* 30 (October 1940): 608–16; Aurelio Porto, *Die deutsche Arbeit in Rio Grande do Sul* (São Leopoldo: Rotermund, 1934), 64–91, 181–87. For an example of a single colony, see Klaus Becker, "A fundação e os primeiros 30 anos de Teutônia," in *I. Colóquio de Estudos Teuto-Brasileiro* (Porto Alegre: Universidade Federal do Rio Grande do Sul, 1963), 217–27.

29. Roche, *La colonisation allemande*, 175–82; Leo Waibel, "European Colonization in Southern Brazil," *Geographical Review* 40 (October 1950): 529–47; Terry Jordan, "Aspects of German Colonization in Southern Brazil," *Southwestern Social Science Quarterly* 42 (March 1962): 346–53; Hanns Porzelt, *Der deutsche Bauer in Rio Grande do Sul* (Ochsenfurt am Main: Fritz und Rappert, 1937), 41–43; Smith, *Brazil*, 250–53 and 276–82. Smith makes the further point strongly that the line-village form was by no means limited to German settlements. It became the standard mode throughout the country.

30. For examples of German line-villages in the United States, see Russel L. Gerlach, *Immigrants in the Ozarks: A Study in Ethnic Geography* (Columbia: Univ. of Missouri Press, 1976), 66–70, especially the map on p. 68. The formation of a line-village by German-Russian immigrants in the United States is described in D. Paul Miller, "Jansen, Nebraska: A Story of Community Adjustment," *Nebraska History* 35 (June 1954): 129–31 and figs. 2 and 3.

31. Emílio Willems, *A aculturação dos alemães no Brasil: Estudo antropológico dos imigrantes alemães no Brasil* (São Paulo: Companhia Editora Nacional, 1946), 329. See also Emílio Willems, "Social Change on the Latin American Frontier," in *The Frontier: Comparative Studies*, ed. David Miller and Jerome O. Steffen (Norman: Univ. of Oklahoma Press, 1977), 262–63.

32. For example, see Heinz Dressel, *Der deutschbrasilianische Kolonist im alten Siedlungsgebiet von São Leopoldo, Rio Grande do Sul* (Neuendettelsau, West Germany: Freimund, 1967). The isolation of the typical Teuto-Brazilian family in rural districts is strongly emphasized by Emílio Willems in his books and articles. For a particularly excellent example, see his "Immigrants and Their Assimilation in Brazil," in *Brazil: Portrait of Half a Continent*, ed. T. Lynn Smith

and Alexander Marchant (1951; reprint, Westport, CT: Greenwood, 1972), 209–25.

33. It should be noted that in Brazil, a Catholic country, parochial schools tended to be Protestant, in contrast to the pattern in the United States, a country with Protestant foundations, where they were usually Catholic.

34. A. H. Neiva and M. Diégues, Jr., "The Cultural Assimilation of Immigrants in Brazil," in *The Cultural Assimilation of Immigrants,* ed. W. D. Borrie (Paris: UNESCO, 1959), 221.

35. Emílio Willems, "Some Aspects of Cultural Conflict and Acculturation in Southern Rural Brazil," *Rural Sociology* 7 (1942): 379.

36. Kathleen N. Conzen, *Immigrant Milwaukee, 1836–1860* (Cambridge, MA: Harvard Univ. Press, 1976).

37. Luebke, *Bonds of Loyalty,* 31–32; Edward P. Hutchinson, *Immigrants and Their Children, 1850–1950* (New York: Wiley, 1956), 123–24.

38. Roche, *La colonisation allemande,* 390–92.

39. I have described these disturbances and their consequences in my book, *Germans in Brazil,* chaps. 5, 7, and 8.

Images of German Immigrants
in the United States and Brazil,
1890–1918: Some Comparisons

In the 1890s, following a decade of unprecedented immigration from Europe, the United States experienced a period in which national identity was greatly stressed. The term *Americanization* came into frequent usage as many citizens, privately and through various organizations, stressed conformity to the dominant culture in language, manners, and religious belief.

During these same years a similar development, in some respects stronger than in the United States, could be detected in Brazil. In 1889 the empire of Brazil ended when Pedro II went into exile and Brazilian leaders introduced a republican form of government. During the preceding decade Brazil, like the United States, had experienced heavy immigration from Europe.[1] The abolition of slavery in 1888 had created a labor shortage, chiefly in the central and southern states, that the government had sought to relieve through the recruitment of Italian, Spanish, Portuguese, and German immigrants. During the 1890s the Brazilian Republic, unsure of itself in its first years, experienced a wave of nativism much like that in the United States. The new Brazilian leaders, motivated strongly by doctrines of Comtean positivism, insisted on a new national unity. They felt strongly that immigrants should resist the natural tendency to remain separate. To speak a different language, to wear different clothing, to eat different foods, to attend different schools, and to worship a different god all seemed undesirable because such behavior threatened to alter national identity and to undermine the confidence of the republicans to govern their huge, diverse, and undeveloped country.[2]

German immigrants and their children were conspicuous in both countries. Approximately five million Germans had arrived in the United States during the nineteenth century. In each of the peak years of 1854 and 1882 more than two hundred thousand persons arrived. Although 85 percent of the Germans settled in the northeastern quarter of the country, they could be found in all states of the Union. Two-thirds lived in urban places (a proportion much higher than that for the American population generally at that time), but they were also strongly attracted to agriculture, especially dairy farming in the Midwest. By the end of the century there were about eight million first- and second-generation Germans in the United States, roughly 10 percent of the total population. Unusually diverse in origin, occupation, residence patterns, and religious belief, they were easily the largest non-English-speaking group in America.[3]

The Brazilian pattern was similar but on a much smaller scale. The German immigration to Brazil had begun in the 1820s, largely as a consequence of vigorous recruitment efforts sponsored by the Brazilian government. The annual totals seldom exceeded two thousand, yet after seventy-five years the Germans had multiplied and prospered until they numbered nearly four hundred thousand persons, mostly Brazilian-born and German-speaking. Although important colonies developed in the large cities and seaports of Brazil, the majority of Teuto-Brazilians (as they were called) settled in rural regions, where they founded exclusive settlements chiefly in the two southernmost states of Rio Grande do Sul and Santa Catarina, in which they accounted for one-fifth of the population by 1910. There, even more than in the United States, they created a society within a society—a large, isolated, diverse, structured community with its own values, attitudes, language, and folkways. They adapted their agricultural practices to subtropical realities, raised large families, and built churches, schools, and towns. Like the German-Americans, the Teuto-Brazilians were of diverse provincial origins and were divided between the Catholic and Protestant faiths. Like their American counterparts, the Teuto-Brazilians developed a substantial German-language press and an amazing array of voluntary associations.[4]

Stereotypes naturally developed in both countries. Each receiving society tended to regard the Germans in their midst as a unified group with common characteristics. Provincial differences, linguistic variations, religious divisions, and social and political distinctions were usually lost on the native-born, who tended to lump all German immigrants together on the basis of their presumably common language. Because Germany did not exist as a unified state until 1871, a German was simply someone who spoke the German language.

There was no uniform or consistent content to the images of the German immigrant. Wealthy and educated Americans, for example, generally registered more favorable impressions than did the lower classes. Rarely rubbing shoulders with ordinary newcomers, these Americans more often encountered persons who had adapted quickly to American ways and who, like themselves, were educated and successful. Moreover, their impressions were conditioned by notions about Germany itself, such as the preeminence of German learning. In the nineteenth century, approximately ten thousand Americans had studied in various German universities. They discovered a quality of scholarship, a depth of thought, and an appreciation for learning and academic freedom that led them to place Germany on a cultural pedestal. Although such impressions of Germany and its institutions must be separated from ideas about German immigrants, they contributed to a generally high regard for them among the upper strata of society.[5]

Ordinary Americans of the nineteenth century, however, had little contact with the products of German universities and still less with their books and essays. Instead, impressions of things German were gained from ordinary contacts with German-born barbers, bartenders, cobblers, cooks, and seamstresses, or with immigrants who lived next door or on a nearby farm, worked in the same factory, or deposited savings in the same bank.

Perhaps the most prominent elements in the American stereotype of German immigrants were industriousness, thrift, and honesty—admirable virtues in the American value system. The German male seemed strongly attached to his family; he was orderly, disciplined, and stable. A bit too authoritarian by American standards, he was nonetheless admired for his ability to achieve material success through hard work. Similarly attractive was his reputation for mechanical ingenuity. The Germans were usually perceived as an intelligent people, although somewhat plodding in their mental processes. And if they tended to be unimaginatively thorough, they sometimes also seemed stubborn and graceless in manner. But the German wife and mother was commonly regarded as a model of cleanliness and efficiency; her daughter was valued as a reliable house servant or maid. Although some native Americans thought that the Germans treated their women badly, on the whole they considered these newcomers desirable additions to the American population.

But there were negative elements in the image as well. Some felt that Germans were unwarrantably proud of their origins and culture. Others had ambivalent feelings about German festivities. It seemed as though the Germans had a celebration for every occasion, complete with parades and contests both athletic and cultural. Even their church affairs often took a festive air. Especially offensive was what puritanical Americans perceived as abandoned dancing and boorish swilling of beer, especially on the Sabbath, the day that God had set aside for worship, rest, and spiritual contemplation. Still others were put off by the apparent radicalism of German immigrants. The American labor movement seemed to have among its leaders an unusually large number of Germans who preached alien doctrines of communism, anarchism, and varying degrees of socialism. Impressions drawn from such unfortunate and widely publicized affairs as the Chicago Haymarket Riot of 1886 strengthened the image of at least some Germans as dangerous revolutionaries.[6]

Clashes between native and immigrant cultures produced some of the most potent political issues of the late nineteenth century. Although many German immigrants were interested in political reform, economic development, and the tariff and currency questions, they responded more strongly to issues related to ethnocultural conflict. In addition to political and economic liberties, they wanted social and cultural freedom. By the 1890s prohibition had become the dominant political manifestation of cultural conflict. Women's suffrage, Sabbatarianism, and efforts to regulate (if not close down) parochial school education were closely related issues that were capable of producing remarkable, although temporary, levels of uniformity in the voting behavior of German immigrants.[7]

Ethnocultural politics had an impact on nativist attitudes. Awareness of ethnic group identities was greatly intensified among immigrants and nativists alike. Thinking in stereotypes and symbols was encouraged; tolerance and understanding diminished. The live-and-let-live attitudes common in earlier decades were weakened by organized political action. Changes in attitudes toward immigrants were also fostered by some of the most respected social scientists of the day, whose study of the immigration question led them to conclude that socially undesirable characteristics were hereditary and were more typical of some ethnic groups than of others. Both negative and positive qualities were thus thought to be fixed or rigid.[8]

Still, as such ideas gained currency at the end of the nineteenth century, the German Americans fared well. Although there were dissents from the general view, most Americans considered the Germans to be a desirable people. Moreover, as racial thinking became increasingly common early in the twentieth century, some German-American intellectuals were stimulated, in countless speeches and articles, to laud and magnify the achievements of their group, ranging from such early contributions as those of Baron von Steuben in the Revolutionary War to the more recent accomplishments of such engineers as John Roebling and his American-born son, who designed and built the Brooklyn Bridge. This indulgence in cultural chauvinism was partly an effort to lay claim to a share in American greatness, but it was also intended to balance Anglo-Saxonist notions of racial superiority and preeminence in world affairs.[9]

By the beginning of World War I, the leaders of the rapidly assimilating German element in the United States, understandably proud of their cultural heritage, were encouraged in their ethnocentrism by the stereotypes native-born Americans generally held of them. Some were even prompted to promote their heritage as a culture counter to the dominant Anglo-American. But this was a dangerous course in a period of resurgent nativism. Deviations from American norms were but lightly tolerated by persons unwilling or unable to distinguish cultural chauvinism from the political or nationalistic variety.

In Brazil, German immigrants were generally perceived favorably in the nineteenth century, especially by the ruling classes, who regarded them as desirable additions to Brazilian society. The Germans, they thought, would not only bring valued skills to Brazil but would also "whiten" the population, which in 1890 was only 44 percent white. The Brazilian elite, like the American, was strongly influenced by racist theories based on presumably scientific criteria that gave the highest rating to so-called Nordic peoples, which, of course, included the Germans.[10] As in the United States, they were admired for their industry, orderliness, and stability.

Even though the Germans were welcomed and valued for the contributions they were making to Brazilian development, the Brazilian image, even more than the American, rested on inadequate and distorted information, rhetorical exaggeration, and myth[11] because the multiracial Brazilian society was considerably more divided than the American between rich and poor, the literate and the illiterate. German immigrant society in Brazil was both more concentrated spatially and more isolated socially than in the United States, especially in the rural settlements. Moreover, the German enclaves in the Brazilian cities were often dominated by wealthy, educated *Reichsdeutsche* (subjects of the German kaiser). Such persons—bankers, industrialists, merchants, journalists, technicians, and various representatives of large German firms—frequently considered life in Brazil to be temporary. Moreover, they were often contemptuous of Luso-Brazilian culture,[12] an attitude that did not go unnoticed by the Brazilians with whom they were in frequent contact.

Some Teuto-Brazilian leaders also shared this attitude of condescension for Brazilian culture. Feeding on ethnocentric German nationalist propaganda of the turn of the century, they considered Brazilian culture to be decidedly inferior to their own. In one example of such literature, a German writer on Brazil recommended stout resistance to assimilation on the ground that Brazilian culture was worthless. "What the Lusitanians have created in America," he wrote, "is a country that has produced nothing memorable in any field, including economics and culture; in the economic sphere . . . this state . . . is crippled, . . . a poorly organized community of seventeen million people. And these seventeen million, who rule over a rich and productive area the size of Europe, are unable to colonize anything, nor are they able to establish a properly functioning means of transportation and communication, regulate their financial affairs, guarantee justice, build a fleet, nor maintain an army other than one that is really nothing more than a privileged band of robbers."[13] This statement is so extreme, of course, that it cannot be considered typical. Still, many Teuto-Brazilians regarded Brazilian culture as weak and ineffectual; the Luso-Brazilians themselves seemed to combine indolence and ignorance with ridiculous conceit. The Portuguese language was useful to know for practical reasons, they thought, but it seemed to offer few literary treasures compared to the German.[14] Like the most extravagant of German-American cultural chauvinists, some Teuto-Brazilians insisted that the Germans would perform their best service as loyal citizens by infusing the culture of their adopted country with their presumably superior German qualities. If German language and culture were allowed to fade from use, they argued, Brazil would be deprived of the invaluable German sense of duty and commitment to the work ethic. Many felt that the chances for successful maintenance of German language and culture were greater in Brazil than in the United States, where, they believed, Anglo-American Protestant culture was so strong that German immigrants were virtually unable to withstand its assimilative power.[15]

The status of the Germans in Brazilian society was not a topic of national debate. At most it was a regional issue discussed in the states where the Germans were concentrated and where upper-class perceptions were drawn primarily from the behavior of unrepresentative persons who perpetuated immigrant culture because it served their economic interests and psychological needs. Hence most educated Brazilians had little comprehension of the diversity of the German immigrant group, such as the differences that divided Catholics from Protestants or the disparate values and behaviors that distinguished the rural farmers from the urban workers and the economic and social elite. Moreover, they failed to understand how the physical environment, in conjunction with unique events in Brazilian history, promoted German isolationism. They were often mystified by the German spirit of separatism. They could not understand why the Germans would want to perpetuate their own language and culture indefinitely, especially since Brazilian culture was so attractive. In their view, Brazilian culture was open, tolerant, hospitable, adaptable, nonideological, humane, and free of rigid stratification. Brazilians, they believed, were motivated by a spirit of conciliation that sought compromise and rejected extremist measures. Above all, they considered themselves to be a nonviolent people.[16]

It is not possible to determine the extent to which the illiterate and unskilled classes in Brazilian society shared the concerns of the elite. Because of the isolated character of most German rural settlements, the social interaction of the Germans with other Brazilians was infrequent and often superficial. Furthermore, the Germans, like any other social group, differed widely in education, skills, health, and working habits, and large numbers experienced a deterioration in social and economic circumstances as they struggled to survive in the Brazilian environment. But the prevailing image was that the Germans were better housed and fed; that their system of private and parochial schools was often superior to what passed for public education in Brazil at that time; and that their homes and persons were cleaner and healthier. The Germans also seemed willing to work very hard, at least in contrast to the impoverished *caboclos* (persons of mixed Indian and Portuguese descent), among whom labor was intermittent and subject to frequent and long interruptions. One may assume that some Brazilians of the less privileged classes regarded the Germans with resentment and jealousy, but even so, there is no record of persistent cultural conflict based on ethnic differences.[17]

Of course, most Brazilians, rich or poor, white, black, mulatto, or *caboclo*, rarely thought about the Germans at all, much less in any systematic way. Similarly, the ordinary Teuto-Brazilian people went about their daily business, adapting to their surroundings and rarely giving the problems of assimilation any consideration. Like any other immigrant group, the Germans included many persons who were favorably disposed toward the language and culture of the host society and wanted to become part of it as quickly and painlessly as possible. Through daily contacts at work, at the store, at church, in school, or even in the home, they learned Portuguese readily. Whether they learned quickly or slowly depended upon individual circumstances and whether they had good or poor opportunities for interaction with speakers of Portuguese. Obviously, the isolated, exclusive rural colonies offered few such chances.

The existence of colonies where there were no Portuguese-language schools and where hundreds of second- and third-generation children had only rudimentary knowledge of Portuguese began to concern members of the Brazilian elite as the nineteenth century drew to a close. When they tried to identify typical German attitudes they naturally paid attention to the most conspicuous persons—the articulate German-Brazilian idealists who made speeches and wrote editorials, essays, and letters demanding their right to maintain their cultural separatism. Some persons in government were eager to break up the rural German enclaves, especially in Rio Grande do Sul, and to guarantee that new settlements would consist of a mixture of ethnic groups. Several efforts were made on both the state and national levels to restrict the growth of the colonies, but none were effective. In Santa Catarina the attack on immigrant institutions centered on private schools. For example, a law enacted in 1913, mild by present-day standards, ordered inspection by state officials and required that statistics of attendance be reported. It further specified that any schools that accepted subventions from either state or local governments were required to use Portuguese as the language of instruction.[18]

Luso-Brazilian fears that the Germans in the southern states were becoming so numerous that they could never be assimilated were heightened by much discussion of the so-called "German peril"—a commonly held belief that Germany had set itself upon a course of worldwide imperialism, based in part on the presence of German immigrants in various underdeveloped countries, including Brazil. At the same time, German aggressiveness was observed in the South Pacific, China, the Philippines, and the Caribbean. When in 1904 the Germans threatened the integrity of Venezuela in a debt-collection controversy, alarmists saw the first steps in a plan designed to create a German protectorate over southern Brazil and possibly a state that would be German in language and culture.[19]

Meanwhile in Germany the noisy, supernationalistic Pan-German League fueled new fears of German imperialism. In its widely distributed publications, this organization emphasized the cultural kinship of Germans all over the world and agitated vociferously for a colonial empire, for an enlarged navy, for war as an instrument of national policy, and for the preservation of German language and culture in German settlements overseas. A symptom rather than a cause of the rampant nationalism of the time, the Pan-German League was identified by English and French propagandists as the coordinating agency of German imperialism. Although the league's importance was grossly exaggerated, a flood of articles exposing the alleged Pan-Germanist conspiracy soon appeared in newspapers and periodicals in Europe and America. In Brazil, the noted Brazilian literary critic Sylvio Romero produced a lengthy tract entitled *O allemanismo no sul do Brasil* (1906). Although he welcomed the influx of German immigrants, Romero warned his countrymen of the German peril, outlined steps that could be taken to combat the threat, and urged that measures be taken to assimilate the German colonists into Brazilian society.[20] Other Brazilian writers expressed similar fears.

When world war engulfed Europe in 1914, the governments of both the United States and Brazil declared their neutrality. For most ordinary people in both countries, but especially in Brazil, the war in Europe was a distant affair of no particular consequence. It seemed to affect their daily lives in no direct or discernible fashion. Still, the war tended to evoke sympathies for one side or the other. Immigrants and their descendants naturally felt an emotional bond with their ancestral homeland and were convinced of the justice of its cause. Leaders of the German ethnic groups in both countries tended to be extravagant in their partisanship for Germany. Opinion among the educated or "established" groups in both the United States and Brazil, however, tended to favor the Allied powers. In Brazil, even more than in the United States, the press was disposed against Germany.

In 1917 the neutrality period came to an end when both the United States and Brazil declared war on Germany, ostensibly because vessels in their respective merchant marines had been torpedoed by German submarines. Although there were strong similarities in the behavior of Brazilians and Americans toward the Germans in their midst, the differences are striking.

In the United States, the war introduced a period of persecution for German Americans. Many citizens of German origin were suspected of disloyalty. Individuals were harassed in various ways as the American people were swept up in a wave of anti-German feeling. In effect, there was a war against German language and culture. The climate of suspicion produced such measures as bans on German-composed music and the renaming of persons, foods, streets, parks, and towns. German-language instruction in the schools was restricted or eliminated, and German-language newspapers were closely regulated. There were scores of patriotic demonstrations in which German Americans were forced to kiss the American flag, buy war bonds, or sing the national anthem. Ceremonies were held at which German-language books were burned. There were frequent instances of vandalism, beatings, arrests for allegedly unpatriotic utterances, and even a lynching of a German alien in Illinois.[21]

But the American behavior pales in contrast to the Brazilian. Following the Brazilian break in diplomatic relations with Germany in April 1917, German Brazilians were victims of numerous destructive riots. Property damage was enormous as hundreds of residences, German-language newspaper offices, churches, schools, clubhouses, businesses, factories, and warehouses were damaged or destroyed by mobs. Six months later, following Brazil's declaration of war in October, a second series of riots resulted in more destruction. Martial law was declared in Rio de Janeiro and all southern states, where the great majority of the Teuto-Brazilians lived. All publications in the German language were forbidden. All instruction in the German language was banned in all schools at all levels. All German-language church services were outlawed. The president was empowered to seize the property of enemy aliens and to sell all goods consigned to them. Enforcement of these repressive measures was inconsistent and sometimes haphazard, but Brazilian behavior was remarkably violent and repressive compared with the American.[22]

It is easy to explain the Brazilian response to the German problem in terms of the classic stereotype of the Latin temperament as irresponsible, unrestrained, volatile, emotional, and spontaneous. But such a simple interpretation would explain very little. It is more useful to compare Teuto-Brazilian circumstances with the American. Although Germans represented a much smaller proportion of Brazilian society than of the American, their settlement patterns were more highly concentrated, exclusive, and isolated in Brazil. Usually better educated and often wealthier than the average Brazilian, the Germans were more slowly assimilated than in America. As northern Europeans, the Teuto-Brazilians, in contrast to the more numerous Italian, Spanish, and Portuguese immigrants in Brazil, had a language and a culture that were significantly different from those of the host society. Differentness in turn promoted a heightened sense of minority group identity in addition to a full complement of ethnic institutions—churches, schools, social organizations, a German-language press—that tended to be more closely tied to Germany than were their equivalents in the United States. All these elements combined to promote a general sense of cultural superiority that had no equal in the United States. Moreover, leadership was more often vested in *Reichsdeutsche*, whose bonds with Germany were close. Finally, compared to their American cousins, the Germans in Brazil wielded greater economic power, but their political influence was weaker.

The comparison should be carried a step further. Brazilian society, compared to the American, was more highly stratified: its rich were richer and its poor poorer. Its economy was less developed and its political institutions less democratic; it had no long-standing constitutional tradition. Illiteracy was pervasive. In such a social setting, the relatively prosperous Germans naturally tended to evoke antagonism, the Brazilian reputation for tolerance and goodwill notwithstanding.

As the spirit of nationalism swelled early in the twentieth century, the Brazilians, like the Americans, naturally acted on the basis of stereotypes that obscured individual differences and beclouded interpersonal relationships. Lacking both knowledge and understanding of the separatistic German subsociety, its manners and institutions, they demanded an unprecedented measure of conformity to established Brazilian ways. When war came in 1917, they treated their Germans with a severity surpassing anything generally experienced by Germans in the United States. Had the German Americans been as divergent from the American norms as the Teuto-Brazilians were from Brazilian, it is likely that they too would have suffered from destructive riots, as did nineteenth-century Chinese in mining camps of the American West, or American blacks in Chicago, East St. Louis, Tulsa, and elsewhere in the immediate postwar period. Had their number been small enough, they might have been herded into concentration camps, as were Japanese Americans in World War II.

NOTES

1. For the Brazilian portion of this essay, I have relied heavily on my article "A Prelude to Conflict: The German Ethnic Group in Brazilian Society, 1890–1917," *Ethnic and Racial Studies* 6 (January 1983): 1–17. For accessible statistics of German immigration to Brazil, see Imre Ferenczi, comp., and Walter F. Willcox, ed., *International Migrations*, vol. 1: *Statistics* (New York: National Bureau of Economic Research, 1929), 695, 700–701.

2. Gilberto Freyre, *Order and Progress: Brazil from Monarchy to Republic*, ed. and trans. Rod W. Horton (New York: Knopf, 1970); E. Bradford Burns, *A History of Brazil* (New York: Columbia Univ. Press, 1970), 250–54; Fernando de Azevedo, *Brazilian Culture* (New York: Knopf, 1966), 159–60, 414–18; Gilberto Freyre, *New World in the Tropics: The Culture of Modern Brazil* (New York: Knopf, 1966), 154; José Honório Rodrigues, *The Brazilians: Their Character and Aspirations* (Austin: Univ. of Texas Press, 1967), 96. European immigration is placed within the context of racist thought and Brazilian nationalism in Thomas E. Skidmore, *Black into White: Race and Nationality in Brazilian Thought* (New York: Oxford Univ. Press, 1974), 38–68, 124–44.

3. For the American portion of this essay, I have drawn extensively on my book *Bonds of Loyalty: German Americans and World War I* (DeKalb: Northern Illinois Univ. Press, 1974), esp. chap. 2. See also U.S. Bureau of the Census, *Historical Statistics of the United States, Colonial Times to 1957* (Washington, D.C.: U.S. Government Printing Office, 1960), 57; Edward P. Hutchinson, *Immigrants and Their Children, 1850–1950* (New York: Wiley, 1956), 123–24.

4. The most comprehensive study of Germans in Brazil is by Jean Roche, *La colonisation allemande et le Rio Grande do Sul* (Paris: Institut des Hautes Études de l'Amerique Latine, 1959). Among useful surveys is Karl Fouquet, *Der deutsche Einwanderer und sein Nachkommen in Brasilien: 1808–1824–1974* (São Paulo: Instituto Hans Staden, 1974). See also Karl H. Oberacker, Jr., *Der Deutsche Beitrag zum Aufbau der brasilianischen Nation* (São Paulo: Herder, 1955); Oberacker, "Die Deutschen in Brasilien," in *Die Deutschen in Lateinamerika*, ed. Hartmut Fröschle (Tübingen: Erdmann, 1979), 169–300.

5. Walter P. Metzger, *Academic Freedom in the Age of the University* (New York: Columbia Univ. Press, 1955), 93–107, 119–24; Clara E. Schieber, *The Transformation of American Sentiment toward Germany, 1870–1914* (Boston: Cornhill, 1923), 256.

6. Luebke, *Bonds of Loyalty*, 59–63.

7. A considerable literature has been produced on ethnocultural conflict in the last decades of the nineteenth century. See, as examples, Paul Kleppner, *The Cross of Culture: A Social Analysis of Midwestern Politics, 1850–1900* (New York: Free Press, 1970); Richard Jensen, *The Winning of the Midwest: Social and Political Conflict, 1888–1900* (Chicago: Univ. of Chicago Press, 1971); and Frederick C. Luebke, *Immigrants and Politics: The Germans of Nebraska, 1880–1900* (Lincoln: Univ. of Nebraska Press, 1969).

8. See the writings of Josiah Strong, Edward A. Ross, John R. Commons, Edward Channing, John W. Burgess, and many others. The voluminous reports of the Immigration Commission, published in 1911, also reflect these attitudes.

9. Luebke, *Bonds of Loyalty*, 47–51.

10. Skidmore, *Black into White*, 38–77. See especially the tendency of Brazilian writers to compare the Brazilian experience with that of the United States (pp. 69–77).

11. Egon Schaden, "Die Deutschbrasilianer—Ein Problem," *Staden-Jahrbuch: Beiträge zur Brasilkunde 2* (1954): 184.

12. Portuguese-Brazilian. The term derives from Lusitania, the name of the ancient province virtually coterminous with modern Portugal. Its usage is comparable to Anglo-American in the United States.

13. Walter Kundt, *Brasilien und seine Bedeutung für Deutschlands Handel und Industrie* (Berlin: Siemenroth, 1903), 18.

14. *Deutsche Zeitung* (Porto Alegre), October 20, 1917; Oskar Canstatt, *Brasilien: Land und Leute* (Berlin: Ernst Siegfried Mittler, 1877), 251, 416; Ernest Tonnelat, *L'expansion allemande hors d'Europe* (Paris: Armand Colin, 1908), 125, 141; Clarence H. Haring, *The Germans of South America* (New York: Oxford Univ. Press, 1920), 43.

15. Schaden, "Die Deutschbrasilianer," 183–84; Emílio Willems, "Immigrants and Their Assimilation in Brazil," in *Brazil: Portrait of Half a Continent*, ed. T. Lynn Smith and Alexander Marchant (1951; reprint, Westport, CT: Greenwood Press, 1972), 209.

16. Rodrigues, *The Brazilians*, 60–61; A. H. Neiva and M. Diegues, Jr., "The Cultural Assimilation of Immigrants in Brazil," in *The Cultural Integration of Immigrants*, ed. W. D. Borrie (Paris: UNESCO, 1959), 185.

17. Although Emílio Willems is in no way responsible for my interpretation here, I have relied in part on his numerous works and have modified my views in consequence of private correspondence with him. See Emílio Willems, *A aculturação dos alemães no Brasil*, 2d ed. (São Paulo: Companhia Editora Nacional, 1980). Among his English-language articles, see his "Assimilation of German Immigrants in Brazil," *Sociology and Social Research* 25 (1940): 125–32, and "Some Aspects of Cultural Conflict and Acculturation in Southern Rural Brazil," *Rural Sociology* 7 (1942): 375–84.

18. G. Entres, ed., *Der Staat Santa Catharina in Vergangenheit und Gegenwart unter besonderer Berücksichtigung des Deutschtums* (Florianopolis: Livraria Central, 1929), 223; Ferdinand Schröder, *Brasilien und Wittenberg: Ursprung und Gestaltung deutschen evangelischen Kirchentums in Brasilien* (Berlin: Walter de Gruyter, 1936), 356; Martin Braunschweig, "Die rechtliche Stellung des deutschen Schulwesens in Südbrasilien," in *Die Kulturbedeutung der evangelischen Kirche in Brasilien*, ed. Bruno Geissler (Leipzig: Hinrichs'sche Buchhandlung, 1922), 51.

19. Schieber, *Transformation of American Sentiment*, 88, 136, 171, 177, 178.

20. Mildred S. Wertheimer, *The Pan-German League, 1890–1914* (New

York: Columbia University, 1924), 65, 74, 117, 126; Sylvio Romero, *O allemanismo no sul do Brasil, seus perigo e os meios de os conjurar* (Rio de Janeiro: Ribeiro, 1906). See also Skidmore, *Black into White,* 32–37, 56.

21. Luebke, *Bonds of Loyalty;* Carl Wittke, *German-Americans and the World War* (Columbus: Ohio State Historical Society, 1936); Donald R. Hickey, "The Prager Affair: A Study in Wartime Hysteria," *Journal of the Illinois State Historical Society* 62 (Summer 1969): 117–34. A variety of other studies on the local level have been published during the past decade. See also Phyllis Keller, *States of Belonging: German-American Intellectuals and the First World War* (Cambridge, MA: Harvard Univ. Press, 1979).

22. Detailed accounts of the Brazilian riots may be found in various metropolitan newspapers, April 16–18, 1917, for example, *A Federação* and *Correio do Povo* of Porto Alegre and *Jornal do Commercio* of Rio de Janeiro. For summary accounts of the April riots in the German-language press, see *Deutsche Post* of São Leopoldo, April 24, 1917, and *Germania* of São Paulo, April 25, 1917. Because publication in the German language was forbidden in November 1917, comparable accounts for the November riots do not exist. The *New York Times* published numerous translations of dispatches from Brazilian newspapers. The full text of *Lei da guerra* (War Law) is given in English translation in Andrew Boyle, ed., *The Brazilian Green Book: Consisting of Documents Relating to Brazil's Attitude with Regard to the European War, 1914–1917* (London: George Allen and Unwin, 1918), 99–102. For a useful survey of Brazil's role in the war, see Percy Alvin Martin, *Latin America and the War* (Baltimore: Johns Hopkins Univ. Press, 1925), 30–106.

The German Ethnic Group in Brazil: The Ordeal of War War I [1]   8

In April 1917, shortly after Brazil broke off diplomatic relations with Germany, Brazilians of German origin or descent were victims of numerous, destructive riots. Although death and personal injury were minimal, property damage was enormous as hundreds of residences, business houses, factories, and warehouses were damaged or destroyed by mobs gone out of control. Porto Alegre was the scene of the worst riots, but disturbances occurred almost simultaneously in São Paulo, Pelotas, and other cities of the South, where large numbers of German Brazilians lived. Six months later, following Brazil's declaration of war against the German Empire, another series of riots resulted in more destruction in the German districts of Rio de Janeiro, Petrópolis, Curitiba, and elsewhere.[2]

Like most riots, these outbursts of violence may be attributed to immediate causes. In this case, intergroup tension was intensified by genuine dismay and anger over Germany's having torpedoed Brazilian merchant vessels, by virulent anti-German propaganda, and by the rhetorical excesses of pro-Ally politicians. But that is like saying that World War I itself was caused in 1914 by the Serbian nationalist who assassinated the Archduke Franz Ferdinand in Sarajevo. The anti-German riots in Brazil are better understood within a larger context of ethnic history: The behavior of the dominant Luso-Brazilians (persons of Portuguese language and culture) and the minority Teuto-Brazilians (as the Germans were often called) may be best interpreted if examined historically in terms of ethnic group relations, perceptions, and images.[3]

Germans were among the earliest and most numerous of non-Portuguese Europeans to settle in Brazil. Beginning in the 1820s, a small stream of Germans entered the country, largely as a consequence of vigorous recruitment efforts sponsored by the Brazilian government. The number of German immigrants seldom exceeded two thousand in a single year. Yet after nearly a century they had multiplied and prospered until they numbered approximately 400,000 persons, mostly Brazilian-born and German-speaking.[4]

Although colonies of German immigrants developed in several of the large cities and seaports in Brazil, the majority sought new homes in rural regions that had been ignored or bypassed by earlier Portuguese or Azorean settlers. Locating chiefly in the southern states of Rio Grande do Sul and Santa Catarina and to a lesser extent in Paraná, they built a new society, different from what they had known in Germany and different as well from that of the receiving Luso-Brazilian society. The Teuto-Brazilians adapted their agricultural practices to subtropical realities, raised large families, and built churches, schools, and towns. They were the dominant group in some provincial cities, notably São Leopoldo, Blumenau, and Joinville, and became an influential minority in such major cities as Porto Alegre, São Paulo, and Rio de Janeiro.[5]

Because of the accidents of time and place, the Germans in Brazil had been allowed to develop their own society without much interference. By the 1880s, the last years of the Brazilian Empire, they had become a society within a society—a large, diverse, and structured community with its own values, attitudes, language, and folkways. In general, they were well received, respected, and valued for the contributions they were making to Brazilian economy and culture.[6]

With the advent of the republic in 1889, however, attitudes toward the Teuto-Brazilians began to change. The difference was partly a matter of confidence: The republic had to demonstrate its authority and its ability to govern, a task made more difficult by the diffusion of political power among the states and the development of political parties on a state basis. The abolition of slavery had its own repercussions as many thousands of new immigrants were recruited in Italy, Spain, and Portugal to supplement the labor supply. At the same time, the modernization of the economic structure of Brazil was under way, especially in the South. With the expansion of industry in relation to the production of agricultural commodities came economic and social dislocations that were new to Brazilian experience. As the world has witnessed so often in the twentieth century, modernization produced new social problems and tensions, especially in the cities. Some Brazilians, doubting the capacity of their society to absorb the flood of immigrants, demanded that the newcomers learn to conform to Brazilian ways.[7]

A measure of nativism also invaded Brazilian thought and attitude. Nativism was consonant with the doctrines of the Comtean positivism to which many of the new republican leaders subscribed. The commitment of the Brazilian positivists was not merely to *progress*, but also to *order*, which they understood to include a harmony among the classes, races, ethnic groups, and sexes. They could applaud the diverse origins of Brazilian society and culture and yet insist that a new unity—a distinctively Brazilian unity—had to be achieved, by force of dictatorship, if necessary.[8]

During the decade before the outbreak of World War I, many Brazilians in all levels of society, but especially among the ruling classes, began to perceive the Germans as a problem—an element that threatened the equilibrium of Brazilian society.[9] The Germans seemed rich and powerful, socially exclusive, and unwilling to be assimilated. To the more suspicious, they were eager accomplices in a vast Pan-Germanic plot to extend the power of the German Empire and with it German language and culture to all parts of the world, especially the southern states of Brazil.[10]

The Brazilian image of the Germans, like most stereotypes, rested on insufficient and distorted information, rhetorical exaggeration, and myths.[11] There was little comprehension of the diversity within the group, such as the differences that divided Catholics from Protestants or the disparate values and behaviors that separated rural farmers from urban workers and businessmen, or Teuto-Brazilians from *Reichsdeutsche*. Perceptions were drawn primarily from the behavior of the ethnic elite— the articulate, educated clergy, journalists, and businessmen who perpetuated immigrant culture because it served their economic interests and satisfied their psychological needs.

To the most ethnocentric among the German elite it seemed obvious that Luso-Brazilian culture was inferior to their own. They found little in it that they deemed worthy of adaptation or imitation. Brazilian culture was thought to be weak, and Luso-Brazilians themselves seemed to combine indolence with ridiculous conceit. As for their Portuguese language, it seemed useful to know but unimportant in terms of world culture. Compared to German, they thought, it offered few literary treasures.[12]

At the same time, however, these same Teuto-Brazilians sought acceptance and recognition. They were eager to be considered an essential element in their adopted country's history and they wanted Brazilians to understand and appreciate how extensive their contributions had been to Brazil's development. Thus the literature of Teuto-Brazilian filiopietism describes how individual Germans had participated in the exploration of the land, the independence movement, and the preservation of Brazilian territorial integrity through the wars with Argentina and Paraguay. Moreover, they insisted that German leaders had helped to initiate the renewal of national intellectual life through their defense of liberty of conscience. Filiopietists also stressed the role of the Germans in placing new value and dignity on work and in condemning slavery as morally and socially obnoxious; they had contributed significantly to the elevation of moral, cultural, and material standards in Brazil; and they could take credit, at least in part, for the emergence of the middle class in Brazil.[13]

For a substantial proportion of the German subsociety in Brazil, this kind of ethnocentric talk was pointless. Like any other immigrant group, the German included persons who were favorably disposed toward the language and culture of the host society and wanted to become a part of it as quickly and painlessly as possible.[14] Unlike the cultural idealists who insisted that it was their right to maintain their immigrant speech and folkways and who denied the right of the government to demand that they learn the language of the country, such rapid assimilators were eager to abandon the marks of immigrant status because they had become a source of social and economic deprivation.

Between these two—the cultural chauvinists at one extreme and the rapid assimilators at the other—was the majority, who saw no problem at all. They went about their daily business gradually adapting to their surroundings and rarely giving the problem of assimilation any thought. If their assimilation was unusually slow, it was because they had further to go, culturally speaking, than, for example, the Italians, to whom they were frequently and negatively compared. Because of this cultural distance, they tended to cluster in separate communities. Since they were so numerous, they could create the institutions that maintained their distinctive cultural forms. Yet through daily contacts at work, in school, at church, or at the store, they learned Portuguese more or less automatically. Whether they learned quickly or slowly depended upon individual circumstance and whether provided good or poor opportunities for interaction with speakers of Portuguese. For most of them, however, the ability to speak Portuguese became the symbol of higher social status; it was the avenue to social and economic progress, especially for the young.[15]

When governmental personnel began to object to the exclusiveness of the rural German colonies and the slowness of the Germans to assimilate, as they did in the two decades preceding World War I, they thought first of the extreme cases—the highly isolated districts where there were no Portuguese-language schools and where hundreds of second- and third-generation children could be found whose knowledge of Portuguese was rudimentary at best. Similarly, when they tried to identify typical German attitudes, they naturally paid attention to the most conspicuous persons—the noisy idealists who made speeches and wrote editorials, essays, and letters demanding the right to maintain their cultural separatism.

Thus the Luso-Brazilian majority acquired a distorted image of the Teuto-Brazilians. Some elements of the composite picture were correct, others were out of proportion, and a few were simply wrong. For decades in the nineteenth century, the Luso-Brazilian majority had ignored the question of German assimilation, probably because it had not seemed important enough to demand action. Then, when the failure of the Germans to assimilate began to be perceived as a problem, some Brazilian leaders tended to overreact and to press for extreme or far-reaching measures that were intended to enforce greater conformity.

When national rivalries exploded into world war in 1914, Luso-Brazilian sympathies were strongly with France and her allies and their tolerance for the loyalty Teuto-Brazilians naturally felt for Germany was correspondingly reduced. Influential political and cultural leaders then attacked Brazil's German ethnic group as a menace to national security and recklessly charged them with a full range of subversive activity. The subsequent anti-German riots of 1917 were thus the natural children born of intergroup tensions in conjunction with the accidents of world history.

The long neutrality period from 1914 to 1917 was generally a period of incubation for these tensions. Circumstances in Brazil were much like those in the United States. Germans in both countries felt a strong bond of loyalty to the land of their fathers; the host societies leaned toward the Allies. In Brazil, the Portuguese-language press quickly became a vehicle for intensely anti-German atrocity propaganda; the Germans in Brazil vigorously countered with propagandistic efforts of their own. The effect of this verbal conflict was to rejuvenate the German ethnic community and invest it with a new sense of self-esteem, if not strength. The German-language press thrived and voluntary organization experienced new surges of vitality as they shared in the new chauvinism.[16]

German ethnic behavior was not, of course, uniform. This was especially true of the churches. The leading Protestant denomination was the Evangelical church, which was organized in several synods. Especially strong in Rio Grande do Sul, it claimed as members about half of all Teuto-Brazilians. In the nineteenth century the Evangelicals (plus certain Lutheran groups) developed strong institutional ties with the Prussian state church, from which they received most of their clergy in addition to significant financial support. Not surprisingly, it became a central doctrine among Evangelicals that German language and culture were inseparable from religious belief. In the neutrality period, therefore, Evangelical parishes and other institutions became powerful agents for the promotion of pro-Germanism. They raised funds for the German Red Cross, bought German war bonds, sponsored bazaars and rallies to aid German victims of war; special prayer services were held to implore the deity for the success of German arms.[17]

In contrast to the Evangelicals, the Lutherans, especially those affiliated with the North American Lutheran Church—Missouri Synod, were much less chauvinistic. Their subsidies came not from Germany but from the United States. Even though this church still used German as its basic language, it believed that a transition to Portuguese was essential to survival. Hence it never offered a word of defense for Germany or for the preservation of *Deutschtum*. These Lutherans saw the European conflict as a judgment of God upon a sinful people—punishment for wickedness, unbelief, failure to pray, contempt for God's word, and the idolatry of human wisdom as revealed especially in modern science and theological liberalism.[18]

The German Catholics in Brazil provided a third pattern of behavior. That Catholicism was the religion of the vast majority of Brazilians made their situation fundamentally different from the Protestants. The German Catholics were nearly as numerous as the Evangelicals but were much less chauvinistic. Because the Catholic church was universal and multiethnic, it tended to unite its German adherents with other Brazilians— persons of Italian, Portuguese, and Spanish origins—rather than to separate or isolate them from the rest of society. Even when a Catholic parish consisted largely of Teuto-Brazilians, it usually was not a ready agency for raising either money or enthusiasm for Germany's cause. Moreover, the preeminent German in the Brazilian Catholic hierarchy, Archbishop João Becker of Porto Alegre, was determined to align his administration with the dominant attitudes and behaviors of Luso-Brazilian society. Nevertheless, there were individual German Catholics who were outspoken in their partisanship for Germany.[19]

In contrast to the churches, secular ethnic societies, especially the umbrella organizations, were more likely to lend themselves consistently to active or vocal pro-Germanism. Brazil had no national organization like the National German-American Alliance in the United States, but early in 1916 a German agent, ostensibly working as a fund-raiser for the German Red Cross, founded the short-lived *Germanischer Bund für Süd-Amerika*. Widely publicized, this organization inevitably generated suspicion and alarm among partisans of the Allies; but even within the German subsociety it also earned much opposition because it represented a challenge to the established ethnic leadership, especially the Evangelical clergy.[20]

The *Germanischer Bund* unintentionally stimulated the growth of patriotic organizations among Luso-Brazilians, the most important of which was the Liga pelos alliados (League for the Allies). Led by the brilliant Brazilian orator and statesman Ruy Barbosa, this organization bore a striking resemblance to the National Security League in the United States. Both organizations defended the Allies, advocated preparedness, protested alleged German atrocities, raised funds for the British and French Red Cross, and sought to hasten the assimilation of immigrants through educational means—literacy programs, instruction in the language of the host society, and in the promotion of patriotism. A special target of the Liga pelos aliados was Brazil's distinguished foreign minister, Lauro Müller, a thoroughly assimilated second-generation Teuto-Brazilian who was finally forced out of office in May 1917.[21]

Following Germany's decision to resume unrestricted submarine warfare on February 1, 1917, anti-German propaganda was intensified in Brazil. It was repeatedly charged that Germany was plotting to use the Teuto-Brazilian colonies in the southern states as the base for its imperialist designs. Similarly, the German-language newspapers persisted in their intense pro-Germanism, despite many ominous signs that Luso-Brazilian tolerance for such behavior was weakening.[22]

The breaking point came on April 5, 1917, when a German submarine torpedoed a small Brazilian freighter, the *Paraná*, off the coast of France. Official confirmation of the sinking came on the same day the United States declared war on Germany.[23] Brazilian newspapers stormily protested the loss and demanded that the government take decisive action; the Liga pelos aliados urged an immediate declaration of war and several prominent dailies swelled the chorus.[24] Patriotic rallies and demonstrations attracted huge crowds in Rio de Janeiro, São Paulo, Porto Alegre, and elsewhere. In several cities these demonstrations were transformed into ugly anti-German affairs. Allegedly impelled by patriotism, crowds of people surged to prominent German business establishments, clubhouses of German societies, and German-language newspapers. Despite genuine efforts of municipal governments to maintain order, several demonstrations degenerated into riots causing enormous losses due to arson and looting.[25]

On Saturday, April 14, and continuing through to Tuesday, April 17, Porto Alegre experienced the worst of these riots, as much of its German district was burned. Mobs consisting largely of waterfront riffraff, enlivened by alcoholic drink, pillaged the district. At the end of three days of riot, nearly three hundred buildings lay in various stages of ruin. Factories, warehouses, restaurants, schools, newspaper offices, plus many private residences were damaged or destroyed.[26]

Riots plagued other cities in Rio Grande do Sul, most notably Pelotas, located near the southern tip of Brazil. Although the heavily German state of Santa Catarina was mostly spared, other cities from Curitiba in Paraná to Pernambuco far to the north experienced disturbances. Governments on all levels attempted to cope with the problem of civil disorder as efficiently as possible, yet in the weeks that followed, superpatriots continued their intolerant and inflammatory rhetoric. The press also continued to print, as it had before the riots, the wildest of rumors, including one that an army of 80,000 armed Germans were gathering in Santa Catarina, where the governor was Felippe Schmidt, another Brazilian-born German, a cousin of Lauro Müller, the foreign minister.[27]

The range of reaction among the Germans of Brazil following the April riots was as varied as the people themselves. A few fled to the exclusive German colonies in the interior, but most were willing to accommodate their behavior to the newly narrowed standards of patriotic conduct. Some decided that the best course would be to make overt gestures of assimilation. This could be done most obviously by changing German names to something acceptable in Portuguese. Others dropped their memberships in the numerous *Vereine* or withdrew their children from the German schools. The German-language newspapers suspended publication for a couple of weeks, but by the end of April most had resumed publication, with government approval. A sharp division of opinion emerged regarding the proper course to follow. Some die-hard chauvinists were more determined than ever to maintain their ethnicity and to assert the justice of the German cause, but others advised a more moderate course.[28] Even though the majority of the ordinary German-speaking Brazilians had been indifferent to the war in Europe, many persons had now been touched by it in a frightfully direct way. Given the unrestrained character of the riots and the hatred they seemed to project, many Teuto-Brazilians wondered what would happen to them if Brazil actually declared war.

That did not occur until another six months had passed. On October 25, 1917, following the news that another Brazilian vessel, the *Macao*, had been torpedoed, the Brazilian president asked Congress to declare war, which it promptly did the following day. Nearly as promptly, Brazil subjected itself to another round of riots. This time Rio Grande do Sul remained relatively free of trouble, although this was not true of the city of Pelotas. Santa Catarina suffered serious disorders in Itajaí and Florianópolis. But the worst excesses occurred in the cities farther north, beginning on October 28 in Curitiba, spreading to Petrópolis, and climaxing in Rio de Janeiro on November 3. As in April, property damage was extensive but there was no loss of life.[29]

Government repression of its German ethnic citizens began immediately after the declaration of war. The minister of the interior ordered an end to all publications in the German language, including newspapers, periodicals, and books, even prayer books and textbooks for teaching German speakers to learn Portuguese. Another decree ordered the closing of all German schools in which Portuguese was not the language of instruction. The Brazilian postal service announced that it would no longer handle materials printed in the German language. There were also injunctions against the use of the German language in public meetings, including worship services in the immigrant churches.[30]

Congress also enacted special wartime legislation, the most significant of which was the *Lei de guerra*, enacted on November 16, 1917. This law chiefly treated economic problems and was aimed directly at the great German-owned banks and coffee-exporting firms. By it the president of the republic was empowered to seize the property of enemy aliens and to sell all goods consigned to them. Superpatriots in the Congress also demanded and received a provision granting the president the authority to declare any part of the country to be under a state of siege. The next day the president announced that Rio de Janeiro and the southern states were in such a state of siege. Martial law was imposed, German aliens were interned, and detachments of the Brazilian army were billeted in the German colonies. Inevitably, German aliens were required to register with police; passes with fingerprints and photographs were issued; and mail was censored.[31]

The total prohibition against any publication in the German language was far more severe than any wartime restrictions imposed by the United States upon its German-speaking minority. In Brazil economic survival for the publishers was possible only if they switched entirely to Portuguese, which many of them did. Such Portuguese-language substitutes almost always were considered to be temporary expedients but inevitably most newspapers experienced sharp reductions in the number of their subscribers.

Like the newspapers, the German-language schools were shut down immediately—267 in Santa Catarina alone. They were not allowed to open until they could demonstrate that they were staffed with teachers competent in Portuguese and that instructional materials in Portuguese were going to be used.[32] In the United States there was nothing comparable to Brazil's nationwide closure of private and parochial German-language schools, although German-language instruction was generally curtailed in the public schools. Even though enforcement was lax in some districts, many schools never reopened. Because public schools had never been established in many areas of German settlement, the regulation meant that thousands of Teuto-Brazilian children were simply deprived of education during the war.

It was also ‹a difficult time for many of the German churches, especially in the larger towns and cities, where superpatriotic pressures were felt most strongly. Inevitably, the Evangelicals suffered the most because of their insistence on the linkage between religion and German language and culture. A few congregations simply suspended all public functions for several months. Others tried to make the requisite transition to Portuguese. Some that were located in remote rural districts ignored the wartime restrictions entirely and continued undisturbed. Enforcement was thus inconsistent or haphazard. Higher government officials often tended to be tolerant and understanding, but local authorities were sometimes harsh and unyielding. Still other officials enforced the anti-German decrees only when superpatriots in a local community demanded it. Individual preachers and parishes endured harassment, but the most important general consequence of the war for the Evangelicals was that it cut off the source of financial support and the supply of well-trained clergymen. They were thus forced to become more independent, more self-reliant.[33]

In contrast to the Evangelicals, the Catholics and the Missouri Synod Lutherans fared reasonably well. Again, individual clergymen and congregations suffered, sometimes deservedly. The Lutherans, because of their connections with the United States, actually prospered during the war and, by all accounts, suffered no depredations during the riots, even though their congregations included virtually no one who was not German. In the numerically dominant Catholic church, the ranking Brazilian prelate (the archbishop of Rio de Janeiro) issued a pastoral letter urging understanding and tolerance of the Teuto-Brazilians, but the German-born archbishop of Porto Alegre, João Becker, imposed his own prohibition against the use of the German language in his diocese, closed all Catholic schools administered by German priests, and replaced parish priests of German birth. When individual German parishes were attacked in the superpatriotic press, Becker failed to defend them, fearing the wrath of superpatriots within Brazil's ruling class, and earning thereby the contempt of many Teuto-Brazilian Catholics.[34]

It was relatively easy for the numerous *Vereine* to accommodate to the new restrictions, compared to the churches, schools, and newspapers. Large numbers changed their names to something in Portuguese; some revised and rewrote their governing documents and opened their doors to persons other than Germans. Even so, most such organizations lost many members during the war and some simply voted themselves out of existence.[35]

Brazil's actual participation in the war was limited. Its navy patrolled a part of the Atlantic but no soldiers were sent to the battlefields of Europe. Agricultural production was greatly stimulated, but the impact of war was almost imperceptible for most persons. Under such conditions, the intense anti-German feelings that prevailed during the fall months of 1917 were bound to dissipate. Some of the severest federal restrictions were relaxed and a few were removed by spring 1918, although the ban on publication in the German language remained in force through most of 1919. On the state level there was much variation. In Santa Catarina, for example, restrictions against German-language schools remained in force until 1921.[36]

After the war, the Germans of Brazil quickly returned to their old patterns of cultural chauvinism and self-imposed separation. German-language schools reopened, newspapers resumed publication, German sermons were heard again in the churches, and the *Vereine* resumed their activities as before the war. Teuto-Brazilian businessmen and industrialists prospered. Nevertheless, the forces of assimilation inevitably eroded ethnic consciousness in many persons. It is impossible to determine how many Teuto-Brazilians were absorbed into the Brazilian mainstream because of war-born influences. But in the isolated, rural colonies, bastions of German ethnicity remained intact, if not untouched. The cultural distance between Teuto-Brazilians and the rest of society, enhanced by the strong sense of German cultural superiority, remained much greater in Brazil than in the United States, where the decline of German ethnicity was almost precipitous.[37]

Even though a general spirit of tolerance prevailed in Brazil in the postwar decade, a residue of bitterness remained. Just as some Luso-Brazilian patriots continued to insist that national unity demanded programs of forced assimilation, there were Teuto-Brazilians who felt more disillusioned and more alienated from political life than ever before.[38] Some newspapers, such as the *Germania* of São Paulo, resumed preaching the gospel of ethnic chauvinism immediately upon resumption of publication in 1919. Still, this journal also insisted that Germans owed their Brazilian fatherland love and loyalty and that they had the responsibility to work for its progress and welfare.[39] Nevertheless, the sense of resentment remained keen in many Teuto-Brazilian hearts. Their sense of ethnic distinctiveness had been intensified by the war; it was further strengthened by political unrest in the southern states of Brazil during the 1920s, when self-protection against revolutionary bands became necessary in some communities. Taken together, these experiences caused many German Brazilians to be receptive to the siren song of *Volkspolitik*. When the Nazi variations on that theme were played in the 1930s, some Teuto-Brazilians found the music irresistible.[40] Given this history, it should come as no surprise that the programs of forced assimilation undertaken by the Brazilian government under the Vargas regime and thereafter were more intense and prolonged than anything attempted during World War I.

NOTES

1. The first several paragraphs are taken from my article, "A Prelude to Conflict: The German Ethnic Group in Brazilian Society, 1890–1917," *Ethnic and Racial Studies* 6 (January 1983): 1–17, and are reprinted here with the permission of the publisher, Routledge and Kegan Paul, Ltd., Oxford, United Kingdom.

2. Detailed accounts of the riots may be found in various metropolitan newspapers of Brazil, April 16–18, 1917; for example, see *A Federação and Correio do Povo* of Porto Alegre and *Jornal do Commercio* of Rio de Janeiro. For summary accounts in the German-language press, see *Deutsche Post* of São Leopoldo, April 24, 1917, and *Germania* of São Paulo, April 25, 1917; the *New York Times* published numerous translations of dispatches from Brazilian newspapers; see similar sources for the later riots, which occurred from October 28, to November 2, 1917.

3. Compare my account of the impact of World War I on the German ethnic group in the United States, *Bonds of Loyalty: German Americans and World War I* (DeKalb: Northern Illinois Univ. Press, 1974).

4. Imre Ferenczi, comp., and Walter F. Willcox, ed., *Statistics*, vol. 1. *International Migrations* (New York: National Bureau of Economic Research, 1929), 695, 700–701.

5. The most comprehensive study of Germans in Brazil is by Jean Roche, *La colonisation allemande et la Rio Grande do Sul* (Paris: Institut des Hautes Études de l'Amérique Latine, 1959). A large number of filiopietistic histories have been published in German, the most useful of which is by Karl Fouquet, *Der deutsche Einwanderer und seine Nachkommen in Brasilien: 1808–1824–1974* (São Paulo: Instituto Hans Staden, 1974). The most important English-language writer on the Germans in Brazil is the anthropologist Emílio Willems, who has published a half dozen or more excellent articles in American journals since 1940. Willems is also the author of *A aculturação dos alemães no Brasil: Estudo antropológico dos imigrantes alemães e seus descendentes no Brasil* (São Paulo: Editora Nacional, 1946). For examples of recent scholarly, monographic work in Portuguese, see the published proceedings of three symposia, each entitled *Colóquio de estudos teuto-brasileiros* (Porto Alegre, 1963; Pernambuco, 1974; Porto Alegre, 1980).

6. Gilberto Freyre, *Order and Progress: Brazil from Monarchy to Republic*, ed. and trans. Rod W. Horton (New York: Knopf, 1970), 56–57, 123–24, and 188–89. Freyre has noted that, of all the immigrant groups, the Italians were the most desired, the most imitated, and the most highly praised by Brazilian leaders who in those years hoped the influx of European immigrants would "whiten" the population. Since Italians were closer than Germans to Luso-Brazilians on a sociocultural distance scale, they were less separatistic and thus more capable of producing the desired genetic effect (see pp. 256–57).

7. Ibid., 123 and 197; E. Bradford Burns, *A History of Brazil* (New York: Columbia Univ. Press, 1970), 250–54.

8. Freyre, *Order and Progress,* 13; Fernando de Azevedo, *Brazilian Culture* (New York: Knopf, 1950), 159–60 and 414–18.

9. Martin Fischer, "O problema da conservação da cultura alemã," in *Colóquio de estudos teuto-brasileiros* (Porto Alegre: Centro de Estudos Sociais da Faculdade da Universidade Federal do Rio Grande do Sul, 1963), 339–56; Egon Schaden, "Der Deutschbrasilianer—Ein Problem," *Staden-Jahrbuch: Beiträge zur Brasilkunde* 2 (1954): 181–94.

10. See, for example, Sylvio Romero, *O allemanismo no sul do Brasil: Seus perigos e os meios de os conjurar* (Rio de Janeiro: Ribeiro, 1906). A decade later Edgardo de Magalhães wrote a piece for English readers, but it merely repeated typical anti-German propaganda of the war period. See his "Germany and South America: A Brazilian View," *Nineteenth Century and After* 81 (January 1917): 67–80.

11. Schaden, "Der Deutschbrasilianer," 184.

12. *Deutsche Zeitung* [Porto Alegre], October 20, 1917; Oskar Canstatt, *Brasilien: Land und Leute* (Berlin: Ernst Siegfried Mittler, 1877), 251 and 416; Ernest Tonnelat, *L'expansion allemande hors d'Europe* (Paris: Armand Colin, 1908), 125 and 141; Clarence H. Haring, *The Germans in South America: A Contribution to the Economic History of the World War* (New York: Oxford Univ. Press, 1920), 43.

13. Arpad Szilvassy, "Participação dos alemães e seus descendentes na brasileira," in *Colóquio de estudos teuto-brasileiros* (Porto Alegre), 247–61. A classic example of Teuto-Brazilian filiopietism is Karl H. Oberacker, Jr., *Der deutsche Beitrag zum Aufbau der brasilianischen Nation,* 3d ed., rev. and expanded (São Leopoldo: Federação dos Centros Culturais 25 de Julho, 1978). The second edition appeared in the Portuguese language under the title, *A aculturação teuta a formação da nação brasiliera* (Rio de Janeiro: Editora Prensença, 1968).

14. Fischer, "O problema da conservação," 344.

15. Schaden, "Die Deutschbrasilianer," 189–93.

16. These generalizations are based on both the Portuguese- and German-language press of the period, including such representative newspapers as *Jornal do Commercio* [Rio de Janeiro], *A Federação* [Porto Alegre], *Deutsche Zeitung* [Porto Alegre], and *Germania* [São Paulo]. See also Hans Gehse, *Die deutsche Presse in Brasilien von 1852 bis zur Gegenwart* (Münster: Aschendorffsche Verlagsbuchhandlung, 1931) and Georg Königk, *Die Politik Brasiliens während des Weltkrieges und die Stellung des brasilianischen Deutschtums* (Hamburg: Hans Christian, 1935).

17. Joachim Fischer, "Geschichte der Evangelischen Kirche Lutherischen Bekenntnisses," in *Es begann am Rio dos Sinos: Geschichte und Gegenwart der Ev. Kirche Lutherischen Bekenntnisses in Brasilien,* ed. Joachim Fischer and Christoph Jahn (Erlangen: Verlag der Ev.-Lutherischen Mission, 1970), 85–186; Erich Fausel, *Dr. Rotermund: Ein Kampf um Recht und Richtung des Evangelischen Deutschtums in Sudbrasilien* (São Leopoldo: Verlag der Rio Grandenser Synode, 1936); *Deutsche Zeitung* [Porto Alegre], August 1914.

18. *Evangelisch-Lutherisches Kirchenblatt für Süd-Amerika* [Porto Alegre],

August 15, 1914, and November 15, 1915; *Lutherische Kirche in Brasilien: Festschrift zum 50-jährigen Bestehen der lutherischen Synode* (Joinville: n.p., [1955]).

19. Roche, *La colonisation allemande*, 517–24; Petrus Sinzig, *Nach dreißig Jahren* (Curitiba: Verlag des Franziskanerprovinzialat, 1922); Hugo Metzler, *Die St. Josefsgemeinde der deutschen Katholiken zu Porto Alegre während des Weltkrieges* (Porto Alegre: n.p., 1918).

20. See the entire run of the *Bund* publication, *Monatsblätter des Germanischen Bundes für Süd-Amerika* [Porto Alegre], 1916–17, in the Institut für Auslandsbeziehungen, Stuttgart, West Germany.

21. These generalizations are based on scores of references to *Liga pelos alliados* in *Jornal do Commercio* [Rio de Janeiro] and other newspapers. See also *New York Times*, May 4, 1917; *Germania* [São Paulo], May 4, 1917.

22. See especially *Deutsche Zeitung* [Porto Alegre] and *Germania* [São Paulo] for the period.

23. *Jornal do Commercio*, April 6, 1917; *New York Times*, April 7–9, 1917.

24. *New York Times*, April 8–14, 1917.

25. *Jornal do Commercio*, April 12, 1917; *New York Times*, April 14 and 15, 1917; *Deutsche Zeitung*, April 13, 1917.

26. See note 2.

27. *Correio do Povo* [Porto Alegre], April 20, 1917; *Jornal do Commercio* April 23, 1917; *New York Times*, April 20 and 25, 1917.

28. *Jornal do Commercio*, April 19, 26, and 30, and May 3, 1917; *Correio do Povo*, April 25, 1917; *Fünfzig Jahre Deutscher Verein Germania und Deutschtum in Bahia* (Berlin: Emil Ebering, 1923), 153; *Deutsche Post* [São Leopoldo], April 24, 1917.

29. *O Paíz* [Rio de Janeiro], November 3 and 4, 1917; *A Federação*, October 31, and November 1 and 9, 1917; *Jornal do Commercio*, November 4 and 5, 1917; Sinzig, *Nach dreißig Jahren*, 100–03, 143–44; Wilhelm Fugmann, *Die Deutschen in Parana: Das deutsche Jahrhundert-Buch* (Curitiba: Empresa Editora Olivera, 1929), 87, 121, 127, and 192.

30. *Correio da Manha* [Porto Alegre], October 27 and 28, 1917; *A Federação*, October 30, and November 5, 1917; Königk, *Die Politik Brasiliens*, 52; *O Paíz* [Rio de Janeiro] November 5 and 6, 1917; *Jornal do Commercio*, October 25, to November 16, 1917; Percy A. Martin, *Latin America and the War* (Baltimore: Johns Hopkins Univ. Press, 1925), 81; Percy A. Martin, "Brazil," in *Argentina, Brazil, and Chile since Independence*, ed. A. C. Wilgus (1935; reprint, New York: Russell and Russell, 1963), 256; *Fünfzig Jahre Deutscher Verein Germania*, 157.

31. *Jornal do Commercio*, November 17, 1917; *A Federação*, November 17, 1917; *Hundert Jahre Deutschtum in Rio Grande do Sul, 1824–1924* (Porto Alegre: Typographia do Centro, 1924), 384.

32. Martin Braunschweig, "Die rechtliche Stellung des deutschen Schulwesens in Südbrasilien," in *Die Kulturbedeutung der deutschen evangelischen*

Kirche in Brasilien, ed. Bruno Geißler (Leipzig: Hinrichs'sche Buchhandlung, 1922), 50; *A Federação,* November 9, 1917; *O Paíz* [Rio de Janeiro], November 9, 1917.

33. Wolfgang Ammon, *Chronik von São Bento in Santa Catharina, 1873–1923* (Joinville: Boehm, 1923), 230; *75 Jahre Deutschtum: Santo Angelo-Agudo* (São Leopoldo: Rotermund, 1932), 129; *Lutherische Kirche in Brasilien,* 140, 151, and 176; Fritz Wüstner, *Kirchengemeinde Joinville* (Joinville: privately printed, 1951), 51; Fausel, *Rotermund,* 148–50, 153, and 154; Fischer, "Geschichte der Evangelischen Kirche Lutherischen Bekenntnisses," 150; Rudolph Becker, *Deutsche Siedler in Rio Grande do Sul* (Ijuhy: Verlag der Serra-Post, 1938), 79.

34. Pfarrer Radlach, "Die Einwirkungen des Weltkrieges auf die deutsch-evangelischen Gemeinden in Santa Catharina," in *Die Kulturbedeutung der deutschen evangelischen Kirche in Brasilien,* 26; Haring, *The Germans of South America,* 48; Roche, *La colonisation allemande,* 515; *Der Familienfreund: Katholischer Hauskalender und Wegweiser für das Jahr 1918* (Porto Alegre: Hugo Metzler [1917]), 124; Sinzig, *Nach dreißig Jahren,* 100–101 and 144–45; *A Federação,* November 9, 1917; *Correio do Povo,* November 27, 1917; Metzler, *St. Josefsgemeinde.*

35. Roche, *La colonisation allemande,* 539; *Jornal do Commercio,* November 6, 1917; Heinrich Hinden, *Deutsche und deutscher Handel in Rio de Janeiro: Ein hundert-jähriges Kulturbild zur Zentenar-Feier der Gesellschaft 'Germania,' 1821–1921* (Rio de Janeiro: Gesellschaft Germania, 1921), 524.

36. Ferdinand Schröder, *Brasilien und Wittenberg: Ursprung und Gestaltung deutschen evangelischen Kirchentums in Brasilien* (Berlin: Verlag Ev. Hauptverein für Deutsche Ansiedler und Auswanderer, 1936), 357; Gottfried Entres, ed., *Der Staat Santa Catharina in Vergangenheit und Gegenwart unter besonderer Berücksichtigung des Deutschtums* (Florianópolis: Livraria Central, 1929), 223.

37. *Koseritz' Deutscher Volkskalender für Brasilien auf das Jahr 1921* (Porto Alegre: Krahe, 1920), 120; Max Dedekind, *Brasilien, das Ziel deutscher Auswanderer und die Deutsche Evangelische Kirche in Brasilien* (Elberfeld: Evangelische Gesellschaft für die protestantischen Deutschen in Südamerika, 1924), 25. Compare Luebke, *Bonds of Loyalty,* 309–31.

38. Fouquet, *Der deutsche Einwanderer,* 181; Erwin Buchmann, "Die deutsch-sprachige Presse in Brasilien," *Staden-Jahrbuch* 4 (1956): 221.

39. *Germania,* August 19 and 22, 1919; *Koseritz' Volkskalender, 1921,* 33.

40. Joseph L. Love, *Rio Grande do Sul and Brazilian Regionalism, 1822–1930* (Stanford: Stanford Univ. Press, 1971), 199–215; Becker, *Deutsche Siedler,* 83; Königk, *Die Politik Brasiliens,* 66.

Turnerism, Social History, and the Historiograpy of European Ethnic Groups in the United States

9

I

During the past century an enormous number of books and articles have been written on European ethnic groups in American history. Mainly produced by amateur historians, this extensive literature consists of articles in state and local history journals and collections, books published by obscure and sometimes private presses, church or denominational histories, diaries, and reminiscences. Primarily factual in character and descriptive of separate ethnic group experience, most of these materials fail to illuminate either internal social structures or the intricate relationships of minorities to each other and to the dominant or host society. Moreover, they tend to be filiopietistic; their purpose often is to praise the great deeds of the ethnic fathers who led their people through the wilderness to establish new homes in a strange land. They recount in loving detail how this group or that settled here or there, established their distinctive institutions, and perpetuated their special cultural forms. They record the bravery, fortitude, imagination, and skill with which ethnic groups braved environmental hardship to become solid and respectable citizens. Analyses of failure, incompetence, mismanagement, intragroup conflict, and stubborn refusal to adapt are less common in this literature.

Filiopietistic accounts that concentrate on the accomplishments of ethnic group leaders or prominent members of the subsociety have a special tendency to mythologize the past. The history of ethnic groups in America is first of all the story of large numbers of ordinary persons, not dramatic tales of colorful or unusually talented leaders. To focus on an ethnic elite without treating the character of the masses or examining the relationships between leaders and followers is automatically to distort the history of immigrant people. Some leaders, because of their own personal background and psychological needs, identify much more strongly with the ethnic group than do the rank-and-file members. Other persons, prominent because of individual accomplishments in the business, political, or intellectual worlds, tend to have exceptional social experiences and hence may have few meaningful ties with the ethnic group associated with them in the public mind. They may, in fact, shed ethnic attitudes and behaviors with remarkable speed. In either case, it is a mistake to apply generalizations drawn from leadership or elite experience to the minority group as a whole, as often has happened in immigration history.

If the writings of amateurs and filiopietists tended to lack adequate conceptual foundations, the work of academic or professional historians early in our century was often influenced strongly by a point of view that tended to minimize the importance of ethnic history. I refer to the frontier thesis of Frederick Jackson Turner (1861–1932) and his considerable influence on the concepts and methods employed by American historians during his lifetime and after.

Turner's impact on immigration historiography, as I try to make clear in the pages that follow, also had its positive aspects, particularly with respect to methodology. In the early development of this subfield, Turner's emphasis on the environment as a force leading irresistably to the assimilation of millions of immigrants infused the writings of academic historians. Then, in the 1950s, when the work of Oscar Handlin stamped the field with insights drawn from sociology and other social sciences, the historiographical emphasis shifted from environmentalism to social conflict or, in other words, from rapid assimilation to the persistence of immigrant cultural forms. By the 1970s the Turnerian thread virtually disappeared as attention shifted first to ethnocultural variables in political behavior and then to a variety of social analyses that stress the pluralist character of American society. Finally, in the 1980s, in the work of historians who trace the patterns of international migration, there has been a renewed recognition of environmental factors. This essay concludes with some discussion of a neo-Turnerian conceptual framework that interprets ethnic history as emerging from the interaction over time of immigrant culture with specific physical and social environments.

II

The central assumption of Turner's overarching schema—his celebrated frontier thesis—is that the exigencies of life in primitive circumstances forced people, regardless of their origins or culture, to adapt their ways to the physical realities of the place they had chosen for their new home. The frontier environment is thus assumed to have been a crucible in which the cultural characteristics of newcomers were melted away. Out of the heat of this refining process, wrote Turner, emerged a new type, an American, who was different and probably superior in his or her strengths, qualities, values, and virtues, compared to his or her forebears and contemporaries in Europe. Where environmental forces are assumed to be especially powerful, as in the American West with its barren deserts, rugged mountains, and treeless, semiarid plains, ethnocultural distinctions could be easily eradicated. Thus Turnerism, it appears, predisposed the historian to emphasize the ease and rapidity with which ethnic groups were assimilated into American society and to ignore ethnocultural conflict and the persistence of immigrant attitudes, values, and behaviors.

Turner was a master whose sweeping imagination and romantic style inspired scores of followers to write histories patterned on his famous thesis with its dominant strain of environmental determinism. Many historians of the American frontier writing in the Turnerian mode tended to treat their subject as the story of an undifferentiated, English-speaking majority on a steady, civilizing march from the time of exploration and settlement toward the present, with its allegedly high levels of accomplishment. This is not to say that racial groups were absent from these accounts, which often describe how progress was generally obstructed by Indians, sometimes noble but usually savage, and in lesser ways by Mexicans and Chinese. But questions of the past were seldom framed in terms of the differing cultures in collision and even more rarely in ways that fostered the analysis of ethnocultural variations within white society.

But Turner also stressed the importance of method. Because he produced so few books and essays of a monographic character in his own lifetime, his methodology does not emerge clearly from his published works. In his seminars, however, Turner led his students to data stored in census reports, commercial records, church registers, and the multifarious tabulations compiled by county, city, and township governments; he taught them to sort, classify, and interpret quantitative evidence. Moreover, he emphasized the spatial differentiation that may be discovered in economic, social, and cultural evidence. Turner's workshop contained numerous maps that plotted election data, ecological information, differences in soils, ethnic settlement patterns, literacy rates, church memberships—anything that might reveal geographical variation.[1] This was the Turner who stressed the significance of sections. In contrast to the frontier thesis, which worked against the study of the ethnic variable, Turner's sectionalist doctrines were based on a methodology that was ideally suited for the study of ethnic minority groups in America.[2]

Nevertheless, it is a fact that Turner himself never pursued ethnocultural variables in a more than superficial way. He understood that ethnicity was capable of modifying a region's character to such an extent that it could be distinguished from the rest of the nation. Moreover, he often charted ethnic and religious groups on his maps, and he even wrote a series of popular articles on several immigrant groups for the *Chicago Record-Herald* in 1901.[3] Yet he never penetrated the subject deeply enough to analyze the significance of the variables he had discovered. This could emerge most readily through the study of group conflict, but for Turner conflict occurred chiefly between regions rather than within them. Because of his preoccupation with variation on a sectional scale, he tended to slight class and group conflicts that were not fundamentally related to spatial distribution.[4]

But it took no great leap of the imagination to substitute ethnic minority groups for regions in Turner's sectionalist theories. Ethnic groups, like the people of each region in the United States, considered their culture to be superior and they expected the rest of the country to tolerate their ways, if not to emulate them. If, as Turner had taught, the American political system provided a forum for the definition of regional interest and an arena for the resolution of sectional conflict through accommodation and compromise, it could also be understood as serving the same function for ethnic minority groups, although on a more local level. The question therefore arises whether any of Turner's students analyzed immigration or ethnic history in a way that transcended the confinements of the frontier thesis by employing the research methods Turner had fostered in his pursuit of sectionalism.[5]

Turnerian methodology is ably illustrated in the several works by Joseph Schafer, a Turner Ph.D. who became superintendent of the State Historical Society of Wisconsin in 1920. Although not an immigration historian, Schafer was much interested in the acculturation of Wisconsin's numerous ethnic groups, especially the Germans. During his two decades as superintendent, Schafer produced a series of microcosmic studies under the general title of *The Wisconsin Domesday Book*. It was an ambitious enterprise. Ultimately he produced five volumes, of which three are attempts to understand the history of carefully defined areas in Wisconsin—four lakeshore counties, the lead region, and a river basin—in terms of the interaction of the people, including the many immigrants, with their specific environments. Schafer treated topography, soils, land use, migration and settlement, agriculture, politics, and population changes. Ethnic groups were always integral parts of his analysis, but as a devoted Turnerian committed to the frontier thesis, Schafer tended to emphasize the Americanization of the immigrants—how rapidly they were assimilated in the frontier environment, not how tenaciously they retained ethnic cultural characteristics.[6]

Schafer also tended to overstate the striving of immigrants toward the ideal of the socially acceptable American citizen, but he admitted that it was not necessary for them to discard all ethnic traits in order to become "good Americans."[7] No filiopietist, Schafer had a keen understanding of the assimilation process, its ethnic group variations, and the role in it of language, religion, and exogamy, even though he tended to overestimate the rate at which these variables operated. He employed census data, land office records, and surveyor reports to calculate for each immigrant group such variables as spatial diffusion, attitudes toward land, occupational distributions, family size, marriage rates, and income patterns compared with native-born persons. In short, Schafer's analysis was remarkably comprehensive for its time. He provided a model for research that has been all but ignored by later generation of historians interested in ethnic history.

One of the last of Turner's students at Harvard, Merle Curti, followed Schafer a generation later with a far more comprehensive and systematic case study. *The Making of an American Community* was designed to test objectively Turner's frontier thesis, most specifically the idea that the frontier experience promoted American democracy. This included the increasing participation of immigrants in the political process and the expansion of opportunities for them in economic and cultural affairs. Curti chose Trempealeau County, Wisconsin, as the subject for his study at least partly because its frontier population included significant numbers of German, Norwegian, and Polish immigrants. Thus Trempealeau provided a laboratory in which to verify Turner's metaphor of the frontier as a crucible in which the immigrants were to have been fused into a mixed race. Curti and his associates analyzed mobility data, indices of success in various occupations, changes in occupational structures, and measures of leadership, political participation, school attendance, and marriage patterns. He concluded that frontier conditions had in fact stimulated democracy in Trempealeau and that "decade by decade the foreign-born, including those from non-English speaking countries, were increasingly represented in political and also in cultural activities."[8]

Whether these findings supported Turner's general position, as Curti claimed, is less clear. He had in fact merely demonstrated that "Americanization" had occurred in Trempealeau; he had not proved that this process occurred because of frontier conditions. It is possible that in an urban setting, for example, these same persons might have assimilated more rapidly than they did on the Wisconsin frontier. Moreover, the possibility remains that the frontier conditions masked, or were mistaken for, variables with greater power to explain the process by which ethnic groups gradually lost their distinctive character and became indistinguishable from the majority. What was missing in Curti's research design was a series of comparisons with other appropriate communities; what was needed was a conceptual framework to replace the powerful imagery of Turner's frontier thesis.

If Schafer and Curti were microscopic in their approaches, another Turner student, Marcus Lee Hansen, was telescopic. Hansen's perspective was intercontinental as he shifted attention in immigration history from the cultural contributions of immigrant leaders to the phenomenon of mass migration from Europe to America. This he achieved chiefly through two posthumously published books, *The Immigrant in American History* and *The Atlantic Migration, 1607–1860*. The latter book in particular laid the foundation for the sophisticated studies of the 1980s that treat migration chains and community formation in rural America. Like Schafer, Hansen was the son of an immigrant, a great advantage in assessing immigrant experience.

Hansen's work represents a laudable accomplishment, but he was also a source of a misconception about immigrants on the frontier. Hansen taught that newcomers from Europe were not commonly found on the fringe of settlement because they lacked experience in coping with the problems of such an environment. The immigrant was not a frontiersman, wrote Hansen, and "had, in fact, an innate aversion to the wilderness with its solitude and loneliness and primitive mode of life. . . . Neither by experience nor temperament was the immigrant fitted for frontiering."[9] This notion is partly founded on the fact that from 1775 to 1830 European immigration practically ceased. Hence few immigrants from any country could possibly have participated in the settlement of the American frontier as it existed in those decades. After the 1830s, however, immigration increased spectacularly. Thus when the trans-Mississippi West was settled, immigrants were present on the northern and western frontiers in proportions that were usually in excess of that registered for the United States as a whole.

The purpose of this discussion about Turner, his students, and their treatment of ethnic history is to suggest, first, that the frontier thesis is conceptually inadequate for the study of ethnic minorities because it assumes the dominance of environments over culture and therefore predisposes the historians to emphasize the rapid assimilation of immigrants. It does not offer a framework for the study of the frontier as a place where environment and culture interact.[10] Instead, it postulates that the frontier is more powerful than the culture brought to it. It stimulates the consideration of evidence that supports the thesis and tends to ignore the rest. In effect, it makes a judgment before the evidence is brought forth.

My second point is positive in character. Unlike the frontier thesis, Turnerian methodology fosters the search for interpretive frameworks—alternatives to the frontier thesis—that encompass evidence for the persistence of ethnic culture as well as its disappearance, for slow assimilation as well as rapid, for the study of masses of immigrants as well as their leaders, for inquiry into conflict as well as accommodation to established norms. Above all, Turnerian methodology encourages the study of ethnicity in its relationships to environment, whatever they may be, rather than assuming the dominance of environment over ethnicity.

III

At about the same time that Marcus Lee Hansen was drafting his *Atlantic Migration,* Oscar Handlin was completing his doctoral dissertation at Harvard under the direction of Arthur Schlesinger, Sr. Published in a revised form in 1941 as *Boston's Immigrants: A Study in Acculturation,* Handlin's work reflected the influence of social science—more sociology than the geography that was implicit in Turnerian thought.[11] Instead of rapid assimilation into American life as the Turnerians perceived it, Handlin emphasized conflict between immigrant groups and the receiving society. He focused on social process—the process of change that grew out of the interrelationships between immigrants and native stock. He made extensive use of aggregated census data and, like most recent students in this field, he concentrated on a local community, in this case, Boston. By any standard, *Boston's Immigrants* was an impressive achievement.

Yet Handlin is best known for his Pulitzer Prize winner, *The Uprooted,* which was first published in 1951. Radically different from *Boston's Immigrants,* this book, which is based entirely on impressionistic sources, treats the effect of the immigrant experience on the individual.[12] Although Handlin continued to draw on sociology, here he concentrated on the psychological dimension—how the individual immigrant experienced trauma and alienation, how immigrant culture crumbled and communal life disintegrated in the new social environment. He wrote ethnic history in terms of the ghetto model: rejected by the host society, the newcomers were more or less forced into segregated areas where they had to work out their own problems and gradually learn to adapt to American ways. *The Uprooted* is essentially a romanticized account, emphasizing tragedy and pathos in the lives of immigrants. Ultimately, however, Handlin's emphasis is on adjustment, accommodation, and assimilation—not on the persistence of ethnocultural forms and the retention of ethnic identity among countless Americans of the second and third generations.

Throughout the 1950s Handlin's interpretation reigned unchallenged in immigrant historiography. Then, in the early '60s, important criticisms were published. In an influential article Rudolph Vecoli asserted that whatever validity *The Uprooted* had for other groups, it had little applicability to Italian immigrants. Their "Little Italies" were formed voluntarily, not forced by circumstances; their family and communal ties remained strong; their lives were not filled with trauma; they did not rely on the immigrant church as the one remaining pillar in their crumbling house of culture. In short, they did not feel uprooted.[13] Other critics pointed out that Handlin's view, if valid, applied to urban settings and that it had little relevance for rural and small-town experience. Indeed, most studies of international migration and community formation published in the 1970s and '80s describe a society fundamentally different from that outlined by Handlin.

Handlin had not in fact solved the central historiographical problem in immigration history. The Turnerians had emphasized the experience of immigrants who had assimilated rapidly into American life and tended to ignore the rest. At the other extreme, Handlin had concentrated on individuals for whom immigration had been traumatic. What was needed was a new point of view that could encompass the full range of behavioral response—both extremes and the majority who fell between. Merle Curti's study of Trempealeau filled this prescription in methodology, but it was weakened by its Turnerian purposes and preconceptions.

IV

The most important new work in ethnic history published in the 1960s and '70s emerged from other sources. Its roots lay in political history, for it was in this field that the implications of ethnocultural persistence could be most readily observed. In 1961 Lee Benson's *Concept of Jacksonian Democracy: New York as a Test Case* revealed that ideologies, specifically Jacksonian democracy, had relatively little to do with voting behavior when that phenomenon is observed on the local level. Instead of economic issues influencing voter decisions primarily, Benson found that ethnic and religious identities were paramount.[14] In other words, cultural factors appeared to be more significant than class in explaining political history.

The key to the new political history was the systematic analysis of data on the local level in which detailed comparisons could be made with related data in terms of space, time, and rate of change. Moreover, the emphasis was now placed on group behavior rather than on the attitudes of ethnic leaders. Immigrant voters, it was discovered, tended to vote with much consistency regardless of the changing issues. When issues on the local level were investigated, it was found that ethnoreligious concerns were usually more salient than such economic questions as the tariff, trusts, and railroads—issues that dominated political discourse on the national level in the late nineteenth century. Issues that touched lives directly were debates over prohibition, women's suffrage, Sabbatarian legislation, naturalization laws, and the regulation of parochial schools. Probably no historian was more successful than Samuel P. Hays in bringing these matters to the attention of scholars. Through a series of theoretical articles Hays showed that ethnic groups maintained separate identities and distinctive behaviors, sometimes for generations—and that they voted accordingly.[15] During the late 1960s and '70s a new generation of historians put the ideas of Hays, Benson, and other scholars, including social scientists, to the test and produced many books treating the relationships of ethnic groups to the political history of various regions and states.[16]

V

Since the development of the ethnocultural school of American political historians in the early 1970s, there has been a great expansion of immigration studies, consisting of the usual dissertations, articles, monographs, and syntheses. Even though contemporary concerns focus mainly on the huge influx of Latin Americans and Asians, the majority of these works, as in the past, treat European groups in the nineteenth and early twentieth centuries. Like the political studies, they are usually informed by concepts and methods drawn from the social sciences, and therefore often incorporate comparative analyses as they pursue data relating to occupation, class, social mobility, family patterns, religion, education, assimilation, voluntary associations, and the development of ethnic group consciousness and strategies to succeed in a new social and economic environment. Some treat one ethnic group in one place; others effectively analyze the entire complex of immigrants comparatively in an urban setting and thus are more closely related to the concepts and methods of urban history than to those traditionally associated with immigration history. Still other historians include ethnic groups in their studies of American labor history.

This substantial corpus of historical literature has been perceptively analyzed by John Higham. After briefly differentiating assimilationist historians from the pluralists, Higham distinguished "soft pluralists" from "hard pluralists." The former include historians whose books are categorized above. In most cases the family is identified as the conserving agent of cultural persistence, and immigrant groups usually are seen to cut vertically across the class structure. The latter group of historians, Higham observed, are radical in orientation and write from the perspectives of labor history. Not interested in the preservation of ethnicity, the "hard pluralists" consider ethnic culture to be significant, not for its own sake, but for the way it functions as an impediment or a stimulus for class consciousness. Higham further pointed out that the two versions of pluralism lack a common theory of social integration and hence neither can provide a general synthesis of ethnic history in the United States.[17]

Soon after Higham published that essay a new synthesis appeared—*The Transplanted: A History of Immigrants in Urban America*, by John Bodnar. By conceptualizing ethnic history in a way that transcends the agendas of pluralism, Bodnar has provided the best general interpretation of American immigration history since Maldwyn Jones's Turnerian *American Immigration* appeared in 1960.[18] Although he limits himself to immigrants in urban settings, a field in which he personally excels as a historian, Bodnar bases his interpretation on the only commonly shared experience all immigrants in the cities had — finding a place in an unfamiliar economic order based on capitalism.

Bodnar's interpretation allows him to leap the hurdles of both the hard and soft pluralist schools identified by Higham. He argues that the central commitment of immigrants was neither to their class nor their ethnic group, but rather "to secure the welfare and well-being of their familial or household base." In any industrial setting, ethnic communities were too deeply fragmented by social, economic, or cultural variables to command loyalty to anything else. At the same time, ethnic group culture, Bodnar contends, did not condition the immigrant's response to capitalism as much as did its continuous interaction with class experience. Instead of the traditional view of the immigrant progressing "from a premodern, holistic community to a modern, atomistic one" emerging from clashes between immigrant and American urban cultures, Bodnar sees "a process of social change" conditioned by class, ideology, and culture (including religion) — a continuum of interaction "between economy and society, between class and culture." Thus he goes beyond the idea of immigrants as clinging together as either aliens or workers to argue that immigration history emerges at all points "where immigrant families met the challenges of capitalism and modernity: the homeland, the neighborhood, the school, the workplace, the church, the family, and the fraternal hall."[19]

Like some other writers in the field of immigration history, Bodnar chose a title — *The Transplanted* — that is entirely appropriate in itself, but nonetheless implicitly challenges Handlin's *Uprooted* and its emphasis on immigrant trauma and alienation.[20] As bold as Handlin in his willingness to generalize, Bodnar offers a synthesis that is better balanced, more comprehensive, and more firmly grounded on scholarly research (as one should expect of a work written three decades later). But its greatest strength rests in its unity of conception. Structured on a carefully articulated foundation, the book includes nothing that fails to contribute to its thesis. Unlike countless textbooks, it casts no crumbs from the master's table to feed the dogs of special interest groups.

Still, *The Transplanted* has its limitations. Its thesis is applicable to the nineteenth and early twentieth centuries, not to the colonial era or the decades since World War II. It treats immigrant societies in urban settings, not in rural or small-town America, even though many of its observations are applicable there. And like most recent works in ethnic history, whether organized in terms of assimilation, cultural persistence, urban history, or labor history, its treatment of spatial variables is incidental rather than systematic. Bodnar readily recognizes the importance of such relationships. For example, he differentiates ethnic ghettoes from other parts of the city and he observes that cities in different parts of the United States often offered contrasting *milieux* for immigrant success. Yet the assessment of space and place does not emerge naturally from his conceptual framework, as it did in Turnerian methodology and does in the work of recent students of international migration.

VI

Although intercontinental movement received its first effective treatment fifty years ago in Marcus Lee Hansen's *Atlantic Migration, 1607–1860*, it was not until the 1980s that this topic has received systematic treatment. Drawing their inspiration from the English historian Frank Thistlethwaite, and perhaps to a lesser extent from the Uppsala University project in Sweden headed by Sune Åkerman, a trio of scholars—Jon Gjerde, Walter Kamphoefner, and Robert Ostergren—have analyzed patterns of transatlantic chain migration. Working primarily on microcosmic scales and paying equal attention to conditions in communities of origin and of destination, they study intensively the process of emigration from specific communities in Norway, Germany, and Sweden, and their dispersion and reconstitution in states of the Midwest.[21]

These studies of international migration in the Thistlethwaitean mode illustrate additional possibilities for ethnic history when it is released from old agendas and conceptual schemes. The Turnerians emphasized the study of ethnicity in relation to the physical environment, but neither the ethnocultural political historians nor the pluralists, hard or soft, paid heed to the limitations imposed by place or space as they examined ethnicity in its social relationships. As suggested above, Bodnar's synthesis offers a new conceptual scheme based on the ongoing interaction of ethnicity with class, ideology, and culture, but again spatial relationships are not part of his model, even though he is mindful of the fact that urban geography was often conditioned strongly by ethnic values.

But the "Thistlethwaiteans," if we may label them so, emphasize the need to understand immigrant societies as products of the interaction of their imported culture with both the physical and social environments of their new homes. Spatial relationships are central, especially in the work of Robert Ostergren, a historical geographer who charts patterns of movement and communication back and forth between two discrete places separated by an ocean, as well as the changes inspired in each community by the axes of migration.[22] Ostergren, more effectively than any other contemporary student of immigration history, supplies the conceptual framework that was missing in the Turnerian schema. Like Bodnar, these students of international migration see history as emerging from a continuous interaction among variables of time and culture, but whereas Bodnar emphasizes ideology in his model, Ostergren integrates spatial relationships and the conditioning variables of specific physical environments.

VII

One may conclude from the work of these students of international migration that if ethnic groups in the United States are to be understood, the historian should employ a conceptual framework sufficiently broad to discover who the immigrants were, where they came from, and when and why they emigrated. One must comprehend the culture that immigrants brought with them—group values, attitudes, folkways, religions, and languages. The enormous variation possible with each group as well as among different groups must become part of the equation. Further, one must understand the physical and social environments in which the assimilative process occurred.[23] It was one thing, for example, for Norwegian immigrants to settle in the vast, sparsely populated prairies of North Dakota; it was quite another for them to join the Scandinavian stream to the Mormon Zion in the deserts of Utah; it was still another to participate in the development of Washington State, with its great forests and bustling seaports. In each environment Norwegian immigrants had different assimilative histories. Similarly, Ostergren demonstrates that the experiences of Swedish immigrant farmers from Rättvik parish in Upper Dalarna varied considerably between forested Isanti County in Minnesota and the grasslands of Clay County, South Dakota.[24]

The mode of settlement is also an essential part of immigration history. Did the immigrants come individually or in colonies? Did they come directly or in stages, living temporarily elsewhere in the United States before permanent settlement? For example, the collective experiences of the Germans from Russia, a large proportion of whom came directly to the Great Plains states in colonies, were significantly different from those of Germans from Germany, for whom the classic pattern of chain migration and resettlement was standard. What patterns of distribution in space where established by a given group? Were they farmers? Were they townsfolk? Were they overwhelmingly urban? To what extent were distributive patterns influenced by the physical environment and to what extent by immigrant culture? Among Black Sea Germans, for example, inheritance customs were such that a high proportion of immigrants were enabled to reestablish themselves on farms on the Great Plains, but among the Volga Germans a different inheritance custom had the effect of reducing the number of potential farmers and forcing a large proportion to seek employment in cities, thereby creating a strikingly different settlement pattern.[25]

The question of the density of ethnic population holds special importance for places where the small numbers of people are thinly spread over areas. In order for ethnocultural forms to be sustained over time, they must have the support of institutions such as churches, schools, and immigrant-language press, social and cultural institutions of all kinds, mutual benefit or insurance societies, and businesses that cater to the ethnic trade. A certain level of concentration in the ethnic population—a "critical mass"—must be attained before the supportive institutions can be generated. If they appear, ethnic language and culture will be maintained for a longer period of time. Without their support, immigrants will lose their ethnocultural characteristics and assimilate rapidly.[26] Richard Etulain has shown, for example, that even among the Basques, a small group that has an unusually keen sense of identity, assimilation takes place more rapidly in small ethnic enclaves than in large ones.[27] Obviously, the required auxiliary institutions cannot be easily created or maintained in areas where the physical environment dictates a sparse population. In this context the religious characteristics of a given group are especially important. Churches were commonly the easiest of immigrant institutions to create. Often they were the only ones in rural areas, where they frequently provided the nucleus of ethnic life and functioned as substitutes for the array of social and cultural societies that were available in urban centers. Moreover, they almost always functioned effectively as conservators of ethnocultural values.

The degree of concentration necessary for the maintenance of ethnic language and culture is also related to the social distance perceived by an ethnic group between its own distinctive way of life and what it discerns as the culture of the host or receiving society. In the United States the core culture may be described as having emerged from English and pietistic Protestant origins. The greater the difference perceived between immigrant group characteristics and those of the mainstream society, the greater the tendency for clustering. For example, we may expect that late-nineteenth century Polish immigrants, as adherents of Roman Catholicism and speaking a Slavic tongue, tended to congregate more readily than Swedes, whose language is a Teutonic relative of English and whose Lutheran Protestantism in America savored strongly of pietism. If the cultural difference were accompanied by discernible differences in physical appearance, as among Japanese or blacks, then the numbers of migrants required for the maintenance of ethnic language and culture will be reduced.

"Critical mass" is thus also related to the internal cohesion of an ethnic group, its homogeneity, and its sense of peoplehood.[28] English immigrants have almost no sense of themselves as an ethnic group, but the Chicanos speak of themselves as *La Raza*. Whereas one hundred ordinary German immigrants in a rural setting was rarely enough to produce a strong sense of communal identity, a hundred is near the maximum size of the colonies of German-speaking Hutterites, a radical Protestant group from Russia that still organizes itself into communally owned agricultural societies in South Dakota, Montana, and the Canadian prairie provinces.[29] Other variables also condition critical mass, among them a population large enough to permit a high level of marriage and family formation within the group.

Finally, the greater the differences between immigrant and core cultures, the greater will be the potential for conflict. For this reason the Hutterites try to avoid contact (and hence conflict and assimilation) by living in isolated colonies in areas of low population density. Even so, historical accident is capable of shattering the communal peace, as it did in World War I, when Hutterite pacificism clashed so intensely with American superpatriotism that a majority temporarily abandoned South Dakota for Canada.[30]

VIII

The history of an immigrant group in America is the story of its assimilation into the mainstream. Assimilation is an interactive process in which the both the immigrant and the receiving societies are changed. The phenomenon is infinitely complex and varies from time to time and from place to place as opportunities, economic and otherwise, are presented to the individual in both contexts or structures.[31] So long as the ethnic group sustains a separate identity it will have an ongoing history. As individual identities are increasingly shaped by other variables, the identity of the group fades. When it disappears, all that remains is nostalgia. For some groups this process is remarkably brief, and it is shorter in some environments than in others. For other groups the process may be attenuated, and distinctive traits and behaviors may be retained over many generations.

Research into ethnic minority history thus may profitably concentrate on how, why, and in what areas of life assimilative changes have taken place. One may ask how quickly or slowly the immigrant society adopts the dress, language, work habits, political behavior, marriage and family patterns, religion, and ultimately the values and attitudes of the host society. The pressures exerted by the physical and social environments in stimulating or forcing ethnic group adaptation or conformance should be integrated into the research design.

Most important, questions of the past should be framed in ways that permit comparisons in space and time. One must ask how a specific behavior of an immigrant group in a given place compared (1) to that of other groups, native- or foreign-born, in the same or comparable environment; (2) to that of the same group in other environments; and (3) to what it became later in time. It is possible, of course, for excellent histories of ethnic groups to be written without comparisons based on quantitative evidence. But since ethnic history is the study of change in a social grouping that is different from the larger society of which it is part, the evolution of these changes often may be discovered and analyzed most efficiently in this way.

Since the mid-1960s there has been an enormous growth in the number and quality of studies treating historical aspects of ethnic minority life in the United States. Although much of this recent work bears similarities in its methods to what Frederick Jackson Turner taught in his famous seminars early in this century, its inspiration lies elsewhere. Turner provided the key to ethnic history in his methodology, but his students fumbled at the door. More attracted by the frontier thesis and its melting-pot corollary, they failed to integrate racial and ethnic minorities into their histories. For decades professionally trained historians left the field to amateurs and filiopietists. Only in the 1960s, when interest in the pluralistic character of American society flourished as it never had before, did the professionals turn to ethnic minority history. Almost none recognized the intellectual debt to Turner, unless it was through his latter-day students Hansen and Curti. Instead, their formulations emerged from the "new social history," "the new political history," urban history, or cross-disciplinary study in cultural geography, sociology, anthropology, and folklore.[32] Still others seem to have been stimulated by a new concern for local history and the changing character of life at the local level. The result of this interest is an array of carefully conceptualized books, the best of which examine the process of change over time in ethnic minority group culture as it interacts with other groups, native and immigrant, within a specific physical and social environment.

NOTES

1. Fulmer Mood, "The Development of Frederick Jackson Turner as a Historical Thinker," *Transactions of the Colonial Society of Massachusetts* 34 (1943): 328–51; Richard Jensen, "American Election Analysis," in *Politics and*

the Social Sciences, ed. Seymour Martin Lipset (New York: Oxford Univ. Press, 1969), 232–35.

2. Merle Curti, "Frederick Jackson Turner," in *Wisconsin Witness to Frederick Jackson Turner*, comp. O. Lawrence Burnette, Jr. (Madison: State Historical Society of Wisconsin, 1961), 202–4; Merle Curti, "The Section and the Frontier in American History: The Methodological Concepts of Frederick Jackson Turner," in *Methods in Social Science*, ed. Stuart Rice (Chicago: Univ. of Chicago Press, 1931), 353–67; Avery O. Craven, "Frederick Jackson Turner," in *The Marcus W. Jernegan Essays in American Historiography*, ed. William T. Hutchinson (Chicago: Univ. of Chicago Press, 1937), 265; Ray Allen Billington, *Frederick Jackson Turner: Historian, Scholar, Teacher* (New York: Oxford Univ. Press, 1973), 209–32.

3. Written in response to a request from the newspaper, six articles treated the immigration of Italians, Germans, Jews, and French-Canadians to the United States. They appeared in August, September, and October 1901. The best analysis of Turner in relation to immigration history is by Edward N. Saveth, *American Historians and European Immigrants, 1875–1925* (New York: Columbia Univ. Press, 1948), 122–37. See also Billington, *Turner*, 171–73 and 486–89.

4. See Richard Hofstadter's criticism of Turner's sectionalism in *The Progressive Historians: Turner, Beard, Parrington* (New York: Knopf, 1968; paper ed., 1970), 95–105; Jackson K. Putnam, "The Turner Thesis and the Westward Movement: A Reappraisal," *Western Historical Quarterly* 7 (October 1976): 377–404; Michael C. Steiner, "The Significance of Turner's Sectional Thesis," *Western Historical Quarterly* 10 (October 1979): 437–66; and Richard Jensen, "On Modernizing Frederick Jackson Turner: The Historiography of Regionalism," *Western Historical Quarterly* 11 (July 1980): 307–22.

5. One of Turner's earliest graduate students at Wisconsin, Kate Everest, effectively studied German immigration to the state. Publication of her earliest work actually preceded the presentation by Turner of his frontier thesis at the American Historical Association meeting of 1893. Unfortunately, Everest's work attracted little scholarly attention then or later. See Kate Asaphine Everest, "How Wisconsin Came by Its Large German Element," *Collections of the State Historical Society of Wisconsin* 12 (1892): 299–334. See also Kate Everest Levi, "Geographical Origins of German Immigration to Wisconsin," *Collections of the State Historical Society of Wisconsin* 14 (1898): 343–50.

6. Clifford Lord and Carl Ubbelohde, *Clio's Servant: The State Historical Society of Wisconsin, 1846–1954* (Madison: State Historical Society of Wisconsin, 1967), 257–63. The volumes in the Domesday series are *A History of Agriculture in Wisconsin* (1922), *Wisconsin Domesday Book: Town Studies* (1924), *Four Wisconsin Counties: Prairie and Forest* (1927), *The Wisconsin Lead Region* (1932), and *The Winnebago-Horicon Basin* (1937), all published by the State Historical Society of Wisconsin.

7. Joseph Schafer, *The Social History of American Agriculture* (New York: Macmillan, 1936), 219.

8. Merle Curti et al., *The Making of an American Community: A Case Study of Democracy in a Frontier County* (Stanford, CA: Stanford Univ. Press,

1959), 444. For an assessment of this seminal work after three decades, see James A. Henretta, "*The Making of an American Community: A Thirty-Year Perspective,*" *Reviews in American History* 16 (1988): 506–12.

9. Marcus Lee Hansen, *The Immigrant in American History* (Cambridge, MA: Harvard Univ. Press, 1940), 65–68; *The Atlantic Migration, 1607–1860* (Cambridge, MA: Harvard Univ. Press, 1940), 13–17. To illustrate Hansen's influence in this regard, see John A. Hawgood, *America's Western Frontiers: The Exploration and Settlement of the Trans-Mississippi West* (New York: Knopf, 1967), 393n.8, and Hawgood's *The Tragedy of German-America* (New York: Putnam, 1940), 22–23. For an assessment of Hansen's importance for immigration history and Turnerian historiography, see Allan H. Spear, "Marcus Lee Hansen and the Historiography of Immigration," *Wisconsin Magazine of History* 54 (Summer 1961): 258–68, and Moses Rischin, "Marcus Lee Hansen: America's First Transethnic Historian," in *Uprooted Americans: Essays to Honor Oscar Handlin*, ed. Richard L. Bushman et al. (Boston: Little, Brown, 1979), 319–47. Two other major historians of American immigration, George Stephenson and Carl Wittke, studied with Turner at Harvard. Neither, however, received encouragement from him to enter this field, nor is their work associated with the frontier thesis or with Turnerian methodology (see Rischin, "Hansen," 334).

10. It should be noted that Maldwyn Allen Jones, a British historian who authored the last synthesis of American immigration history to be fully conceptualized in Turnerian terms, announced in the most concise and explicit terms possible that the theme of his book is "how inheritance and environment interacted." Still, the interpretetive emphasis remained vintage Turner: America was the frontier of Europe that attracted millions of immigrants; it offered an environment in which newcomers quickly lost their distinctive traits, even though American characteristics were altered by them in the assimilative process (see *American Immigration* [Chicago: Univ. of Chicago Press, 1960], 2).

11. Oscar Handlin, *Boston's Immigrants: A Study in Acculturation* (Cambridge, MA: Harvard Univ. Press, 1941).

12. Oscar Handlin, *The Uprooted* (Boston: Little, Brown, 1951).

13. Rudolph J. Vecoli, "*Contadini* in Chicago: A Critique of *The Uprooted*," *Journal of American History* 51 (December 1964): 404–17.

14. Lee Benson, *The Concept of Jacksonian Democracy: New York as a Test Case* (Princeton, NJ: Princeton Univ. Press, 1961).

15. These essays, which date from 1959, have been republished in Samuel P. Hays, *American Political History as Social Analysis* (Knoxville: Univ. of Tennessee Press, 1980).

16. The earliest among the many titles that might be cited are Michael F. Holt, *Forging a Majority: The Formation of the Republican Party in Pittsburgh, 1848–1860* (New Haven: Yale Univ. Press, 1969); my own *Immigrants and Politics: The Germans of Nebraska, 1880–1900* (Lincoln: Univ. of Nebraska Press, 1969); Paul Kleppner, *The Cross of Culture: A Social Analysis of Midwestern Politics, 1850–1900* (New York: Free Press, 1970); Richard J. Jensen, *The Winning of the Midwest: Social and Political Conflict, 1888–96* (Chicago: Univ. of

Chicago Press, 1971; Ronald P. Formisano, *The Birth of Mass Political Parties: Michigan, 1827–1861* (Princeton, NJ: Princeton Univ. Press, 1971.

17. John Higham, "Current Trends in the Study of Ethnicity in the United States," *Journal of American Ethnic History* 2 (Fall 1982): 5–15. Other helpful review essays in this regard are by Richard Jensen, "Ethnometrics," and Milton Cantor, "Work, Industry, and Community: A Review Essay on Labor and Ethnicity," in *Journal of American Ethnic History* 3 (Spring 1984): 67–81.

18. John Bodnar, *The Transplanted: A History of Immigrants in Urban America* (Bloomington, IN: Indiana Univ. Press, 1985); Maldwyn Allen Jones, *American Immigration* (Chicago: Univ. of Chicago Press, 1960). Other useful textbooks produced in this field during the decade, each with its own special emphasis, include Thomas J. Archdeacon, *Becoming American: An Ethnic History* (New York: Free Press, 1983); Leonard Dinnerstein and David M. Reimers, *Ethnic Americans: A History of Immigration*, 3d. ed. (New York: Harper and Row, 1988); Maxine Seller, *To Seek America: A History of Ethnic Life in the United States* (New York: Jerome S. Ozer, 1977); and James S. Olson, *The Ethnic Dimension in American History* (New York: St. Martin's Press, 1979). In addition, there is an excellent synthesis of the European exodus: Philip Taylor, *The Distant Magnet: European Emigration to the U.S.A.* (New York: Harper and Row, 1971).

19. All the quotations are from Bodnar's introduction to *The Transplanted*, xv–xxi.

20. The earliest notable example of a book with an anti-Handlin title is Andrew Rolle's *Immigrant Upraised: Italian Adventurers and Colonists in an Expanding America* (Norman: Univ. of Oklahoma Press, 1968).

21. Frank Thistlethwaite, "Migration from Europe Overseas in the Nineteenth and Twentieth Centuries," in *Xle Congres International des Sciences Historiques*, Rapport 5 (Uppsala, 1960): 32–60. For the Uppsala project see Harald Runblom and Hans Norman, eds. *From Sweden to America: A History of the Migration* (Minneapolis: Univ. of Minnesota Press, 1976). Jon Gjerde, *From Peasants to Farmers: The Migration from Balestrand, Norway, to the Upper Middle West* (New York: Cambridge Univ. Press, 1985); Walter D. Kamphoefner, *The Westfalians: From Germany to Missouri* (Princeton, NJ: Princeton Univ. Press, 1987); and Robert C. Ostergren, *A Community Transplanted: The Trans-Atlantic Experience of a Swedish Immigrant Settlement in the Upper Middle West, 1835–1915* (Madison: Univ. of Wisconsin Press, 1988). Italian migration has also been studied similarly in three recent books, although an intellectual debt to Thistlethwaite is either absent or unacknowledged in them: see John W. Briggs, *An Italian Passage: Immigrants to Three American Cities, 1890–1930* (New Haven: Yale Univ. Press, 1978); Dino Cinel, *From Italy to San Francisco: The Immigrant Experience* (Stanford, CA: Stanford Univ. Press, 1982); and Donna R. Gabaccia, *From Sicily to Elizabeth Street: Housing and Social Change Among Italian Immigrants, 1880–1930* (Albany: State Univ. of New York Press, 1984). Dutch migration has been treated effectively in Robert P. Swierenga, ed., *The Dutch in America: Immigration, Settlement, and Cultural Change* (New Brunswick, NJ: Rutgers Univ. Press, 1985).

22. Ostergren, *A Community Transplanted*, 24.

23. This is the argument of James C. Malin, who insisted that the historian must master the ecology of a region before its history could be written. The study of environmental characteristics and their relationships to human occupance of a region, in his view, is the prolegomenon to history (see *Grassland of North America* (1947; Gloucester, MA: Peter Smith, 1967).

24. Ostergen, *A Community Transplanted*, 155–66 and passim.

25. Timothy Kloberdanz, "Plainsmen of Three Continents: Volga German Adaptation to Steppe, Prairie, and Pampa," in *Ethnicity on the Great Plains*, ed. Frederick C. Luebke (Lincoln: Univ. of Nebraska Press, 1980), 63.

26. Kathleen Neils Conzen, "Historical Approaches to the Study of Rural Ethnic Communities," in *Ethnicity on the Great Plains*, ed. Luebke, 1–18; Kamphoefner, *Westfalians*, 189.

27. Richard Etulain, "Basque Beginnings in the Pacific Northwest," *Idaho Yesterdays* 18 (Spring 1974): 26–32; see also Gordon Hendrickson, "Immigration and Assimilation in Wyoming," in *Peopling the High Plains: Wyoming's European Heritage* (Cheyenne: Wyoming State Archives and Historical Department, 1977), 169–94.

28. Kathleen Neils Conzen, "Immigrants, Immigrant Neighborhoods, and Ethnic Identity: Historical Issues," *Journal of American History* 66 (December 1979): 603–15.

29. Hildegard Binder Johnson has made the additional point that the presence of a church at the nucleus of a rural settlement usually meant growth or expansion; the lack thereof meant atrophy and eventually disintegration ("The Location of German Immigrants in the Middle West," *Annals of the Association of American Geographers* 41 [1951]: 1–41).

30. Allan Teichroew, "World War I and the Mennonite Migration to Avoid the Draft," *Mennonite Quarterly Review* 45 (July 1971): 219–49.

31. See Olivier Zunz, "American History and the Changing Meaning of Assimilation," *Journal of American Ethnic History* 4 (Spring 1985): 53–72, and the comments by John Bodnar and Stephan Thernstrom, 73–81.

32. Kathleen Neils Conzen has pointed out to me that Curti provides a direct link between Turner and "the new urban history." Stephan Thernstrom, a pioneer in the latter field, was clearly aware of Curti's work in Trempealeau County, to which he compared his own discoveries in nineteenth-century urban social mobility (see Stephan Thernstrom, *Poverty and Progress: Social Mobility in a Nineteenth Century City* [Cambridge, MA: Harvard Univ. Press, 1964], 197–98).

I

Several years ago the United States celebrated the 300th anniversary of German immigration to America as marked by the settlement in 1683 of thirteen Quaker and Mennonite families from Krefeld, Germany, in Germantown, a country village that long ago was absorbed by Philadelphia. The president of the United States duly appointed a tricentennial commission, the Postal Service issued an attractive postage stamp, governors and mayors produced suitable proclamations, and across the country local communities staged a wide variety of observances—scholarly conferences, concerts, performances by dance and theater groups, and even picnics and parades, complete with fireworks.[1] Although the tricentennial celebrations seemed to lack popular enthusiasm, scholars—especially historians—responded gladly enough to invitations to lecture and to participate in conferences or symposia.

Such celebrations are in themselves important source material for the study of ethnic group history. They tell us much about how people perceive themselves in relation to American society. For example, in the 1930s, when two important national conferences of Americans of German descent were held, one in New York and one a year later in Philadelphia on the occasion of 250th anniversary of the founding of Germantown, the tone set by the speakers and their topics was in sharp contrast to the one held in the City of Brotherly Love in 1983. A half century ago the conference participants met when the Great Depression was nearly at its worst. They retained fear-filled memories of persecution during World War I and its aftermath. Adolf Hitler's recent rise to power in Germany made some conferees jubilant, others troubled.

The emphasis of the 1932 and 1933 conferences was on the magnificent contributions of German immigrants to America and its culture. Speakers were preoccupied with ethnic recognition and respect; they repeatedly complained that the German "element" had never been accorded its "rightful" place in American society. They were deeply concerned about the preservation of ethnic culture in America, which they saw as suffering devastating erosion. Topics *not* treated by speakers are also instructive. They ignored the crisis in Germany at that time; they avoided questions of relations between the United States and Germany; and they said nothing of the problems faced by the 400,000 German immigrants who had arrived in the 1920s.[2]

Fifty years later the celebrations conveyed a different mood. In contrast to the earlier meetings, when nonacademic ethnic group leaders (journalists, publicists, and the leaders of voluntary associations) dominated the scene, the 1983 commemorative conferences were decidedly academic, and often included a strong representation of scholars from German universities. Although filiopietism was by no means absent from the latter-day festivities, contemporary scholars are not disposed to justify or defend the history of Germans in America. They display no earnest desire to elevate ethnic heroes for German Americans to admire. They seek to understand German-American history, whatever it was, good or bad. Today scholars in both Germany and the United States try to analyze the relations between the two countries dispassionately; they study German emigration as a social or economic phenomenon; they consider assimilation as a social process—a natural adjustment to the social environment—and they also analyze linguistic change within that context. Criticism of German-American literature is no longer inflated with undeserved praise; instead immigrant writings are studied as important manifestations of American culture. German-American settlement patterns, social structures, and political behaviors are analyzed for the ways in which they illuminate the larger patterns of the nation's history.[3] No longer do scholars expand upon the contributions of such figures as Baron von Steuben or Carl Schurz in an effort to burnish the image of Germans in America (or perhaps to compensate for psychological insecurities, collective or individual). In short, German-American studies have finally come of age.[4]

Such changes in conceptualization have led to a restructuring of German-American history. In the pages that follow, I offer a highly condensed version of what historians have learned during the past quarter century about German immigrants and their place in American history. Instead of focusing on ethnic group leaders and their various excellencies, or on the manifold contributions of German immigrants and their children to the greatness of the United States, I use the familiar pattern of German immigration history as a framework to identify some of the most significant discoveries of recent historical research, beginning with the colonial period and continuing through to the substantial immigration of the post–World War II era.

My overview is idiosyncratic in the sense that it reflects my sense of what constitutes satisfying ethnic group history; to treat all significant aspects of German-American history would be discursive and distracting. I concentrate on social history, the conditioning effects of cultural and religious variables, and their consequences for political history. I interpret German immigrants and their children, not as intrusive or foreign elements, but rather as integral parts of American society interacting with other groups, both immigrants and native, in various social processes, the end products of which are usually assimilative. They are thus thought of as full participants in the drama of American history, not probationaries who must complete an acculturation before first-class status can be achieved. Finally, this essay concludes with a brief discussion of the directions in which research in German-American history might go.

II

Let us begin with the thirteen families from Krefeld who founded Germantown three centuries ago. A mixed group whose origins were more Dutch than German, at least as those designations are understood today, these people were not the first Germans to settle in America.[5] A few other German-speaking persons had lived in one or another of the American colonies during the preceding half century, but they had come as individuals and did not form a distinctive settlement, as did the Krefelders of 1683.

The flow of German-speaking immigrants to the British colonies in America during the next century was unsteady, but by the time of the American Revolution about seventy-five thousand had arrived. Although this total was dwarfed by the massive movements of the nineteenth century, it was huge in relation to the size of the receiving population. In the four decades following the founding of Germantown, only a few Germans arrived, but after 1727 the movement was accelerated and regularized as merchants integrated the transportation of migrants into patterns of transatlantic trade. The high point was reached during the late 1740s and early 1750s, when approximately thirty-seven thousand persons disembarked within a six-year period, mostly at Philadelphia. Thereafter the stream from Germany was slowed by reports of adversities suffered by immigrants indebted to merchants for their passage to America and by disconcerting news about Indian uprisings associated with the onset of the Seven Years War.[6]

The great majority of German-speaking migrants of the colonial era came from the Rhine Valley and in America at that time they were usually called Palatines. The Palatinate was indeed an important source of emigration but large numbers came also from Hesse, Baden, and Württemberg. Still others emigrated from Alsace and Switzerland, as well as from lower Rhine districts, including the Netherlands.

The German colonists settled chiefly in Pennsylvania and in neighboring New York, Maryland, and Virginia. Some drifted farther south to found communities in the Carolina Piedmont. Although the majority were farmers (as were most Americans at that time), some lived and prospered in the towns, where they were often shopkeepers and artisans.

Although one must take care not to exaggerate its significance, religious belief formed an important element in the identity of these Germans. At first most were Mennonites, Moravians, Dunkards or Brethren, or members of other sects, and they attracted much attention because of their distinctive manners and beliefs. Later, especially during the 1740s and '50s, Lutherans and Reformed became numerically preponderant and softened the image of the Germans as pietists and religious radicals.

Few of these groups deliberately tried to preserve German languages and customs for their own sakes, but most considered them important for the preservation of the faith. Because the Germans had immigrated in large numbers and naturally tended to cluster together, their settlements often consisted of islands in a sea of English-speaking people. In Pennsylvania, where they were most numerous, their language continued to evolve and later came to be known as "Pennsylvania Dutch." Grammatically this was a Palatine dialect, but as new words were needed, it drew them from English rather than from standard German, as would have been the case had the immigrants remained in Europe. By the end of the colonial period the Germans were easily the largest non-English-speaking group in the thirteen colonies. Albert B. Faust estimated their number at the time of the American Revolution to be 225,000.[7] According to the first United States census, taken in 1790, persons of German birth or parentage constituted about eight or nine percent of a population of about four million persons.

Despite their impressive numbers, most Germans immigrants assimilated rapidly into colonial society. They learned to speak English, at least well enough to get along, often as a matter of practical necessity. Most families were bilingual by the end of the eighteenth century, speaking their German dialect in their homes and English in public settings. Many German names were quickly Anglicized or translated. Schmidt could become Smith, just as Jaeger might become Hunter, even though the bearers of these names might not have been well assimilated either linguistically or culturally.[8] Still, some German communities founded in the eighteenth century retained immigrant traits for many generations, especially in rural areas, but many persons moved quickly into the mainstream because there were few institutions, other than the churches, for the preservation of language and custom.

III

Following the American Revolution immigration from Europe almost ceased for a period of fifty years. Not until the 1830s did the numbers of newcomers from any source begin to swell significantly. The German states of the Rhine Valley then became a leading source again, but with the addition of many from Bavaria, Saxony, and Hanover. Unlike the earlier movement, this immigration included a large proportion of Catholics. Numerically it broke all earlier records, averaging at first about 20,000 persons per year until the late 1840s, when it jumped to more than 60,000. In the early 1850s the annual rate reached nearly 150,000 and then attained a spectacular record of 215,000 in 1854. Thereafter immigration from the German states dropped sharply as news of economic depression and the Civil War restrained many people from leaving.

The causes of this huge migration have been studied in great detail.[9] Political unrest, economic deprivation, crop failures, overpopulation, marriage laws, letters from America, and religious persecution were all part of it, but these factors are hopelessly tangled when applied to individuals. Each adult immigrant had his or her own complex of reasons for wanting to leave and they often included family considerations as well as psychological needs, few of which can be sorted out.

Many older accounts of German emigration ascribed much importance for this early nineteenth century movement to inheritance laws and customs. In most of the German states, impartible inheritance (*Anerbenrecht*) was the rule. That meant that a parcel of land could not be divided among its owner's potential heirs; law or custom dictated that all of it was to go to the eldest son (or youngest, as the case may have been). But in the southwestern German states and later in much of Hesse and the Rhineland—major sources of German emigration—partible inheritance (*Realteilung*) or the division of inherited land among all heirs prevailed. This presumably resulted in the splintering of peasant holdings and, as plots became too small to support a family, thousands of farmers were forced to leave, either to the cities of Europe or overseas to America.[10]

But recent research has demonstrated that rates of emigration were also extremely high in some districts where impartible inheritance was the custom. Obviously, other variables were also at work. Emigration was not merely a result of the mechanical operation of inheritance patterns or, for that matter, of purely economic forces. The American historian Walter Kamphoefner has revealed its complexity by analyzing certain local districts in Westphalia. He has shown that in the neighborhood of Osnabrück a well-developed cottage industry had developed in which linen cloth was woven by rural folk who owned no land. During the second quarter of the nineteenth century, this cottage industry was wiped out by machine competition in the cities, especially in England, northern Ireland, and later Germany itself. Moreover, linen cloth itself came to be replaced by cotton during those same years. By the mid-1840s this decline in linen weaving had reached catastrophic proportions and pushed many thousands of rural lower-class persons to America.[11]

Such landless families of few resources constituted the majority of emigrants from the German states in the pre–Civil War decades. Kamphoefner, among other historians, has also shown that these newcomers were generally less prosperous than had been assumed previously; they were "poor but not destitute."[12] Thus the measure of socioeconomic success that they achieved in America appears all the more dramatic.

Most German immigrants entered the United States at New York, Philadelphia, or Baltimore, but New Orleans also developed as a major port of entry as many newcomers traveled up the Mississippi to settle in the recently organized states of Missouri, Illinois, Iowa, and Wisconsin. Still others moved west to Texas. Although New York never lost its position as the city with the largest number of German-born inhabitants, midwestern cities such as Chicago, St. Louis, Cincinnati, and Milwaukee became centers of huge German-American populations.[13] By 1860, just before the onset of the Civil War, the Census Bureau reported that there were 1,276,000 German-born persons resident in the United States, about four percent of the total population of 31,500,000. Of course, this estimate includes neither the American-born children of the immigrants nor German-speaking persons who emigrated from Switzerland, France (chiefly Alsace), or Austria.

Whatever their number, they, together with the many Irish Catholics who had arrived during the preceding two decades, seemed to represent a frightening challenge to the guardians of the dominant value system of the American society, which was clearly rooted in Anglo Protestantism. Their xenophobic fears were briefly but nonetheless intensely translated during the 1850s into the politics of Know Nothingism, a nativist movement that was more anti-Catholic than anti-immigrant.

The Germans responded defensively. Their leaders, including many of the highly educated, articulate political refugees of the Revolution of 1848 in Europe, now self-consciously sought to develop a common German ethnic identity founded on cultural characteristics shared by the diverse contingents of peasants, artisans, and laborers from the several German states of the Rhineland. Their rhetoric contrasted German idealism with American materialism, to the magnification of the former and the denigration of the latter. Moreover, as Kathleen Neils Conzen has pointed out, this definition of German ethnicity in cultural terms transcended linguistic, political, religious, and socioeconomic distinctions of German *Kleinstaaterei* and stimulated the growth of cultural associations and organizations (rather than political or nationalistic) to the end of the nineteenth century. Thus the ethnopolitical conflicts of the 1840s and '50s and the concomitant development of a German-language press stimulated the emergence of a self-conscious German identity that continue to grow until the end of the century.[14]

Although the American Civil War caused a sharp drop in emigration from the German states, it did not cease entirely, and starting in 1865 it quickly returned to earlier levels. Then, in response to the Panic of 1873, it dropped abruptly to about thirty thousand per year before breaking new records in the early 1880s. The peak year was 1882, when two hundred fifty thousand arrived. Thereafter the rate declined until the end of the century, when it dropped to less than twenty thousand per year. In all, approximately five million Germans had emigrated to the United States by 1900. In the first half of the nineteenth century, when sailing vessels were in use and transatlantic travel was an ordeal, few immigrants ever returned to Europe. But after 1860, when steamships became common, there was an increase in the number of returnees and a decrease in the proportion of families emigrating from Germany. In other words, there was an increase in the proportion of single adult young males who, after a year or two of working in America, could return to Germany with some ease, either to stay or to bring a bride back to the United States.

IV

By the beginning of the twentieth century the number of first- and second-generation Germans in the United States had expanded to about eight million persons—more than ten percent of the entire population. Most Americans tended to think of the Germans in their midst as a unified group with more or less common characteristics. The fact is, however, that the Germans were an extraordinarily heterogeneous group. Provincial differences, linguistic variations, religious divisions, and social and political distinctions were usually lost on native-born Americans, who tended to lump the Germans all together on the basis of their presumably common language. Since Germany did not exist as a unified state until 1871, a German was simply someone who spoke the German language.

In contrast to this stereotype, careful study of census data reveals striking differences in the provincial origins of Germans in America. For example, Württembergers were heavily concentrated in Philadelphia, but they could scarcely to be found in Milwaukee. In contrast, Mecklenburgers were strongly attracted to Milwaukee, but few settled in Philadelphia. Similarly, Hanoverians were common in Cincinnati and St. Louis but relatively uncommon in Wisconsin or Michigan. Lutherans from Franconia (northern Bavaria) settled Frankenmuth, Michigan; Holsteiners concentrated in Grand Island, Nebraska; Nassau was disproportionately represented among the Germans of central Texas; and Oldenburgers clustered in Cincinnati, where they were seven times more numerous proportionately than in the United States generally.[15] The list of such examples might be extended indefinitely. What is clear about this evidence is that, as the German historian Wolfgang Helbich has observed, common region or even neighborhood may have been more important to the immigrants than common language or even religion.[16]

The pattern was the same for both cities and the countryside. Stanley Nadel has examined data from the four wards of *Kleindeutschland* in New York City over three decades to show that important variations were evident even on that level and that changes in provincial origins occurred over time. Nadel also demonstrated that in New York City provincial origins are strongly related to various social and cultural characteristics such as marriage patterns, family structures, and occupation.[17] In studying data from rural Missouri, Kamphoefner has shown that nearly 20 percent of all the Germans in Warren County came from the tiny German principality of Lippe-Detmold. At the same time, there were practically no Lippe-Detmolders in St. Charles County, another heavily German county located a few miles to the east.[18] Similar distributions are evident wherever nineteenth-century Germans settled in the United States.

How did such concentrations develop? Where the first emigrants from a given region in Germany happened to settle in the United States was sometimes purely a matter of chance. Other times migrants were influenced by propaganda. For example, Missouri was popular in the 1830s and 1840s because of a widely read book by Gottfried Duden published in Germany. During those years emigration was especially heavy from northwestern German states; hence the unusually large concentration of Hanoverians and Brunswickers in Missouri. Later on, in the 1870s and 1880s, state boards of immigration, often working cooperatively with western railroad companies with land to sell, convinced thousands of northern Germans to settle in the states of the Great Plains—Kansas, Nebraska, and the Dakotas. German-language materials were prepared and widely distributed by German-speaking agents working both in Germany and in American seaports.[19]

In other cases clergymen provided leadership, as, for example, among the Saxon Lutherans in St. Louis and the Prussian Lutherans in Milwaukee, both of which groups arrived in the late 1830s.[20] In other instances, clergymen were merely instrumental. Knowing that many of his parishioners were determined to migrate to America, a Catholic priest or a Protestant pastor in Germany would direct his people to a certain community in the United States where he knew there was a church or a pastor who would minister to his people. Outstanding leadership in a local German-American settlement also attracted more immigrants, as many articles in the literature of German-American history testify. Similarly, immigration societies such as the *Adelsverein*, which brought the first Germans to Texas, did much to stamp German-American communities with provincial origins.

But the most important factor in determining the location of settlement in America was the pattern of chain migration. For one reason or another, one immigrant and his family would settle in a certain place. Assuming he prospered there, he would write glowing letters to relatives and friends in his hometown about life in America. Helbich, who considers "America letters" to be of preeminent importance in the emigrant's final decision to leave, estimates that about 100 million such letters were dispatched from the United States to Germany in the nineteenth century.[21] Soon the early immigrants would be followed by others and gradually a remarkable concentration would develop in a community. Such informal migration, usually by families, constituted the bulk of German immigration. German emigration societies, even though they have received much attention from historians, were much less important.[22]

Much of this movement of German immigrants, especially to rural and small-town America, was closely connected to churches. This is not to say that the churches were the organizing agents, but rather that immigrants, having generally come from the same place in Germany, tended therefore also to have the same religion. Such patterns help to explain the religious affiliations of many Americans today, not only on the local level but on the state level as well. Wisconsin, for example, has proportionately many more Catholics of German origin than does Nebraska. Wisconsin was settled earlier in the nineteenth century, when the sources of German emigration were concentrated in western and southern German states, where Catholics are numerous. Nebraska was settled later, in the 1870s and '80s, when emigration from the Protestant provinces of northern Germany—Holstein, Mecklenburg, Pomerania— was more important.

This tendency of German immigrants to settle among others of their own kind was by no means unusual. All the immigrant groups did it. But while at least some Germans could be found in all states of the Union, they were concentrated in the Middle Atlantic states—New York, Pennsylvania, New Jersey, and Maryland—and in the North Central states of Ohio, Indiana, Illinois, Michigan, and Wisconsin, plus Missouri, Iowa, and Minnesota. By the end of the nineteenth century, about 85 percent of all German immigrants lived in these states. About 65 percent lived in cities and towns compared to 40 percent for the United States population as a whole at that time. Still, they were strongly attracted to agriculture. By 1900, one-fourth of all gainfully employed German Americans were in farming, a proportion exceeded only by the Scandinavians and the Czechs. They were especially attracted to dairy farming, so much so that they were actually underrepresented in other kinds of farming.

Americans generally perceived the Germans as excellent farmers. Their reputation for industry and frugality was firmly established already in colonial times. Although they generally did not settle on the best land (often it was not available or was beyond their means), they were eager to own rather than to rent their farms. Unlike many native-born Americans, they valued land, not as a speculative investment, but as a permanent home. Proximity to others who shared their language and culture was important. Hence German-American rural life frequently centered on their churches as the easiest and most enduring of institutions that could be created and sustained in such an environment. They rarely made any efforts to duplicate European village patterns—the force of American land law was too strong for that—and their cropping practices were also quickly adapted to locally prevailing norms.[23]

Mobility among German-American farmers was high, but not as high as that registered by the native-born. Much of the movement was accounted for by the out-migration of adult children of the immigrants. This means that the ethnoreligious character of particular German rural settlements has been sustained through several generations to the present time. This persistence has been weakened only in recent decades by technological changes in transportation, communication, and agricultural practice.[24]

In her study of inheritance customs among rural Germans of Stearns County, Minnesota, Kathleen Conzen has demonstrated that a variety of strategies were developed to keep the "home place" within the family, but when that was not possible, they preferred to sell to persons of their own ethnoreligious group.[25] In general, the self-containment and isolation of such family-oriented rural communities nurtured profound conservatism— social, economic, and political.

V

Life in the cities was dramatically different.[26] According to the nineteenth-century stereotype, the typical German immigrant was a skilled practitioner of a craft—a baker, carpenter, brewer, or shoemaker. But that was actually true of only about one-third of the Germans by the end of the century. They were also well represented among the merchant class and among professional people, but until recently the extent of their presence among common or unskilled laborers has been underestimated. In fact, by 1900 more than 40 percent of the gainfully employed among the German-born were in the unskilled worker class, and they were rather more numerous in midwestern cities than in the East.[27]

The importance of ethnicity for urban and labor history has been slighted by many historians. Marxist historians in particular have tended to treat ethnic culture as a negative force that sapped class solidarity in the struggle against capitalist oppression. However, recent historians of German workers in American cities, especially Hartmut Keil and John Jentz, have affirmed the vital importance of German ethnicity in labor history and have sought to define its role in the evolution of working-class culture. Working with evidence from Chicago, they have aimed to comprehend the everyday experiences of immigrant German workers and to understand their adaptations to a new urban and industrial world. In sum, they have analyzed the conflicts that naturally occurred when the verticality of German ethnicity crossed the horizontality of class.[28]

Other studies have concentrated on occupational structures that permit the comparison of Germans with other ethnic groups, notably the Irish, in the nineteenth century. In general, they show that Germans generally fared better than the Irish, although not usually by comparison to native-born Americans. Although the Germans inevitably were under-represented in occupations that demanded a good command of the English language, they more than most immigrant groups displayed a balanced representation in the occupational structure of most cities.[29] Evidence drawn from Poughkeepsie, New York, suggests that, by comparison to most other groups, German shopkeepers and skilled workers experienced exceptional rates of upward mobility, but German immigrants who entered the work force at the unskilled level were less fortunate. Their sons, however, were able to find employment in skilled and white-collar jobs more frequently than were the sons of either Irish-born or native-born laborers.[30]

The distribution of Germans across the occupational spectrum, combined with their huge numbers, permitted urban Germans to create ethnic communities that were virtually self-contained.[31] New York had its *Kleindeutschland*, just as Cincinnati its "Over the Rhine" district. Scores of other American cities had similar enclaves of first- and second-generation German immigrants. The members of such communities could always find a German grocer, carpenter, banker, or doctor; they could often find German employers; they could always attend a German church, read a locally published German-language newspaper, and participate in the affairs of German voluntary associations, which often were familiar forms developed in Germany by middle-class urbanites who transferred them to American cities. In nineteenth-century Milwaukee, Kathleen Conzen has shown, only the German ethnic group had the range and heterogeneity necessary for the development of a genuinely ethnic community with a full complement of supportive functions independent of the host society.[32]

The remarkably heterogeneous German ethnic community in Milwaukee, as elsewhere, functioned effectively as a means to ease the process of adjustment to American life. The very success of first-generation immigrants drew the second generation into the mainstream of American society. That meant that the continued survival of the ethnic community depended upon a continuous stream of new immigrants from Germany. But that flow was dramatically reduced in the 1890s, and at the same time, urban mass transit systems were being developed that permitted upwardly mobile second-generation German Americans to scatter throughout the cities and their suburbs. Although it is true that there were strongly German neighborhoods or wards in most large cities of the United States, the Germans were generally also well distributed by the end of the century.[33]

VI

The Germans were thus remarkably diverse, not only in residence patterns, occupations, and provincial origins, but they also were highly varied in their religious identities.[34] Attitudes, values, and behavior patterns were closely related to religious belief and for many people were more important than economic status. Of all European peoples, the Germans were probably the most deeply divided in religious matters. Naturally they brought their prejudices with them to America. This meant that as concentrations of German Catholics, Lutherans, Mennonites, Evangelicals, or Reformed developed here and there, each group had surprisingly little to do with the others. Of course, this was not universally true, especially during the frontier period, but each group still tended to go its own way and to develop its own religiously oriented institutions—schools and colleges, publishing houses, hospitals, and social organizations for the laity.

The Catholics constituted the largest single religious group among the Germans, accounting for about a third of the total. Although large and important concentrations of German Catholic immigrants could be found in rural areas, the majority lived in cities. According to Jay Dolan, they formed important parts of each stratum of Catholic society, most numerous on the bottom, but present also in the middle and upper levels, although the second generation predominated in the latter category.[35] They were underrepresented, however, in the Catholic hierarchy, and the struggles of German-speaking Catholics with their Irish bishops over issues of governance, language, and property form a familiar part of American Catholic history. German Catholic clergymen were among the strongest advocates of parochial schools, believing that the preservation of the faith required the maintenance of the German language and culture by this means.

In no single city have German Catholics been studied with greater sophistication than in New York, where Jay Dolan has compared them to Irish Catholics on parish level in the mid-nineteenth century. Because the Irish used the same language as the host society, their devotion to the ethnic parish as a solution to the problem of religion and nationality was less intense than among the Germans. There were also distinctive styles of worship, with the Germans displaying more pageantry and ceremony than the Irish. Auxiliary ethnoreligious organizations, which reinforced the sense of community and separatism, seemed to have special prominence for the Germans. Differences also existed in the relationships of priests to people. Whereas the Germans maintained a respectful social distance from their pastors, the Irish developed warm personal and familial bonds with theirs.[36] Despite their impressive numbers, the German Catholics displayed fierce antagonisms against anything that seemed to infringe upon their rights. Inevitably this served to create a heightened sense of identity and to promote a conservative, defensive mentality.

German Lutherans were even more separatistic than the Catholics. They organized themselves into autonomous congregations clustered in a bewildering array of synods, each going its own way, and each representing a different shade of conservatism. They tended to cling tenaciously to the use of the German language and some of the more conservative synods encouraged congregations to establish parochial schools. As late as World War I, about half of the two million German Lutherans in America still conducted worship services exclusively in the German language. Although some of the synods were thoroughly assimilated organizations that had long ago lost their German characteristics, others remained essentially immigrant institutions dedicated to the in-gathering of German newcomers and their children.

Other German Protestant church bodies were smaller in size. Among them were the Reformed and Evangelical synods, Mennonite and Methodist conferences, and many smaller groups, including German Baptists and Presbyterians. Some, such as the Amish, were profoundly separatistic; a few, most notably the Hutterites of the northern Great Plains, organized themselves in self-contained rural colonies or communes. But most were ecumenical in spirit and gradually merged with or were absorbed by English-speaking equivalent organizations, a process that was accelerated in the two decades between the world wars.

The German Jews in the United States were like the various Christian groups in many respects. Numbering perhaps two hundred thousand by the 1880s, they also established their own educational agencies, publications, benevolent institutions, and other auxiliary organizations. Rather more than the conservative Christian sects, the Jews tended to participate actively in German-American institutional life and often provided important leadership. Their loyalty to German language and culture was at least as strong as that of any other German-American ethnoreligious group, even though their struggles with problems arising from their dual identity were inevitably more difficult. Generally their relations with other Germans in America were positive, as one should expect of groups so inextricably bound together. Examples of anti-Semitism among German Americans can be found, but what is striking, Stanley Nadel has observed, is how little of it there actually was.[37]

VII

In general, the church Germans, who were often former peasants or craftsmen, focused their lives around the church and its related activities and took relatively little interest in the broader affairs of the community. In this respect they were quite different from the so-called club Germans, whose values and attitudes tended to be secular. Usually urban in residence and strongly middle class, the latter were often liberal in their politics. But their ranks did not include urban working-class Germans, whose radical ideology placed most "club Germans" and urban "church Germans" in the enemy camp of capitalist oppressors.

Their organizations were rather more diverse than those supported by the churches. They included singing societies, shooting or marksman clubs, fire companies, and veterans organizations. There were benevolent associations for the assistance of the poor and the most recently arrived immigrants. A multitude of mutual benefit societies with primitive insurance programs developed in many cities. There were also clubs for the social elite. Reading societies sprang up whose main goal was the development of subscription libraries of German-language books. Many cities had associations for various professional and business groups. There were lodges as well; some were affiliated with national organizations such as the Masons and the Odd Fellows, others were strictly German, notably the Sons of Hermann and the German Order of Harugari. Still other societies were organized on the basis of the German state or province from which its members had emigrated. As Kathleen Conzen has observed, these were the people who defined, for both themselves and outsiders, what the characteristics of German immigrant culture were. It was they more than the church people who gave coherence and content to what became identified as the German life-style, and who defined the German-American political agenda.[38] These were the people who, in most nineteenth-century American cities with substantial German populations, inspired and directed the pageantry of the great German celebrations, with their festive parades, celebratory speeches, dramatic performances, concerts, and balls.[39]

The "club German" mentality also dominated the German-language press. There were exceptions, of course, chiefly among the religious and the socialist newspapers, but most of the nearly eight hundred German-language newspapers and journals published in the United States by 1890 created a semblance of unity in the German-American community that in fact did not exist. Generally, the publishers and editors were recent immigrants, well educated, and liberal in their politics. Most German-language daily newspapers and many of the weeklies differed little in form, style, and content from English-language papers. In this way the press was a highly effective agent of Americanization. It explained American ways to the newcomers and kept them informed of developments in America, thereby easing the adjustment to life in a strange land.[40]

At the same time, however, the German language became the chief agent for the perpetuation of immigrant cultural forms. Especially after the drastic reduction in number of new arrivals from Germany at the end of the nineteenth century, the press endeavored to sustain its readership among second-generation Germans, few of whom were dependent in a linguistic sense on the German language. The device used by the press to hold its readers was the promotion of German-Americanism, that is, a self-conscious identity among German Americans as participants in a subsociety that was expressive of a superior culture. This meant that the press tended to lose the earlier, critical character that it had when it was dominated by refugees of the Revolution of 1848. Early in the twentieth century, it tended to give full, uncritical support to the institutions of the ethnic community, to all efforts aimed at the maintenance of German language and culture, and to political measures and movements that could be defined as being in the German-American interest.[41]

The diversity and fragmentation of German ethnic society in America also guaranteed political weakness. The variety reflected in the press, voluntary associations, the churches, occupational structures, wealth patterns, and provincial origins meant that ordinarily the Germans could never be rallied behind one political party. Only for brief periods and in times of special stress could they be provoked to effective political action as an ethnic group. Unlike the Irish, who were overwhelmingly Democratic, or the Norwegians, who were strongly Republican, the Germans tended to divide between the two major parties. The result was that they were often perceived as being politically apathetic.

Only when issues impinged directly on the interests of the Germans did they respond with a high level of political unity. In the pre–Civil War era, when the reform impulse expressed itself in nativism, German-American voters, particularly the Catholics, often felt that their language and culture were under attack. The Democratic party, with its Jeffersonian emphasis on minimal government, seemed the more congenial. Still, the Democratic party condoned slavery at that time, and most Germans perceived that institution as morally repugnant. Many were temporarily attracted by Abraham Lincoln and the Republican party during the Civil War era, but they tended to return to the Democratic fold later in the century in those places where prohibition, Sabbatarianism, and uniform public schooling were prominent issues.[42]

Early in the twentieth century there was a concerted effort to achieve united political action among Germans in America through the creation of the National German-American Alliance. Essentially a middle-class organization led by businessmen, journalists, clergymen, and professors, it was unable to attract the active participation of most church organizations. German labor leaders and the socialists generally were disdainful of its program. Supported financially by brewing and liquor interests, the National Alliance was especially interested in fighting prohibition and in promoting German-language instruction in the public schools. As World War I approached, it became a vehicle for much pro-German propaganda. It ultimately fell victim to the hatred generated by World War I, like thousands of other German-American voluntary associations.[43]

World War I was a time when the American people were swept up in a wave of anti-German feeling. In effect, there was a war against German language and culture for a short time, as individual citizens of German origin were harassed and persecuted. This phenomenon is partly explained by the behavior of German-American cultural chauvinists who took extravagantly pro-German positions during the period of American neutrality from 1914 to 1917. Then, when the United States declared war on Germany in 1917, many Americans of German birth or descent found themselves under suspicion of disloyalty. The climate of hate produced such outrages as a ban on German-composed music and the public burning of German-language books during patriotic exercises. Foods, streets, and towns, as well as countless persons were renamed to remove the taint of Germanness. There were vandalism, beatings, arrests for unpatriotic utterances, and even a lynching of a German alien in Illinois. German-language instruction in the public schools was restricted or eliminated, hundreds of German-language newspapers ceased publication, and many German-American churches made a rapid transition to the use of the English language.[44]

VIII

Following World War I, there was a dramatic resumption of immigration of Germans to the United States. Beginning in the early 1920s, it reached a high point of 75,000 persons in 1924. It continued at nearly 50,000 per annum until 1929, when federal legislation limiting immigration took effect. In general, the German immigrants of the 1920s tended to be somewhat better educated, more highly skilled, and more urban than their nineteenth century predecessors. In the 1930s, the proportion of both agricultural and industrial workers among the emigrants declined significantly as the unemployed increased.[45]

During the 1920s some German-American leaders made efforts to revive German ethnic life in the United States, but they were not very successful. Filled with bitterness and resentment after the trauma of the war with Germany, some leaders sought to regain respectability through united political action. After this strategy failed repeatedly in the 1920s, they shifted to an emphasis on culture. But this effort also failed because it was founded on elitist values at variance with those of the average German immigrant of the time. Then, during the Great Depression of the 1930s, the German-American Nazis captured public attention with a strategy of blood. This racist quest for ethnic unity was morally repugnant to the vast majority of German Americans and attracted support chiefly among some of the post–World War I immigrants.[46]

When Adolf Hitler came to power in 1933, German immigration dropped to its lowest point in a century, save for the World War I period. A resurgence followed thereafter, peaking in the American neutrality period of 1939 to 1941, as Hitler intensified his anti-Semitic policies. Approximately 100,000 refugees from Germany arrived during those years, at least 80 percent of whom were Jewish. Had it not been for a variety of restrictions imposed or retained by the United States government, the number would have been much larger. In any case, this was an extraordinary immigration. The proportion of academics and independent scientists, mathematicians, physicians, authors, artists, musicians, and composers, as well as lawyers and businessmen, was unprecedented.[47]

When the United States entered the Second World War against Germany in 1941, the government carefully avoided the mistakes it made in the earlier conflict. German-American ethnicity had not been reawakened by the Nazis; there was no repetition of the repression of 1917 and 1918.

The last great wave of German immigration to the United States followed World War II. Modest at first, it swelled rapidly to nearly 130,000 persons in 1950. In all, nearly a million more German-speaking persons arrived during this period, most of them victims of war who hoped to escape the problems associated with economic, social, and political reconstruction of Europe and to find a better life in America. Like the German-Jewish emigration, which had reached its apex in 1939, the postwar movement included a disproportionately large number of scientists, technicians, and other well-educated persons. Others were the brides of American soldiers in Germany; still others were "displaced persons"—ethnic German refugees from eastern Europe who fled to the West before the armies of the Soviet Union in 1945.

Like the immigrants of the 1920s and '30s, this last great wave of German-speaking immigrants has consisted of persons who have been much interested in being drawn into American society and culture as rapidly as possible. Few have wanted to perpetuate German language and culture in the way that the proponents of an organized *Deutschtum* did in the pre–World War I era. But German ethnicity continues to be fostered in an organized way in the local *Vereine* that may be found in major centers of German-American population. A few are organized for political purposes, not on the local level, but rather to oppose the communism that engulfed their homelands in central and eastern Europe at the end of World War II. But such organizations attract the participation of only a small fraction of German-speaking immigrants in the United States. Most are social or sporting associations and provide opportunities for persons to fraternize and to meet others of similar backgrounds.

IX

The total effect of 300 years of German immigration to the United States has been enormous. According to the census of 1980, approximately 52 million persons in the American population of 226 million are descended from German immigrants. They are the largest single group, exceeding both the Irish and the English. Although it is arguable whether that statistic is significant, the fact remains the Germans have had a profound impact on American history. I do not here refer to men and women of towering importance in political, economic, social, and cultural affairs. One need not recount ad nauseam the contributions of famous Americans—statesmen, military leaders, scientists, financiers, industrialists, artists, novelists—of German birth or descent. Instead, I suggest that the admixture of millions of German immigrants and their children in American society has made it into something that it would not otherwise be—that the American character is partly explained, not only by its frontier experience, its plenteous resources, or whatever, but also by the fact that a huge ethnocultural component has German roots.

The same thing can be said, of course, of other major ethnic groups in American society. The United States is culturally what it is because of the people who came here from other parts of the world. Frederick Jackson Turner's famous frontier thesis notwithstanding, the powerful forces of the American physical and social environments have not blended immigrants into an undifferentiated mass. Moreover, present-day American attitudes and behaviors would be different if, let us say, the French had immigrated to the United States in the same numbers as the Germans, or conversely, if the German influx had been as limited as the French.

How can such an ethnic influence be measured or analyzed? Possibilities abound, but none are easy. Although some historians of ethnicity have made good use of the social scientist's tool box of measurement techniques and quantitative devices, they have not exploited data published by sociologists over the past two decades to assess the persistence of ethnicity, German or other, in American life.[48] Much information of this kind, together with survey research data gathered by the Gallup organization and other pollsters, are wonderfully suggestive of opportunities for useful historical analysis.

In any case, the descendants of German immigrants constitute a major ingredient in the American stew, especially in the Midwest, and their importance for recent history remains to be estimated. In Nebraska, for example, nearly half of all inhabitants trace their ancestry to German-speaking immigrants—more than twice the proportion registered by the English, who rank second. Does this knowledge help to explain the stolid, conservative, unadventurous, and perhaps unimaginative character that is part of the Nebraska stereotype? Does the fact that the German proportion in Nebraska's population doubles that of Kansas help to explain the differences that persist between these two states, especially in politics, despite their superficial similarities?[49] Although studies of such questions must begin on the state and local level, they must eventually be transferred to the national level if they are to acquire lasting significance.

The persistence of German ethnicity and culture in contemporary society is largely *terra incognita*, except for limited work in folklore, material culture, and architecture.[50] Similarly, few scholars have undertaken serious study of German immigration in the post–World War II period. Historians in both the United States and Germany have been preoccupied with the nineteenth and early twentieth century migrations; sociologists and political scientists, when they study race and ethnicity in American life, properly consider problems associated with blacks, Asians, American Indians, and the Spanish-speaking groups. Few students of the German language and literature in the United States have considered any topics pertaining to the last four decades.[51]

If one were to produce a list of research possibilities or needs, basic study of the post–World War II immigration would be at the top. Monographic studies of German-speaking immigrants of this period by historians or social scientists scarcely exist. Except for the most generalized sorts of information, we know practically nothing precise about whence these people came, when and how they arrived in the United States, or where they settled and where they have moved since their arrival. Our knowledge of their socioeconomic status, educational levels, religious affiliations, occupational distributions, and associational activities are similarly limited.[52] Yet they too are a major part of the history of Germans in the United States.

But much more needs to be done with the recent decades. Sometimes maps suggest the range of possibilities. For example, when the largest ancestry groups are mapped by congressional district (based on 1980 census data), the Germans blanket the north-central section of the country. The area includes all of Wisconsin, Minnesota, Iowa, North and South Dakotas, Nebraska, Wyoming, and Montana, plus eastern Colorado, most of Kansas, and much of Missouri, Illinois, Indiana, Michigan, Ohio, and Pennsylvania.[53] The implications of this for Midwestern values and attitudes, or for legislative behavior in Congress, have never been explored, presumably on the untested assumption that the ethnicity of groups such as the Germans and other north Europeans is no longer important. But does the Midwest today still reflect a residue of German immigrant values? Are contemporary demands for public morality and concomitant emphases on family values, self-help, and work for its own sake distilled from this source, among others?

The importance of German ancestry for electoral or voting behavior since 1940 also remains unexplored, despite the fact that such nonhistorians as Samuel Lubell and Kevin Phillips long ago have identified its significance or that Michael Parenti, among other political scientists, emphasized two decades ago that, appearances to the contrary, ethnicity continues to condition political behavior, usually unconsciously, among persons who are from families long ago totally assimilated into American life.[54] The argument is not that, for example, German Catholic voters in southern Indiana are anything like German Catholic voters in southern Bavaria, but rather that their values, attitudes, and behaviors are modi-

fied in infinitely subtle and complex ways by their ethnoreligious antecedents and that, in their voting habits, they may well be discernibly different
from other voters with different cultural roots.

If German immigration in recent decades has been neglected, the
same may be said for the colonial period. Research in this era is more
extensive than for the 1950s, but some of it lacks the sophistication of
concept and method that characterizes the studies that professional historians have produced on German immigration in the nineteenth century.

X

As for the nineteenth and early twentieth centuries, much research
in German-American history remains to be undertaken. Although a
systematic review would no doubt reveal a different list, I prefer merely
to cite several interrelated topics that seem to me to be worthy of
investigation. They concern the German immigrant churches, their auxiliary institutions, their rivals, and their relationships to American and
German-American society and politics.

Jay Dolan, in his study of Irish and German Catholic churches in
New York City, has shown us the way. Writing from the perspective of
the pew rather than the pulpit, he has demonstrated the possibilities for
comparative analysis in time and place. Dolan's doctoral student, Joseph
White, has shifted the focus from Catholics to German immigrants generally in his examination of relationships between religion and community
in Cincinnati.[55] Other cities, notably Pittsburgh and Buffalo, have been
studied, but more needs to be done if the relationship of German churches
to urban immigrant life is to be understood.[56] A related topic concerns
the spread of German-immigrant churches as institutions in space and
time.[57]

The relationship of church people to urban labor in particular
needs exploration. In their study of urban working-class culture in Chicago,
Hartmut Keil and John Jentz (and other historians as well) find that the
German immigrant churches had no part in it. This, of course, is to be
expected because of the militant anticlericalism of German labor leaders
and their publications in the late nineteenth century. Yet common laborers
were also on the rolls of the urban churches. We need to know more
about such persons. Were they in fact only a tiny proportion of the
German-American urban working class? What was their relationship to
working-class culture? How do German workers in their relationships to
the churches compare to other immigrant worker groups, such as the
Poles, Slovaks, or Italians?

Our knowledge and understanding of the auxiliary institutions
erected by German-American churches is at best fragmentary. Small-

town and rural churches rarely had the resources (or the need, for that matter) to create much more than choirs, ladies' societies, men's clubs, and occasional social events such as church suppers and picnics. But in the city there was in the late nineteenth and early twentieth centuries strong competition from secular organizations for individual loyalties. How the churches responded to this challenge needs study. Philip Gleason has examined the German Catholic Central-Verein in great detail, but we could learn much from studies of other organizations that emerged in German Protestant settings.[58] Similarly, how church-based fraternal benefit associations evolved into modern insurance companies is imperfectly understood. A sophisticated study of the laity in the Lutheran Church — Missouri Synod has been produced, but professional studies of laymen and their organizations in other German-origin churches would improve our understanding of immigrant institutions.[59] Indeed, we know very little about either German-American fraternal organizations such as the Sons of Hermann or about German-speaking chapters in the Masonic and other orders, which the churches often viewed as competitors.[60]

But the most important of the auxiliary agencies established by the churches were their schools. Although a useful literature exists on German Catholic and Lutheran parochial schools, much of it fails to address seriously questions concerning the social and cultural functions of the schools (intended or otherwise), the social and professional characteristics of the teachers and their roles in the churches, or the relationship of the schools to public education.[61] Similarly, there are histories of individual colleges established by German immigrant church bodies, but no historian has made the effort to study their origins and development collectively and to find their place in the larger history of higher education in the United States.

The schools of the German immigrant churches also should be placed in the context of political history. Language controversies are reasonably well understood, but control of state governments over curricula and teacher certification, for example, needs careful study.[62] The cooperative effort of Catholics and German Lutherans in Wisconsin to repeal the Bennett law of 1889 in Wisconsin is well known. But this unsuccessful attempt to require all schools, public and private, to use English as the language of instruction in reading, writing, arithmetic, and United States history was only a part of a larger, national campaign to obstruct and restrict education in immigrant religious institutions. Its full history remains to be written.

Conversely, little is known of the extent to which German Americans were able to convert public schools on the local level into de facto ethnoreligious institutions by virtue of their electoral control of district school boards and therefore over the hiring of teachers. Such dominance was not infrequent in Wisconsin, Minnesota, and North Dakota. In many of the Russian-German Hutterite colonies of the northern Great Plains, school officials to this day have accommodated idiosyncratic customs and values in precisely this fashion.[63]

Indeed, the German-American churches themselves have not been studied in terms of political history.[64] They must be viewed as integral parts of American society and their representatives as legitimate participants in the political process. They must be analyzed by means of comparisons to other appropriate identifiable religious groups. Place must also become a part of research design. For example, we should not expect German Protestants who in the 1850s lived in the St. Louis or Cincinnati areas at the border between slave and non-slave states to have the same partisan preferences as their counterparts in Chicago, Detroit, or Buffalo. Political activity, whether defined as partisan voting or as attitudes toward issues, must be placed within a developmental context and analyzed as interaction with other elements in society.[65]

Further, the relationships of German immigrant church memberships to patterns of wealth, occupation, marriage, family, fertility, and land inheritance strategies have heretofore received only fragmentary attention.[66] Similarly, research into patterns of horizontal mobility (or persistence) should include relocation movements by church groups, as when, for example, Catholic Germans from Stearns County, Minnesota, established daughter settlements in North Dakota.[67] One sociological study of agriculture among German Catholics and "Yankees" in Illinois has demonstrated that the former operate smaller farms, are more highly motivated to sustain family ownership, and are less driven by entrepreneurial considerations. Yet neither this study nor another, a venture in historical sociology that analyzes German-Russian farmers in Kansas and reveals a positive association of German ethnicity with persistence, controls data for religion or church affiliation.[68]

For many years church historians have been intrigued by the process of assimilation in German-American denominations and have produced a substantial literature treating evolutionary change in theology and governance. Similarly, students of language have traced the transitions from German to English in worship services, church periodicals, educational institutions, and conventions. Nevertheless, these manifestations of assimilation have not often been analyzed systematically in terms of social history. Dennis Engbrecht has demonstrated some of the possibilities in his model study of assimilational change in the Kansas General Conference Mennonites. He has examined transitions in Mennonite education, church customs, architecture, and music, in addition to language usage and such "ordinances of faith" relating to baptism, communion, and footwashing.[69] Similar studies of other German-American church bodies will make new generalizations possible about the role of religion in ethnic history.

Much more remains to be done in other aspects of German-American history. The work of scholars in fields other than history—geography, the fine arts, sociology—suggests some possibilities. Terry Jordan and D. Aidan McQuillan have shown us what can be done in agricultural history. Russel Gerlach has broadened German-American studies through his examination of German-American landscapes in the Ozarks. Charles van Ravenswaay has brilliantly opened the field of German-American architecture and folk arts. Diane Barthel, in her study of the Amana colonies in Iowa, has demonstrated how the process of secularization can be studied in a radical German religious colony.[70]

During the past two decades scholars in several fields have discovered much about the three centuries of Germans in America. This history is long and complicated, often perplexing in its diversity. From a tiny settlement of a few families of Dutch and German origins in Pennsylvania in 1683, the Germans have grown to their present status as the immigrant group in the United States with the largest number of descendants. But how important is that, considering the degree of assimilation that also has occurred in 300 years?

In the nineteenth century German Americans, especially their leaders, took great pride—often chauvinistic—in their language and culture. They tended to exaggerate their own unity and their importance for national history, as they attempted to participate in political affairs and to claim a part of America's heritage. In the twentieth century, however, the natural processes of assimilation were augmented by the negatives that attended the American assault on German culture in World War I and the shame of Hitlerian fascism, anti-Semitism, and international aggression. For many Americans, German ancestry and ethnicity was now perceived as a source of social deprivation. German ethnic consciousness virtually disappeared; German-Americans ceased to function as an ethnic group. Yet behaviors and attitudes rooted in German ethnicity remained. Unidentified or submerged, they moved silently into the behaviors and attitudes of middle-class America, especially in the states of the Midwest from Ohio west to the Great Plains. To understand three centuries of Germans in America is to understand ourselves. The German ingredient flavors the whole American pie.

NOTES

1. For detailed listings of such observances and celebrations, see the calendar and supplement, *Tricentennial Events in the United States*, published by the Presidential Commission for the German-American Tricentennial in 1983; see also the several issues of the *Newsletter* published by the same office.

2. See my comments about these two conferences above in chapter 6, "German-American Leadership Strategies Between the World Wars," 51–78.

3. For a representative sample of recent work being done by historians and other scholars in the field of German-American studies, see the two volumes edited by Frank Trommler and Joseph McVeigh, *America and the Germans: An Assessment of a 300-Year History* (Philadelphia: Univ. of Pennsylvania Press, 1985). These essays were prepared for a multidisciplinary conference held in 1983 at the University of Pennsylvania in commemoration of the Germantown tricentennial. See also the several interpretive essays in Randall M. Miller, ed., *Germans in America: Retrospect and Prospect* (Philadelphia: German Society of Pennsylvania, 1984). Another useful volume to emerge from a tricentennial observance is *Eagle in the New World: German Immigration to Texas and America*, ed. Theodore Gish and Richard Spuler (College Station: Texas A&M Univ. Press, 1986).

4. This is not intended to suggest that all recent books treating the history of Germans in the United States are free of the old filiopietistic bonds. Amateur historians in particular continue to produce books that do not advance beyond the concepts and methods of the first important synthesis of the German-American history: Albert Bernhardt Faust, *The German Element in the United States*, 2 vols. (Boston: Houghton Mifflin, 1909). As an example, see Joseph Wandel, *The German Dimension of American History* (Chicago: Nelson-Hall, 1979). The German-American tricentennial stimulated the publication in Germany of several books of the same variety, including Dietmar Kügler, *Die Deutschen in Amerika* (Stuttgart: Motorbuch Verlag, 1983) and Armin M. Brandt, *Bau deinen Altar auf fremder Erde: Die Deutschen in Amerika—300 Jahre German-town* (Stuttgart-Degerloch: Seewald, 1983). Much more valuable are the popular and well-illustrated essays written by Günter Moltmann and his associates at the University of Hamburg, *Germans to America: 300 Years of Immigration, 1683–1983* (Stuttgart: Institut für Auslandsbeziehungen, 1982).

5. Stephanie Grauman Wolf, "Hyphenated America: The Creation of an Eighteenth-Century German-American Culture," in *American and the Germans*, ed. Trommler and McVeigh, 1:68–70. See also Ingrid Schöberl, "Franz Daniel Pastorius and the Foundation of Germantown," in *Germans to America*, ed. Moltmann, 16–25.

6. Marianne Wokeck, "German Immigration to Colonial America: Proto-type of a Transatlantic Mass Migration," in *America and the Germans*, ed. Trommler and McVeigh, 1:3–13. This succinct essay is based on Wokeck's Ph.D. dissertation, "A Tide of Alien Tongues: The Flow and Ebb of the German Immigration to Pennsylvania, 1683–1776" (Temple University, 1983).

7. Albert Bernhardt Faust, *The German Element in the United States,* 2 vols. (Boston: Houghton Mifflin, 1909), 2: 285.

8. For a particularly insightful study of assimilation in the eighteenth century, see Stephanie Grauman Wolf, *Urban Village: Population, Community, and Family Structure in Germantown, Pennsylvania, 1683–1800* (Princeton: Princeton Univ. Press, 1976), 127–53.

9. The most useful introductions to this topic are Mack Walker, *Germany and the Emigration, 1816–1885* (Cambridge, MA: Harvard Univ. Press, 1964) and Wolfgang Köllmann and Peter Marschalck, "German Emigration to the United States," *Perspectives in American History* 7 (1973): 499–554. See also Peter Marschalck, *Deutsche Überseewanderung im 19. Jahrhundert* (Stuttgart: Klett, 1973) and Wolfgang von Hippel, *Auswanderung aus Südwestdeutschland: Studien zur württembergischen Auswanderung und Auswanderungenspolitik im 18. und 19. Jahrhundert* (Stuttgart, 1984). For historiographical essays treating the German emigration see David Luebke, "German Exodus: Historical Perspectives on the Nineteenth-Century Emigration," *Yearbook of German-American Studies* 20 (1985): 1–17, and Günter Moltmann, "Migrations from Germany to North America: New Perspectives," *Reviews in American History* 14 (December 1986): 580–96.

10. Walter D. Kamphoefner, "At the Crossroads of Economic Development: Background Factors Affecting Emigration from Nineteenth-Century Germany," in *Migration across Time and Nations: Population Mobility in Historical Contexts,* ed. Ira A. Glazier and Luigi de Rosa (New York: Holmes and Meier, 1986), 174–201.

11. Walter D. Kamphoefner, *The Westfalians: From Germany to Missouri* (Princeton, NJ: Princeton Univ. Press, 1987), 12–39. Kamphoefner includes other variables in his analysis in addition to those described here. See his summary, "At the Crossroads of Economic Development," 191–194.

12. Ibid., 40–69.

13. Kathleen Neils Conzen, "Germans," *Harvard Encyclopedia of American Ethnic Groups,* ed. Stephan Thernstrom (Cambridge, MA: Harvard Univ. Press, 1980), 413, table 4.

14. This theme is well developed in the older historical literature of German America, notably John Hawgood, *The Tragedy of German America* (New York: Putnam, 1940), but has been granted a new sophistication by Kathleen Neils Conzen; see her "Patterns of German-American History," in *Germans in America,* ed. Miller, 14–35, and her "German-Americans and the Invention of Ethnicity," in *America and the Germans,* ed. Trommler and McVeigh, 2: 131–47.

15. Kamphoefner, *Westfalians,* 64–85. Many other historians have made similar, although usually less systematic, observations.

16. Wolfgang Helbich, "The Letters They Sent Home: The Subjective Perspective of German Immigrants in the Nineteenth Century," *Yearbook of German-American Studies* 22 (1987): 13.

17. Stanley Nadel, "Kleindeutschland: New York City's Germans, 1845–1880" (Ph.D. diss., Columbia University, 1981), 73–75, 102, 117, 125, and

299–301. Provincial variation is also theme developed by Lesley Ann Kawaguchi, "The Making of Philadelphia's German-America: Ethnic Group and Community Development, 1830–1883" (Ph.D. diss., University of California at Los Angeles, 1983).

18. Kamphoefner, *Westfalians*, 88–89.

19. For an example of such an agent, see Edith Robbins, "Friedrich Hedde: Grand Island's Forty-Eighter, Pioneer and Leader," *Yearbook of German-American Studies* 20 (1985): 101–2.

20. The role of the clergy, notably Martin Stephan and C. F. W. Walther, in the Saxon immigration to Missouri in 1838–39, is clearly delineated in Walter O. Forster, *Zion on the Mississippi: The Settlement of the Saxon Lutherans in Missouri, 1839–1841* (St. Louis: Concordia, 1953).

21. Helbich, "The Letters They Sent Home," 2.

22. See especially Kamphoefner's chapter on chain migration in his *Westfalians*, 70–105. His research methods have been affirmed in Illinois by Robert W. Frizzell, "Migration Chains to Illinois: The Evidence from German-American Church Records," *Journal of American Ethnic History* 7 (Fall 1987): 59–73.

23. The most thorough analysis of German-American agriculture is Terry G. Jordan, *German Seed in Texas Soil: Immigrant Farmers in Nineteenth-Century Texas* (Austin: Univ. of Texas Press, 1966), but see also David Aidan McQuillan, "Adaptation of Three Immigrant Groups to Farming in Central Kansas, 1875–1925" (Ph.D. diss., University of Wisconsin-Madison, 1975), which treats Swedes, French-Canadians, and German Mennonites from Russia; and Bradley H. Baltensperger, "Agricultural Change among Nebraska Immigrants, 1880–1900," in *Ethnicity on the Great Plains*, ed. by Frederick C. Luebke (Lincoln: Univ. of Nebraska Press, 1980), 170–89, which compares native-born American practices with those of Swedes, Germans, and Germans from Russia. German-American farmers are prominent in an unpublished manuscript by Kathleen Neils Conzen entitled "Rural Immigrants in Nineteenth-Century Agricultural History." I have consulted a draft dated October 1988.

24. One of the earliest and still most useful studies of immigrant mobility is embedded in Merle Curti, *The Making of an American Community: A Case Study of Democracy in a Frontier County* (Stanford, CA: Stanford Univ. Press, 1959), 67–73, where data registered for Germans in Trempealeau County, Wisconsin, may be compared to rates for Norwegians, Poles, Irish, English, and native-born Americans. Curti also includes valuable comparative data on literacy, school attendance, and farm acreages and values.

25. Kathleen Neils Conzen, "Peasant Pioneers: Generational Succession among German Farmers in Frontier Minnesota," in *The Countryside in the Age of Capitalist Transformation: Essays in the Social History of Rural America*, ed. Steven Hahn and Jonathan Prude (Chapel Hill: Univ. of North Carolina Press, 1985), 259–92.

26. James M. Bergquist has provided succinct surveys of this topic in "German Communities in American Cities: An Interpretation of the Nineteenth-

Century Experience," *Journal of American Ethnic History* 4 (Fall 1984): 9–30, and in "Germans and the City," *Germans in America*, ed. Randall M. Miller (Philadelphia: German Society of Pennsylvania, 1984): 37–56.

27. Nora Faires, "Occupational Patterns of German-Americans in Nineteenth-Century Cities," in *German Workers in Industrial Chicago, 1850–1910: A Comparative Persepective*, ed. Hartmut Keil and John B. Jentz (DeKalb: Northern Illinois Univ. Press, 1983), 37–51.

28. See especially the collection of documents edited by Hartmut Keil and John B. Jentz, *German Workers in Chicago: A Documentary History of Working-Class Culture from 1850 to World War I* (Urbana: Univ. of Illinois Press, 1988) and the series of essays in their edited volume *German Workers in Industrial Chicago*. See also Keil's "German Immigrant Workers in Nineteenth-Century America: Working-Class Culture and Everyday Life in an Urban Industrial Setting," in *America and the Germans*, ed. Trommler and McVeigh, 1:189–206.

29. See the useful summary of discoveries in this field by Nora Faires, "Occupational Patterns of German-Americans in Nineteenth-Century Cities," in *German Workers in Industrial Chicago*, ed. Keil and Jentz, 37–51.

30. Clyde and Sally Griffen, *Natives and Newcomers: The Ordering of Opportunity in Mid-Nineteenth-Century Poughkeepsie* (Cambridge, MA: Harvard Univ. Press, 1978), 68–72, 217, and 259.

31. This subject is introduced by Agnes Bretting, "Little Germanies in the United States," in *Germans to America*, ed. Moltmann, 145–51.

32. Kathleen Neils Conzen, *Immigrant Milwaukee, 1836–1860: Accommodation and Community in a Frontier City* (Cambridge, MA: Harvard Univ. Press, 1976).

33. A substantial bibliography of excellent books and articles on immigrants in American cities has developed in the last two decades. For an outstanding example, see Olivier Zunz, *The Changing Face of Inequality: Urbanization, Industrial Development, and Immigrants in Detroit, 1880–1920* (Chicago: Univ. of Chicago Press, 1982).

34. The paragraphs that follow are condensed from my more extended treatment of this subject in *Bonds of Loyalty: German Americans and World War I* (DeKalb: Northern Illinois Univ. Press, 1974), 34–47. A substantial bibliography of materials exists for most of the German religious groups, but there is a direct relationship between the extent of these materials and the strength of identity possessed by individual groups (which is usually congruent with the degree to which the religious body diverges from American norms). Thus there is an extensive literature, much of its filiopietistic, on such groups as German Jews, Amish and Mennonite groups, and conservative Lutheran bodies, notably the Missouri Synod. Such churches often support well-maintained archives and in some cases publish historical journals of their own. Other bodies, most of them long since disappeared as separate entities, including German Methodists, Baptists, Presbyterians, and Congregationalists, have rarely been studied by professional historians.

35. Jay P. Dolan, *The American Catholic Experience: A History from Colonial Times to the Present* (Garden City, NY: Doubleday, 1985), 156.

36. Jay P. Dolan, *The Immigrant Church: New York's Irish and German Catholics, 1815–1865* (Baltimore: Johns Hopkins Univ. Press, 1975).

37. Stanley Nadel, "Jewish Race and German Soul in Nineteenth-Century America," *American Jewish History* 77 (September 1987): 24. Nadel's article is a corrective to Naomi Cohen's point that after 1870 German-American Jews tended to allow their Jewish identity to transcend their Germanness. See Scott Cline, "Jewish-Ethnic Interactions: A Bibliographical Essay," *American Jewish History* 77 (September 1987): 140–42; and Naomi W. Cohen, *Encounter with Emancipation: The German Jews in the United States, 1830–1914* (Philadelphia: Jewish Publication Society, 1984). Any serious study of the relationships between German-Americans and German Jews in the United States should begin with the work of Rudolf Glanz. Fifteen of his essays have been translated into English and published as *Studies in Judaica Americana* (New York: Ktav, 1970). See especially "Jews in Relation to the Cultural Milieu of the Germans in America Up to the Eighteen Eighties," 203–55. The general topic of German-Jewish emigration is effectively introduced by Avraham Barkai, "German-Jewish Migration in the Nineteenth Century, 1830–1910," in *Migration across Time and Nations: Population Mobility in Historical Contexts*, ed. Ira A. Glazier and Luigi de Rosa (New York: Holmes and Meier, 1986), 202–19.

38. Conzen, "Germans," 417. The growth of German associational complexes in individual cities has been studied in several recent dissertations. Among them are James S. Lapham, "The German-Americans of New York City, 1860–1890" (Ph.D. diss., St. John's University, 1977); Lesley Ann Kawaguchi, "The Making of Philadelphia's German America: Ethnic Group and Community Development, 1830–1883" (Ph.D. diss., University of California at Los Angeles, 1983); and Andrew Paul Yox, "Decline of the German-American Community in Buffalo, 1855–1925" (Ph.D. diss., University of Chicago, 1983).

39. This topic has been treated brilliantly by Kathleen Neils Conzen, "Ethnicity as Festive Culture: Nineteenth Century German America on Parade," in *The Invention of Ethnicity*, ed. Werner Sollers (New York: Oxford Univ. Press, 1989), 44–75.

40. The most useful recent survey of the German-language press is James M. Bergquist, "The German-American Press," in *The Ethnic Press in the United States: A Historical Analysis and Handbook*, ed. Sally Miller (Westport, CT: Greenwood Press, 1987): 131–59. It supplements rather than displaces Carl F. Wittke's classic *The German-Language Press in America* (Lexington, KY: Univ. of Kentucky Press, 1957). As an index to newspaper sources, see Karl J. R. Arndt and May E. Olson, *The German Language Press of the Americas*, 3d ed., rev. (Munich: Verlag Dokumentation, 1976).

41. These relationships were first articulated in an influential article by Guido Andre Dobbert, "German-Americans between New and Old Fatherlands, 1870–1914," *American Quarterly* 19 (Winter 1967): 663–80.

42. Frederick C. Luebke, *Immigrants and Politics: The Germans of Nebraska, 1880–1900* (Lincoln: Univ. of Nebraska Press, 1969), 122–65. See also works by Richard Jensen, Paul Kleppner, Ronald Formisano, Samuel

McSeveney, and other advocates of the ethnocultural interpretation of American political history.

43. The National German-American Alliance was treated in detail many years ago by Clifton J. Child, *The German-American in Politics, 1914–1917* (Madison: Univ. of Wisconsin Press, 1939). More recently it has been studied on the state level by David W. Detjen, *The Germans in Missouri, 1900–1918: Prohibition, Neutrality, and Assimilation* (Columbia: Univ. of Missouri Press, 1985).

44. Luebke, *Bonds of Loyalty*, 3–26 and 225–59; Phyllis Keller, *States of Belonging: German-American Intellectuals and the First World War* (Cambridge, MA: Harvard Univ. Press, 1979) provides a psychological interpretation based on the experiences of Hugo Münsterberg, George Sylvester Viereck, and Hermann Hagedorn.

45. Hartmut Bickelmann, *Deutsche Überseeauswanderung in der Weimarer Zeit* (Wiesbaden, West Germany: Steiner, 1980), 16, 17, and 151.

46. The best treatment of this topic is Sander A. Diamond, *The Nazi Movement in the United States, 1924–1941* (Ithaca, NY: Cornell Univ. Press, 1974).

47. Donald P. Kent, *The Refugee Intellectuals: The Americanization of the Immigrants of 1933–1941* (New York: Columbia Univ. Press, 1953); Laura Fermi, *Illustrious Immigrants: The Intellectual Migration from Europe, 1930–41*, 2d. ed. (Chicago: Univ. of Chicago Press, 1971). German immigration in the 1930s is introduced by Michael Just, "Emigration from the Third Reich," *Germans to America*, ed. Moltmann, 171–77. The record of the Roosevelt administration in handling the Jewish refugee problem was been treated throughly in several books. For a recent study, see Alan M. Kraut, Richard Breitman, and Thomas W. Imhoof, "The State Department, the Labor Department, and German Jewish Immigration, 1930–1940," *Journal of American Ethnic History* 3 (Spring 1984): 5–38.

48. Sociologists of religion have published much that can be helpful to historians of immigration and ethnicity in American life. A useful introduction with bibliography is Harold J. Abramson, "Religion," *Harvard Encyclopedia of American Ethnic Groups*, ed. by Stephan Thernstrom (Cambridge, MA: Harvard Univ. Press, 1980), 869–75. Most sociologists recognize the need to differentiate Protestant behavior patterns into denominational components. For example, see Charles Y. Glock and Rodney Stark, *Religion and Society in Tension* (Chicago: Rand McNally, 1965) and *American Piety: The Nature of Religious Commitment* (Berkeley: Univ. of California Press, 1968). Others have differentiated ethnic varieties within American denominationalism. An early venture into this field is Charles H. Anderson, *White Protestant Americans: From National Origins to Religious Group* (Englewood Cliffs, NJ: Prentice-Hall, 1970). A comparable study for Catholics is Harold Abramson, *Ethnic Diversity in Catholic America* (New York: Wiley, 1973). For sociological data on members of the several Lutheran church bodies, see Merton P. Strommen et al., *A Study of Generations* (Minneapolis: Augsburg, 1972).

49. One of the most perceptive students of regional political culture is Daniel J. Elazar, who years ago suggested such relationships in his *American Federalism: A View from the States* (New York: Thomas Y. Crowell, 1966), although he does not directly connect the differences to ethnic variables. See also his essay, "Political Culture on the Plains," *Western Historical Quarterly* 11 (July 1980): 261–83 and my "Nebraska: Time, Place, and Culture," in *Heartland: Comparative Histories of the Midwestern States,* ed. James H. Madison (Bloomington: Indiana Univ. Press, 1988): 226–47.

50. An outstanding example of such work is Charles van Ravenswaay, *The Arts and Architecture of German Settlements in Missouri: A Survey of a Vanishing Culture* (Columbia: Univ. of Missouri Press, 1977). As a guide to collections in material culture, see Margaret Hobbie, comp., *Museums, Sites, and Collections of Germanic Culture in North America* (Westport, CT: Greenwood Press, 1980). Kathleen Neils Conzen has discussed theoretical dimensions of the persistence of ethnic traits long after the disappearance of a sense of ethnic group identity in "Immigrants, Immigrant Neighborhoods, and Ethnic Identity: Historical Issues," *Journal of American History* 66 (December 1979): 603–16.

51. A major exception is the sociolinguist Joshua Fishman, whose numerous works include "Demographic and Institutional Indicators of German Language Maintenance in the United States, 1960–1980," in *America and the Germans,* ed. Trommler and McVeigh, 1:251–69. Linguists continue to study the persistence of German dialects in America, but their efforts seems to have limited value for answering the questions historians ask. For examples, see the essays by Jan E. Bender, Andreas Gommermann, Kurt Rein, and Joseph Wilson in *Languages in Conflict: Linguistic Acculturation on the Great Plains,* ed. Paul Schach (Lincoln: Univ. of Nebraska Press, 1980).

52. These observations are based on an examination of bibliographies of German-American history, including Don Heinrich Tolzmann, *German-Americana: A Bibliography* (Metuchen, NJ: Scarecrow Press, 1975); John D. Buenker and Nicholas C. Burckel, *Immigration and Ethnicity: A Guide to Information Sources* (Detroit: Gale, 1977), and Michael Keresztesi and Gary R. Cocozzoli, *German-American History and Life: A Guide to Information Sources* (Detroit: Gale, 1980). A cursory examination of recent annual indexes of *America: History and Life* (Santa Barbara, CA: ABC–Clio Information Services) also demonstrates the dearth of materials on German immigrants of the post–World War II period.

53. "The Geography of Ancestry," *Harper's Magazine,* June 1988, 24. Other maps and atlases are enormously suggestive in other ways. See, for example, James Allen and Eugene Turner, *We the People: An Atlas of America's Ethnic Diversity* (New York: Macmillan, 1988), 54. For the earlier periods in German-American history, see Heinz Kloss, *Atlas of Nineteenth and Early Twentieth Century German American Settlements* (Marburg, West Germany: N. G. Elwert, 1974). On the state level, see J. Neale Carman, *Foreign-Language Units of Kansas. I. Historical Atlas and Statistics* (Lawrence: Univ. of Kansas Press, 1962) and William C. Sherman, *Prairie Mosaic: An Ethnic Atlas of Rural North Dakota* (Fargo: North Dakota Institute for Regional Studies, 1983).

54. I refer here to Lubell's identification of voters of German and German-Russian descent in North Dakota and other states their electoral behavior in the 1940s in *The Future of American Politics*, rev. ed. (Garden City, NY: Doubleday, 1956); Kevin Phillips's observations regarding German Catholic voters in *The Emerging Republican Majority* (New Rochelle, NY: Arlington House, 1969); and Michael Parenti, "Ethnic Politics and the Persistence of Ethnic Identification," *American Political Science Review* 61 (September 1967): 717–26.

55. Jay P. Dolan, *The Immigrant Church: New York's Irish and German Catholics, 1815–1865* (Baltimore: Johns Hopkins Univ. Press, 1975); Joseph Michael White, "Religion and Community: Cincinnati Germans, 1814–1870" (Ph.D. diss., University of Notre Dame, 1980).

56. Nora H. Faires, "Ethnicity in Evolution: The German Community in Pittsburgh and Allegheny City, Pennsylvania, 1845–1885" (Ph.D. diss., University of Pittsburgh, 1981), especially chapter 4; Andrew Yox, "Ethnic Loyalties of the Alsatians in Buffalo, 1829–1855," *Yearbook of German-American Studies* 20 (1985): 114–21; David A. Gerber, "Language Maintenance, Ethnic Group Formation, and Public Schools: Changing Patterns of German Concern, Buffalo, 1837–1874," *Journal of American Ethnic History* 4 (Fall 1984): 31–61.

57. The Lutheran Church—Missouri Synod has been studied in this regard by Judith W. Meyer, "Ethnicity, Theology, and Immigrant Church Expansion," *Geographical Review* 65 (1975): 180–97, but similar analyses should be made of other immigrant churches.

58. Philip Gleason, *The Conservative Reformers: German-American Catholics and the Social Order* (Notre Dame, IN: Univ. of Notre Dame Press, 1968).

59. Alan Graebner, *Uncertain Saints: The Laity in the Lutheran Church—Missouri Synod, 1900–1970* (Westport, CT: Greenwood Press, 1975).

60. Dale T. Knobel has demonstrated the possibilities for research in this field in his "To Be an American: Ethnicity, Fraternity, and the Improved Order of Red Men," *Journal of American Ethnic History* 4 (Fall 1984): 62–87. See my effort to include lodge membership as a variable in political behavior in *Immigrants and Politics*, 56–58 and 67–69. For brief introductions to the Sons of Hermann and the German Order of Harugari, see Alvin J. Schmidt, *Fraternal Organizations* (Westport, CT: Greenwood Press, 1980), 153, 287–89, and 319–21.

61. Two decades ago I explored this theme in a preliminary way for a publication of Concordia College, Seward, Nebraska: "German Immigrants and Parochial Schools: A Look at Institutional Beginnings," *Issues in Christian Education* 1 (Spring 1967): 11–18. For a study of parochial school teachers as a group in the Lutheran Church–Missouri Synod, see Stephen A. Schmidt, *Powerless Pedagogues: An Interpretive Essay on the History of the Lutheran Teacher in the Missouri Synod* (River Forest, IL: Lutheran Education Association, 1972).

62. See especially David Gerber's study of politics and the language question in Buffalo public schools in the mid-nineteenth century, cited in note 56.

63. Victor Peters, *All Things Common: The Hutterian Way of Life* (Minneapolis: University of Minnesota Press, 1965), 138–45; John A. Hostetler,

Hutterite Society (Baltimore: Johns Hopkins University Press, 1974), 218–19 and 345–46.

64. A notable exception to this generalization is James C. Juhnke, *A People of Two Kingdoms: The Political Acculturation of the Kansas Mennonites* (Newton, KS: Faith and Life Press, 1975).

65. I have developed some of these ideas at greater length in my essay, "Politics and Missouri Synod Lutherans: A Historiographical Review," *Concordia Historical Institute Quarterly* 45 (May 1972): 141–58.

66. For an outstanding example of such work, see Conzen, "Peasant Pioneers."

67. See the references to Stearns County Germans in Sherman, *Prairie Mosaic*, 35.

68. Sonya Salamon, "Ethnic Communities and the Structure of Agriculture," *Rural Sociology* 50 (Fall 1985): 323–40; Jan L. Flora and John M. Stitz, "Ethnicity, Persistence, and Capitalization of Agriculture during the Settlement Period: Wheat Production and Risk Avoidance," *Rural Sociology* 50 (Fall 1985): 342–60.

69. Dennis D. Engbrecht, "The Americanization of a Rural Immigrant Church: The General Conference Mennonites in Central Kansas, 1874–1939" (Ph.D. diss, University of Nebraska-Lincoln, 1985).

70. Jordan, *German Seed in Texas Soil*; McQuillan, "Adaptation of Three Immigrant Groups"; Russel L. Gerlach, *Immigrants in the Ozarks: A Study in Ethnic Geography* (Columbia: Univ. of Missouri Press, 1976); Van Ravenswaay, *The Arts and Architecture of German Settlements in Missouri*; and Diane Barthel, *Amana: From Pietist Sect to American Community* (Lincoln: Univ. of Nebraska Press, 1984).

Index

A Note on the Author

Frederick C. Luebke is Charles J. Mach Distinguished University Professor in the Department of History at the University of Nebraska-Lincoln and the author of many books and articles on German immigrants, among them, *Germans in Brazil: The Problem of World War I in Comparative Perspective* (Louisiana State University Press, 1987).